The Campus History Series

Ojai Valley School

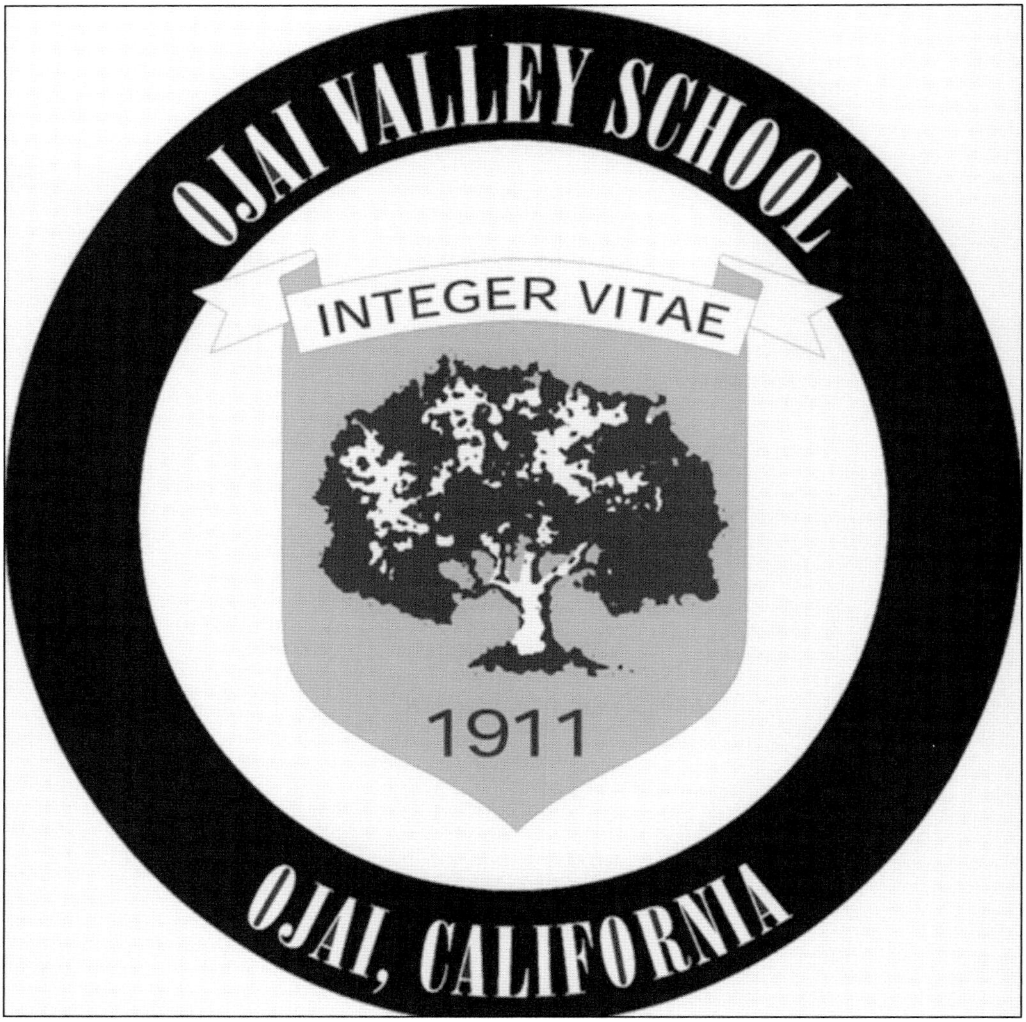

OJAI VALLEY SCHOOL. The seal of Ojai Valley School (OVS) was designed in 1982 by Mary Tilbury. The oak tree stands for strength and courage. As noted by Edward Yeomans, the words *Integer Vitae*—meaning "wholeness of life," "symmetry of life," "soundness of life," and therefore, "poise and strength of life"—are the principles on which he based his school. This book celebrates the first 100 years of Ojai Valley School and its predecessor, the Bristol School. It also recounts the school's progress into the second decade of the 21st century. (Courtesy of the Ojai Valley School.)

ON THE COVER: Children built a replica of Caernarvon Castle in Wales as an English project in the 1930s. The castle was designed by faculty member John Phillip Ascott. The children made cement blocks at a scale of one half inch per foot for the castle's construction. (Courtesy of the Ojai Valley School.)

The Campus History Series

OJAI VALLEY SCHOOL

LYNN YOAKUM TAYLOR

ARCADIA PUBLISHING

ISBN 978-1-4671-3264-0

Published by Arcadia Publishing
Charleston, South Carolina

Printed in the United States of America

Library of Congress Control Number: 2014941888

For all general information, please contact Arcadia Publishing:
Telephone 843-853-2070
Fax 843-853-0044
E-mail sales@arcadiapublishing.com
For customer service and orders:
Toll-Free 1-888-313-2665

Visit us on the Internet at www.arcadiapublishing.com

This book is dedicated to my classmates from the class of 1966, the second graduating class and to my husband, John, whom I met at a Thacher dance in the fall of 1961, when I was in the eighth grade at OVS. We were married in Thacher's outdoor chapel in 1987.

Contents

Foreword		6
Acknowledgments		7
Introduction		8
1.	A Little History	9
2.	Wanting a Little More for the Children	17
3.	The Campus Grows	27
4.	Wallace Burr Arrives	41
5.	The Burr Years	53
6.	The Hermes Legacy	71
7.	Horse Program	87
8.	Outdoor Activities	95
9.	Athletics	105
10.	One Hundred Years and Beyond	117

Foreword

The contributions that OVS alumni have made, both to the school and to the communities in which they live and work, are greatly valued. Each year, new graduates venture into the world and join a global alumni community that is united by warm memories of OVS.

Having celebrated its centennial year in 2011, and preparing to celebrate 50 years at Upper Campus in 2015, the school has reached important milestones and has much for which to be grateful. Thanks to generous alumni and families, there have been many positive developments in programs and facilities over the years, but much also remains unchanged.

The hallmarks of the education that our students experience—high academic standards; supportive teachers; and a small community where young people learn to build character, integrity, and confidence—solidly endure and can be succinctly stated in two words: *Integer Vitae*, meaning "wholeness of life," "symmetry of life," "soundness of life," and therefore, "poise and strength of life."

Such was the vision of our founder, Edward Yeomans, and it was further reinforced by his successors, including my mentor and predecessor, Mike Hermes (L53), who embodied the essence of what it means to be a loyal alumnus: dedication to family and community.

Special thanks go to another loyal graduate and alumna, Lynn Yoakum Taylor (L63, U66), who worked tirelessly and diligently with our alumni office staff in creating this wonderful pictorial history of Ojai Valley School. All of us can take great pride in the images and descriptions she selected to represent the fascinating story of the school's growth and development. From such rich and fertile soil, the family tree of Ojai Valley School has grown and flourished, now with a broad and diverse network of loyal alumni, families, and friends branching out each year.

I encourage you to stay connected to your alma mater, and to one another, by keeping Ojai Valley School updated on your family, career, educational and volunteer pursuits, and other news. Please contact OVS today and be sure to visit campus whenever you find yourself in Ojai.

—Michael J. Hall-Mounsey
President/CEO

ACKNOWLEDGMENTS

The foundational historical work on the school by Patricia Fry, *A Thread to Hold*, and her book on the Ojai Valley, ***The Ojai Valley: An Illustrated History***, were invaluable in the preparation of this book. Two additional books on the Ojai Valley written under the auspices of the Ojai Valley Museum and published by Arcadia Publishing (Images of America: *Ojai* and Postcard History Series: *Ojai*) provided additional images and historical information. OVS publications such as *Family Tree* and various alumni newsletters were also very useful. Edward Yeomans's educational treatise, *Shackled Youth*, provided insight into the founding principles of the school.

Reviews and suggestions by Dok Smith (U65), Spencer Garrett (U65), Ruth Huyler Glass (L63), Kirk Warren (U65), Anne Gottsdanker (U67), and members of the school's administrative team, especially Tracy Wilson, were also much appreciated. (Note that the designations L63, U65, and so forth throughout the book refer to the completion of studies at either the Lower or Upper Campus.)

The author wishes to extend special thanks to John Taylor for his assistance, edits, and advice on computer issues in the development of this labor of love. I also wish to thank the Ojai Valley School alumni staff, led by Will Wyman, and including Malory Taylor and Stacey Sheets, for assisting me in gaining access to the school archives and photographs. My thanks go to each of you for helping me tell this story of a place and time near and dear to me.

All photographs are courtesy of Ojai Valley School unless otherwise noted. Images drawn from the Ojai Valley Museum collection are noted with the initials "OVM."

INTRODUCTION

In his 1921 book *Shackled Youth*, Edward Yeomans lays out the educational philosophy he envisioned and implemented when he founded Ojai Valley School. Yeomans believed that outdoor life was far more stimulating than a structured classroom environment. He dreamed of instilling in students a love of nature, music, shop work, and art by "experiencing instead of telling." He believed that children should live the lesson: if teaching the parts of a horse, use a barn as the classroom; if teaching landforms, take a child mountain climbing and show him or her the layers of the earth in rock formations. Each teacher personified the philosophy of the school as exemplified by the words from Psalm 1:3, carved by Yeomans over the main arch of the old assembly hall: "And he shall be like a tree, planted by the rivers of water, that bringeth forth his fruit in his season." Building on this, OVS continues to demonstrate excellence in education. This book chronicles the history and development of this remarkable educational institution.

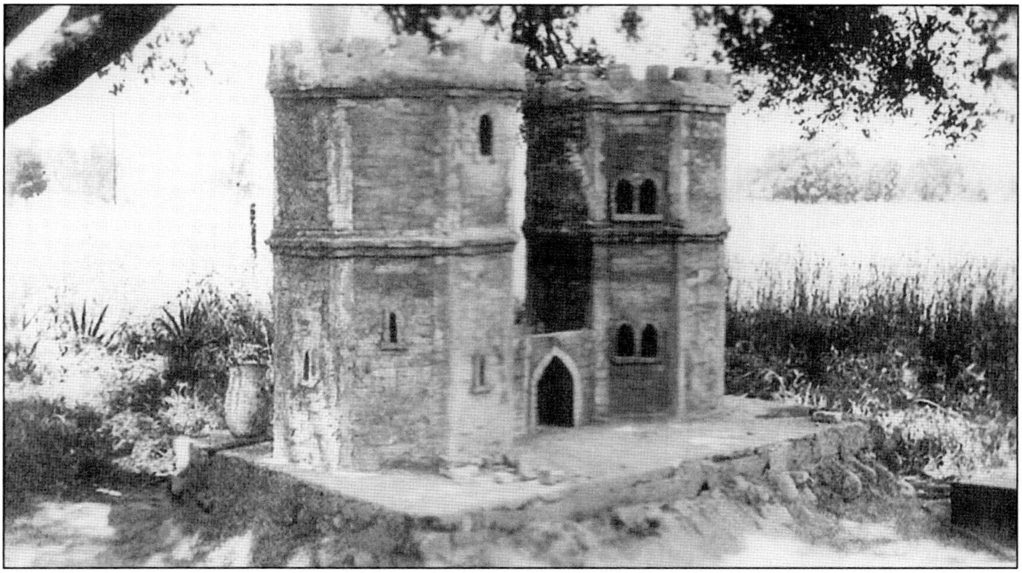

A FOUNDER'S THOUGHTS. Shown here is a model of Caernarvon Castle created by students as an example of Yeomans's philosophy.

One

A Little History

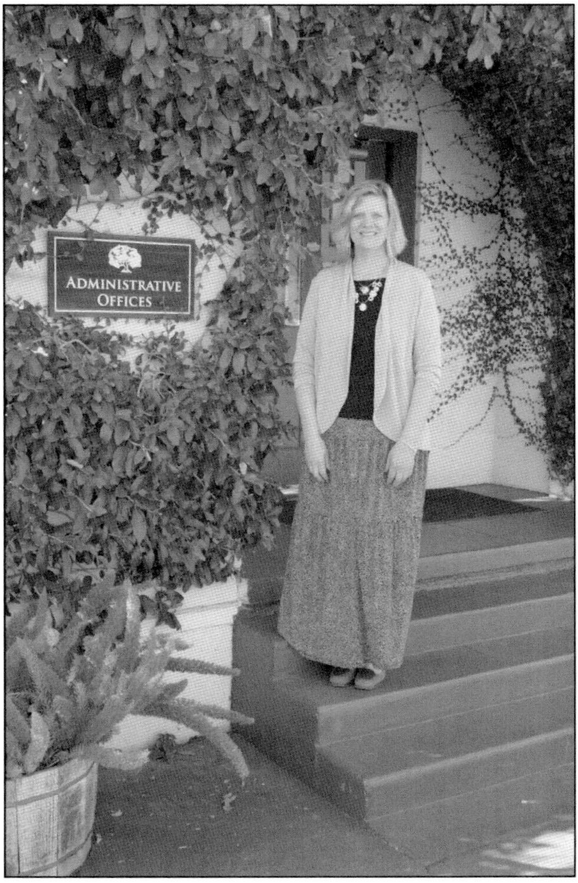

The Threshold. Over the course of OVS's first 100 years, more than 5,340 children have enrolled to be educated by dedicated teachers who measure their own success by the success of their students. Students from 34 countries have come to seek the academic and social guidance that would allow them to contribute to the diverse global community. More than 2,400 students have come from the United States, with the remainder from as far away as China, Japan, Saudi Arabia, Thailand, Vietnam, and South Korea. From its roots in 1911, the school has followed the same motto: "Nothing less than your best." Each student is encouraged to reach his or her full potential, both academically and socially. This book describes the experiences of those students during the school's first century. Over this span of years, there have been 23 heads of school at the Upper and Lower Campuses. Karen Morse, seen here at the threshold of the Lower Campus, became the new head of school of the Lower Campus in 2012.

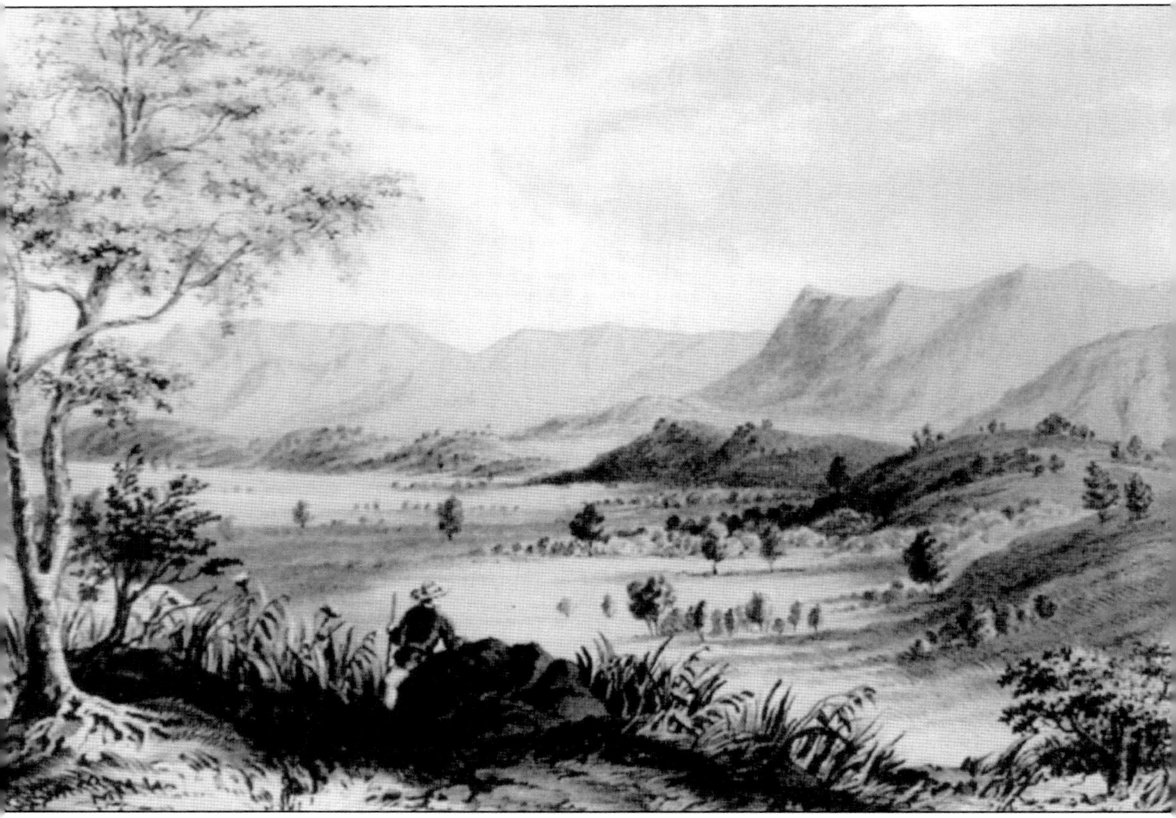

Paradise. The name Ojai, derived from the Chumash Indian word *A'hwai* ("moon"), was given to an inland California valley by early Spanish settlers. A.H. Campbell's 1854 lithograph (pictured), part of a survey for a transcontinental railroad from California to Mississippi, is the earliest known image of the Ojai Valley. The village began in 1874 as the dusty western town of Nordhoff, named for author and journalist Charles Nordhoff. The name was changed to Ojai in 1917 for three reasons: people were already calling the village Ojai; Nordhoff was a German name, unpopular during World War I; and mail was being erroneously delivered to Norwalk, California, instead of Nordhoff. In 1997, Don Weinman noted, "Most residents are sure Ojai means 'nest' in the Chumash language, but experts disagree. They say it means 'moon.' Those of us who live here say it doesn't matter. To us, it means paradise." (OVM.)

Edward Libbey. Edward Drummond Libbey, founder of the Libbey Glass Company of Toledo, Ohio, and his wife, Florence, loved to vacation in the Ojai Valley, staying at the exquisite Foothills Hotel. They and other guests arrived by horse-drawn conveyance, such as Thomas Clark's "six-in-hand" (below). In 1911, the Libbeys built a home on Foothill Road. Thus began the great influence Libbey would have on Ojai and Ojai Valley School. Libbey, a leading benefactor of the Ojai Valley, tried to market 360 acres west of Nordhoff, which he referred to as "the Arbolada," to Easterners. Although The Thacher School for boys had been established about five miles east of Ojai in 1889, people advised Libbey that potential home buyers would be more interested if a private, coeducational school existed in the area. Libbey agreed to donate three acres for this purpose. (Both, OVM.)

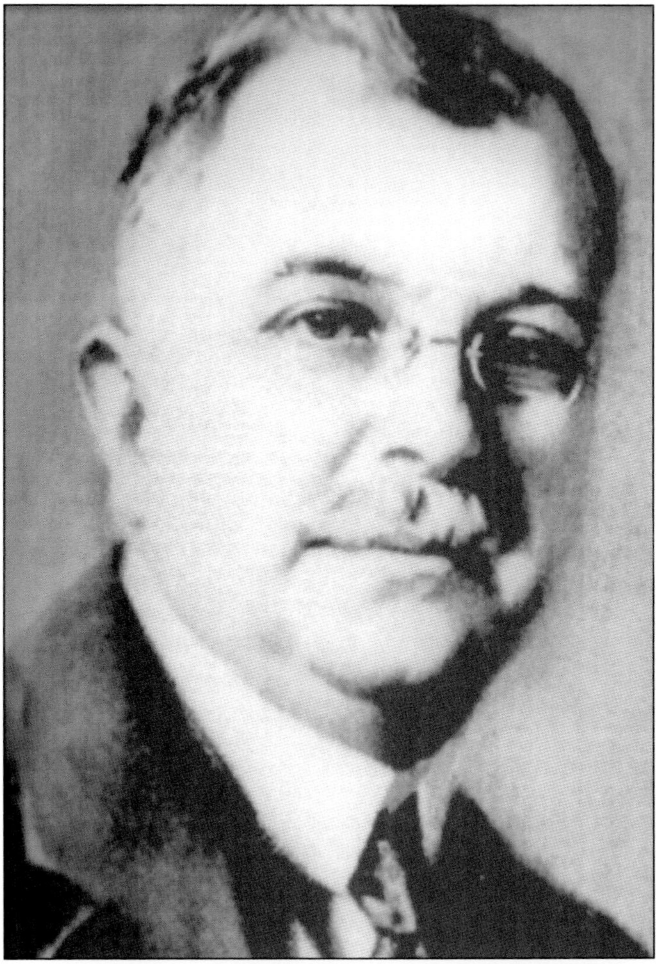

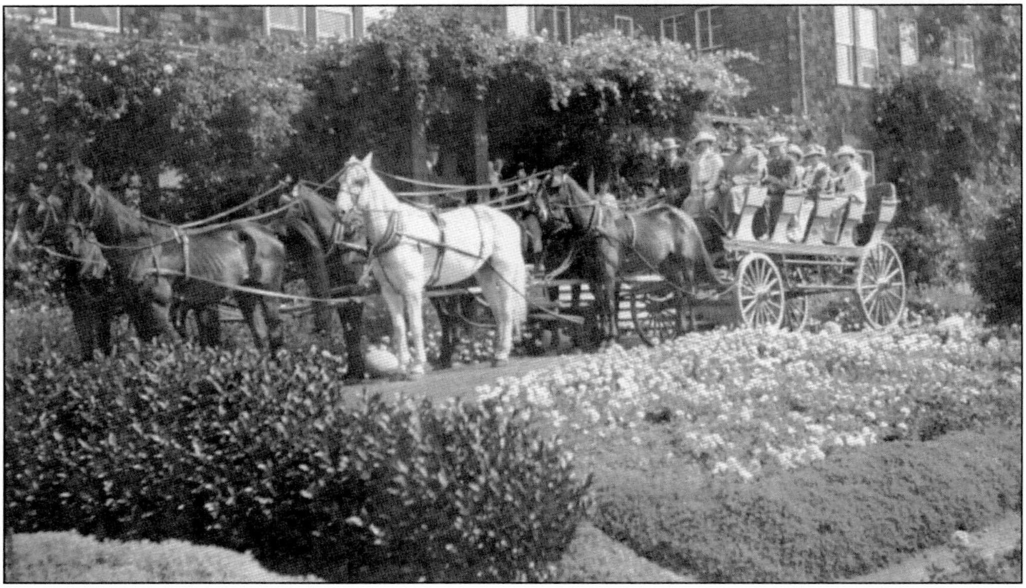

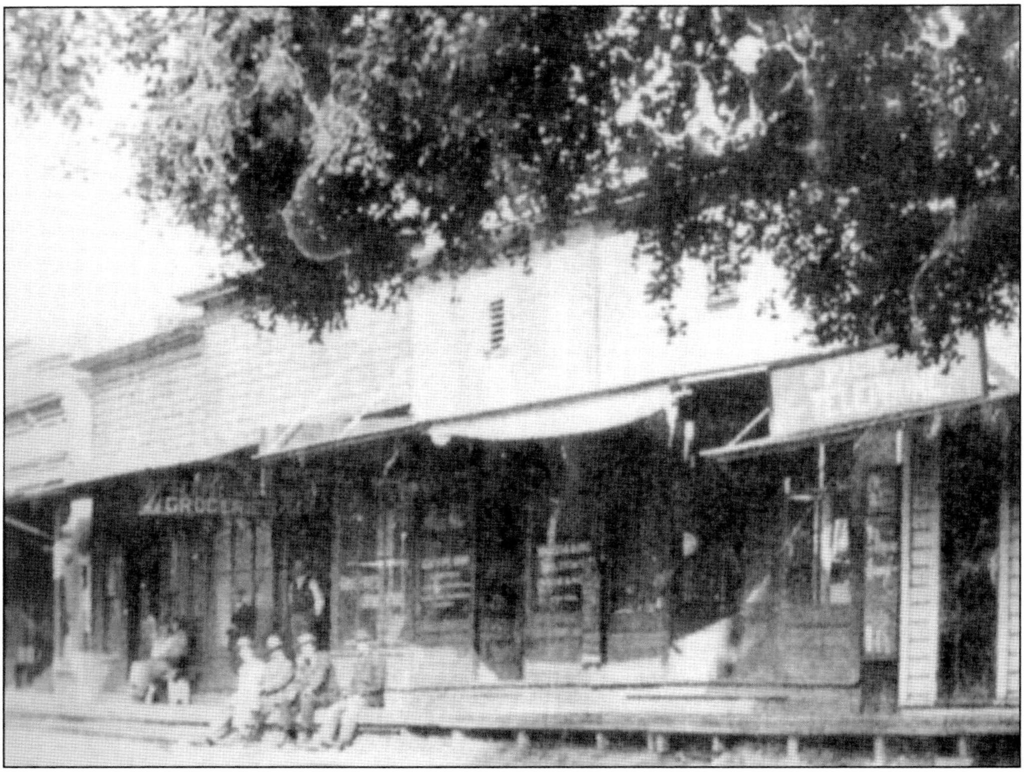

Before the Arcade. The above image shows downtown Nordhoff in 1915 before the arcade was added. Horses and buggies moved lazily down the dirt road that was Main Street, later named Ojai Avenue. The businesses ranged from a drugstore, a barbershop, and a clothing emporium to mercantile stores and a telegraph office. Electricity did not come to the valley until 1913. The arcade, shown below soon after construction in 1917, looks very much the same today. Vehicles of the 1900s parked at an angle to the shops but later had to park parallel to the curb because of increased traffic. Unfortunately, the stately oaks and sycamore trees that Libbey once protected eventually had to be removed for safety reasons. The citizens of Ojai still take pride in keeping their village quaint, minimizing or prohibiting modern developments such as parking meters and fast-food franchises. (Both, OVM.)

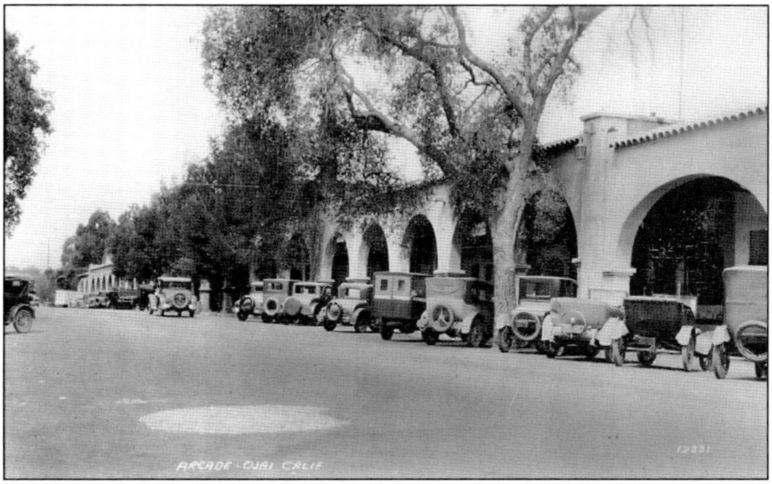

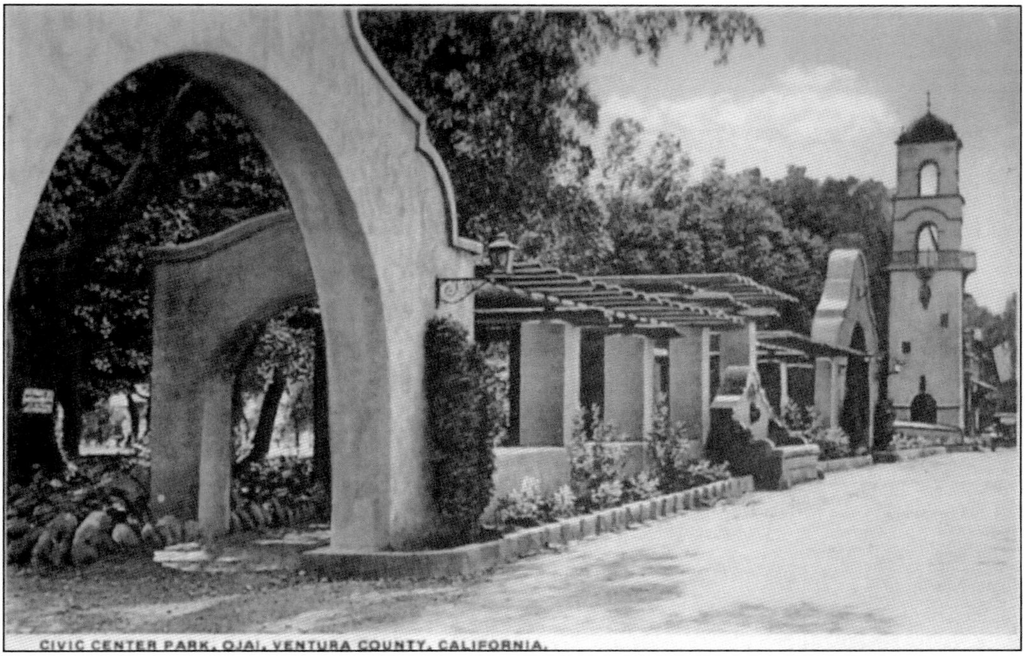

CIVIC CENTER PARK. Edward Libbey, pictured at right with his wife, Florence, around 1901, saw a need to improve the downtown business area, so changes in the valley accelerated sharply after he arrived. His most notable project was financing a face-lift of Main Street. Storefronts were transformed in the Spanish style, a Mission Revival arcaded walkway went down the side of the business area, a Spanish-style tower was constructed for the main post office; and the same style continued with a pergola and a city park across from the arcade. Here, families enjoyed picnics and listened to music. The photograph above, with a view looking west toward the tower, shows the entrance to the park. This became the site of the renowned Ojai Music Festival, which began in 1947 and continues today. (Above, David Mason collection; right, OVM.)

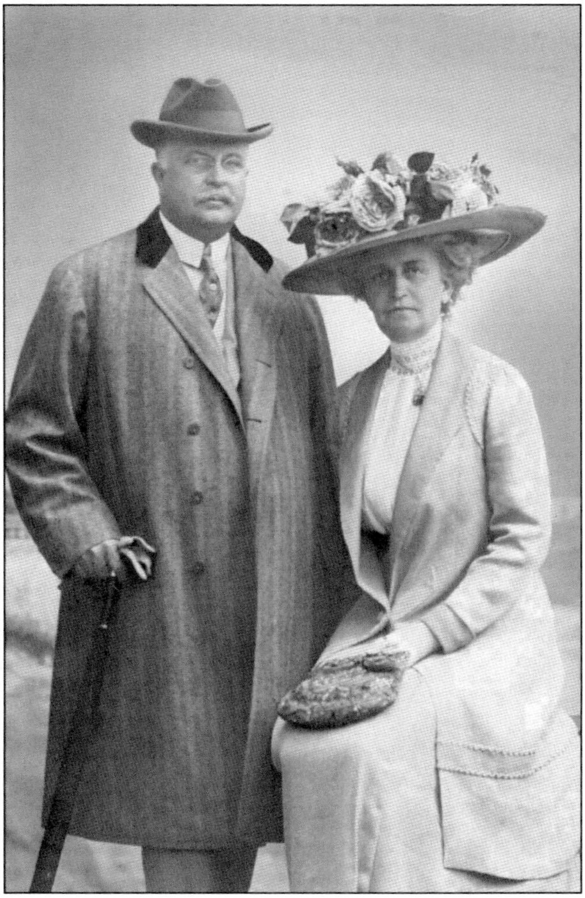

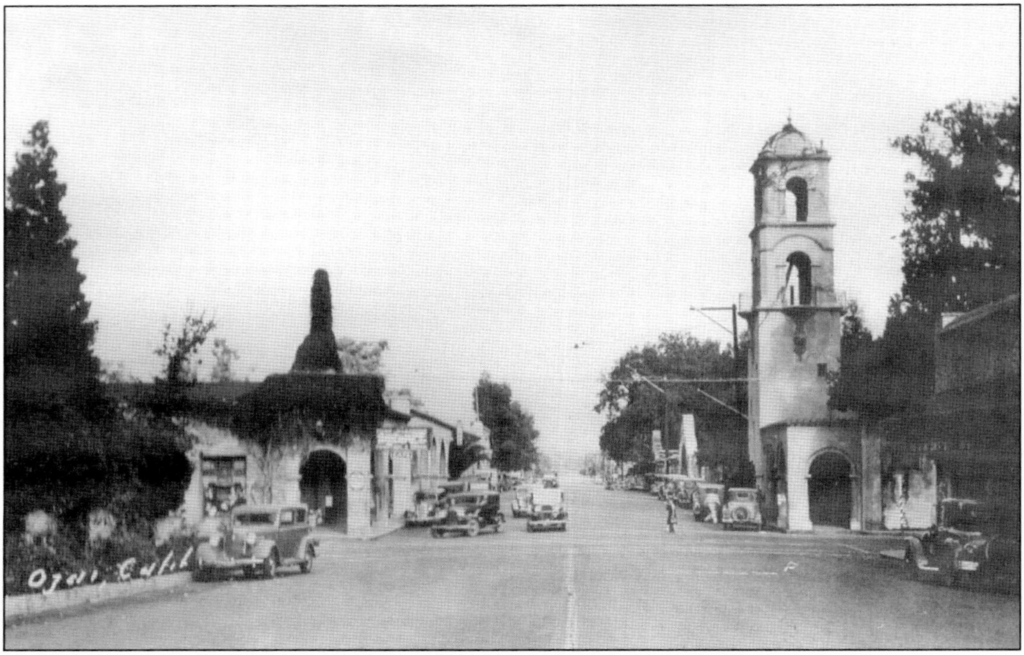

VERY LITTLE CHANGE. When Ojai Valley School opened at its Arbolada location in 1923, the town of Ojai looked very much as it does today. In 1917, the citizens wanted to have a special day to honor Libbey's contributions to the town. The name "Ojai Day" was given to this special occasion, and it is still celebrated. The above image shows the paved Ojai Avenue in 1930. Between 1960 and 1990, the structures and even the park began to deteriorate, but by 1990, there was an increased emphasis on preservation and renovation. The same view in 2011 is shown below. (Above, OVM; below, photograph by author.)

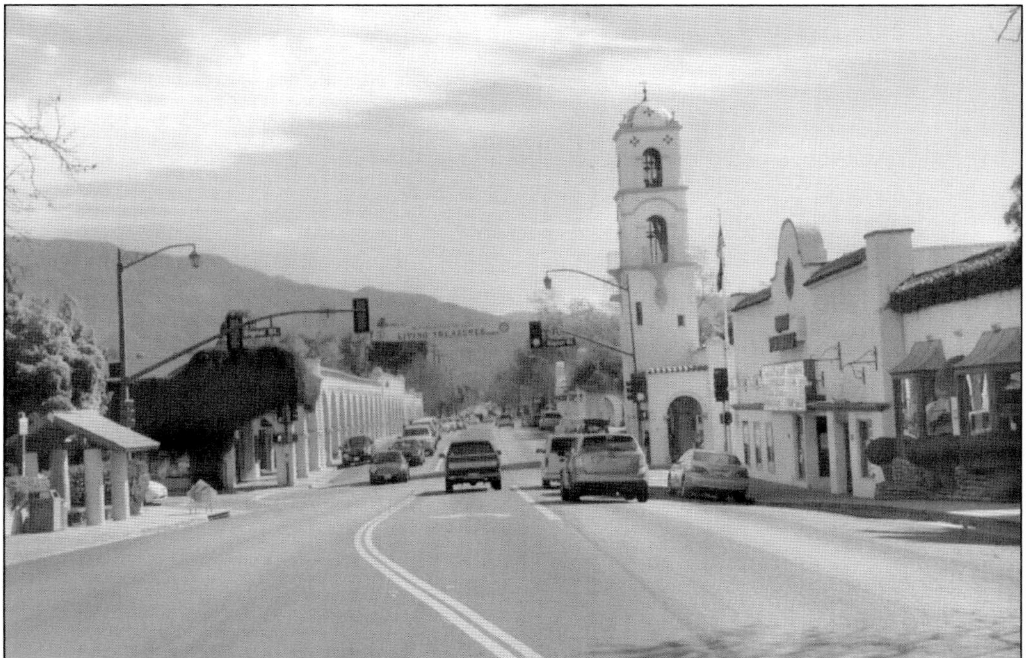

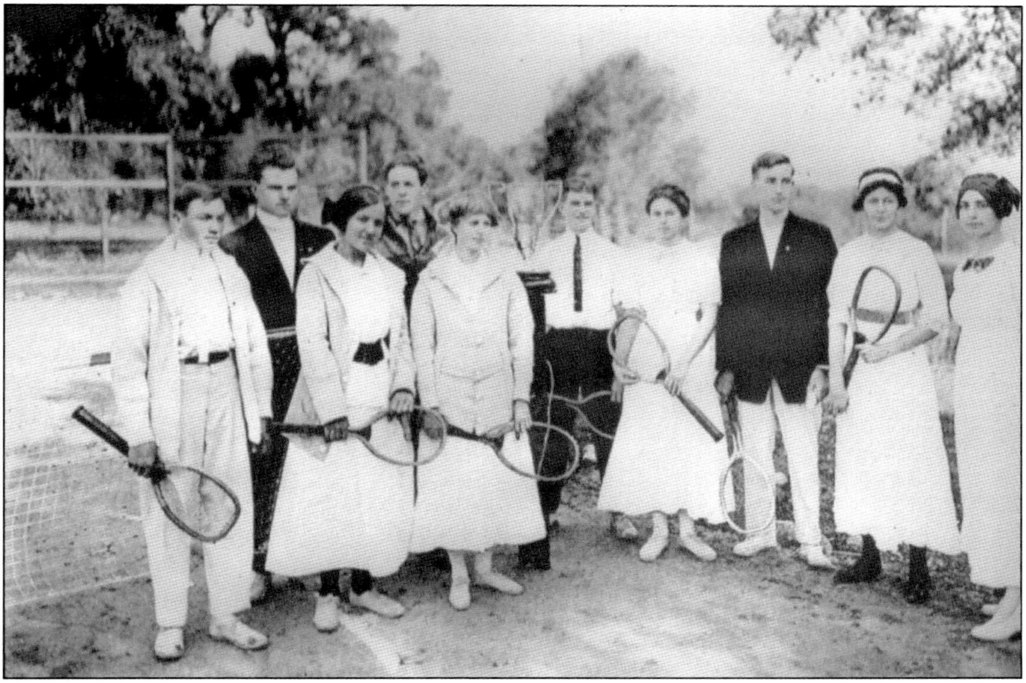

The Ojai. Tennis came to the valley in 1892 when Sherman Thacher and his brother William built the first packed-dirt courts marked with chalk on Thacher property. The first tournament was held there in 1893, and subsequent tournaments began drawing tourists. Men's dress code early in the 20th century required long pants. By 1907, women's interscholastic competition was introduced, and the ladies wore white dresses. By 1912, the Ojai Tournament was the largest amateur tournament held in the United States. In 1917, courts were constructed on land donated by Edward Libbey in the middle of town, and over the years, this tournament, known as "the Ojai," has attained national status. The Ojai tennis tournament celebrated its 100th anniversary in 2000. (Both, OVM.)

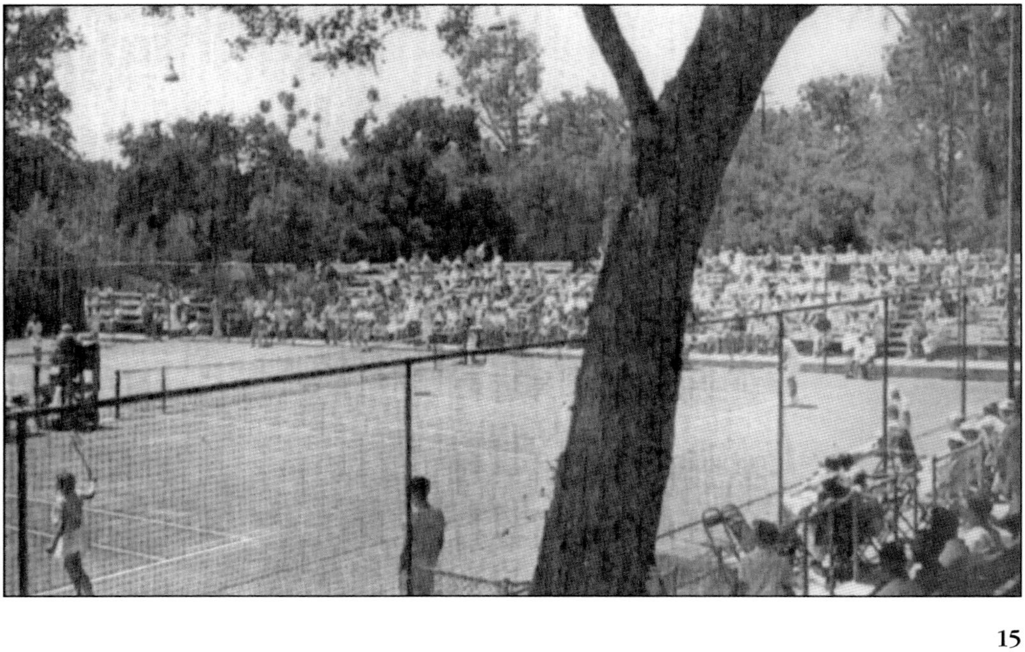

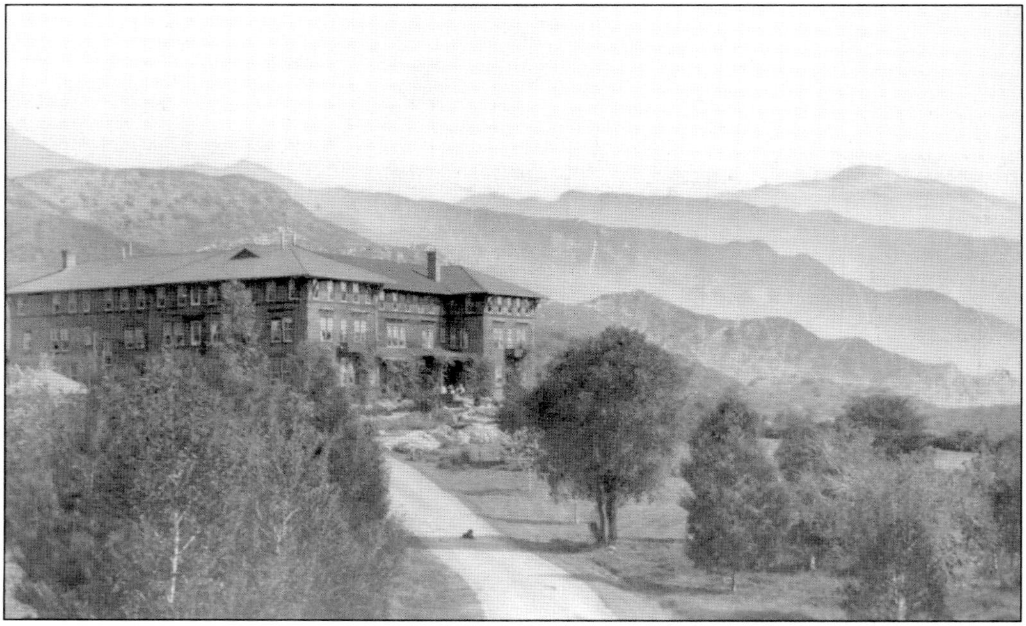

THE FOOTHILLS HOTEL. Given the need for more accommodations, the Foothills Hotel was constructed in the west end of the valley and opened on January 19, 1903. This facility attracted the wealthy clientele that Libbey hoped would purchase property in the Ojai Valley. The hotel burned to the ground in 1917, but was rebuilt in 1918. It continued to flourish until the onset of the Great Depression in 1929. The hotel finally met its demise in 1976, and an Ojai treasure was lost. (OVM.)

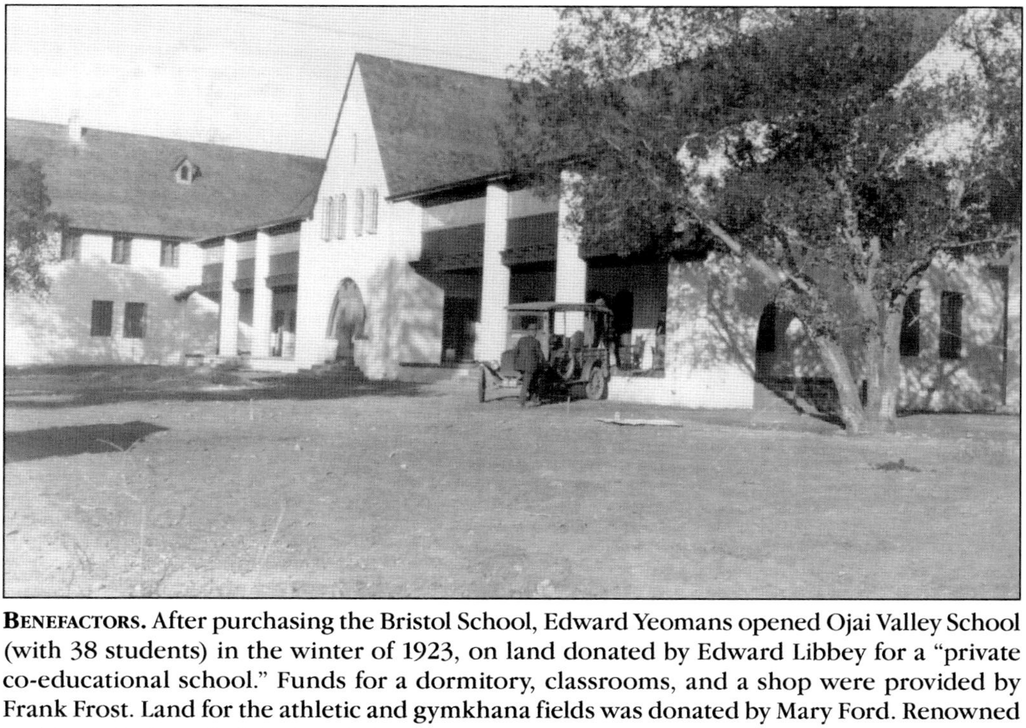

BENEFACTORS. After purchasing the Bristol School, Edward Yeomans opened Ojai Valley School (with 38 students) in the winter of 1923, on land donated by Edward Libbey for a "private co-educational school." Funds for a dormitory, classrooms, and a shop were provided by Frank Frost. Land for the athletic and gymkhana fields was donated by Mary Ford. Renowned architect Wallace Neff designed the new school.

Two

Wanting a Little More for the Children

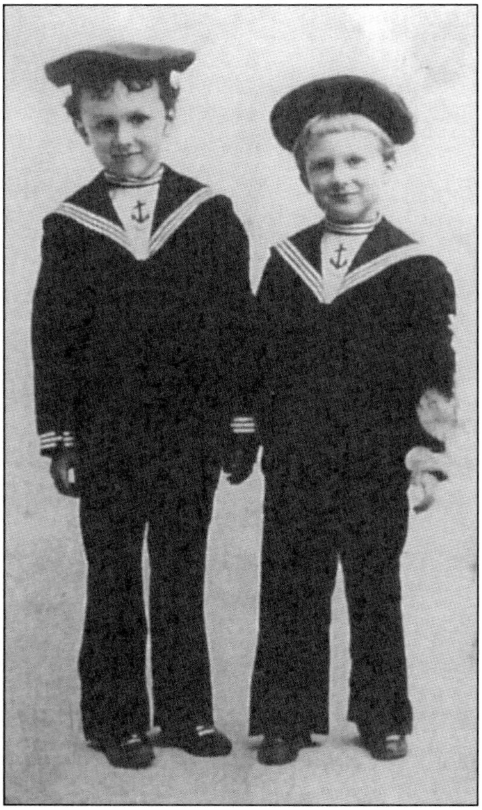

A Simple Beginning. In 1911, Dr. Philip Schuyler Van Patten; his wife, Emily Adams Van Patten; and their two small sons, Philip, age six (left), and Charles, almost four (right), settled in the Ojai Valley. The Van Pattens wanted structure and a broad exposure to life and nature in their sons' lives and thought a small school situation within the home would be ideal. They hired Ida Belle Lamb as a tutor for two hours per day. A year later, Ida Belle, who was getting married, recommended her sister, Olive Bristol, as a teacher for the boys. Olive and her husband, Walter Bristol, taught classes in their own home, located near the present-day northwest corner of Ojai Avenue and Bristol Road. The young boys, along with the Bristols' seven-year-old daughter, Esther, began their studies in the fall of 1912. A large sleeping porch at their home was divided into classrooms to accommodate desks for more pupils. (OVM.)

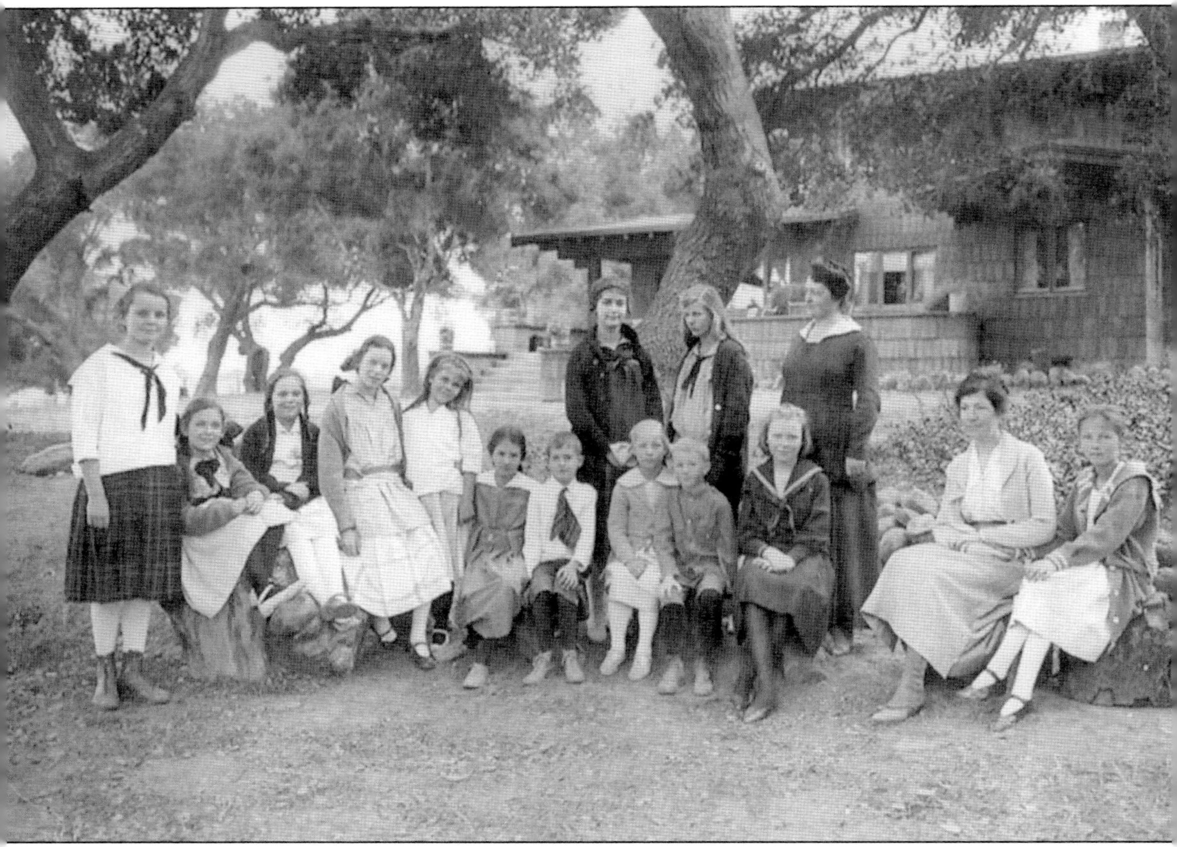

EARLIEST PHOTOGRAPH. This 1914 school photograph is the earliest image of Olive Bristol (standing, far right) and the Bristol School. The school filled a void in many people's plans for their children, and so it continued to grow. By 1915, a small school building was erected to house 12 to 15 pupils, but it was not long until it was bursting at the seams with 25 children. In 1916, at age 11, Philip Van Patten became the first graduate of the Bristol School. The disastrous Ojai fire of 1917 destroyed most of the Bristol School, which was also the family's home. Only the cottages remained, but the Bristols continued educating children. When reconstruction was planned, there was a request for boarding accommodations for six girls. In 1922, Olive retired, and Edward Yeomans bought the school. He reopened it as Ojai Valley School in 1923 on land donated by Edward Libbey between El Paseo Road and Ojai Avenue. While the dorm and classrooms were being constructed, the children remained at the Bristols' home.

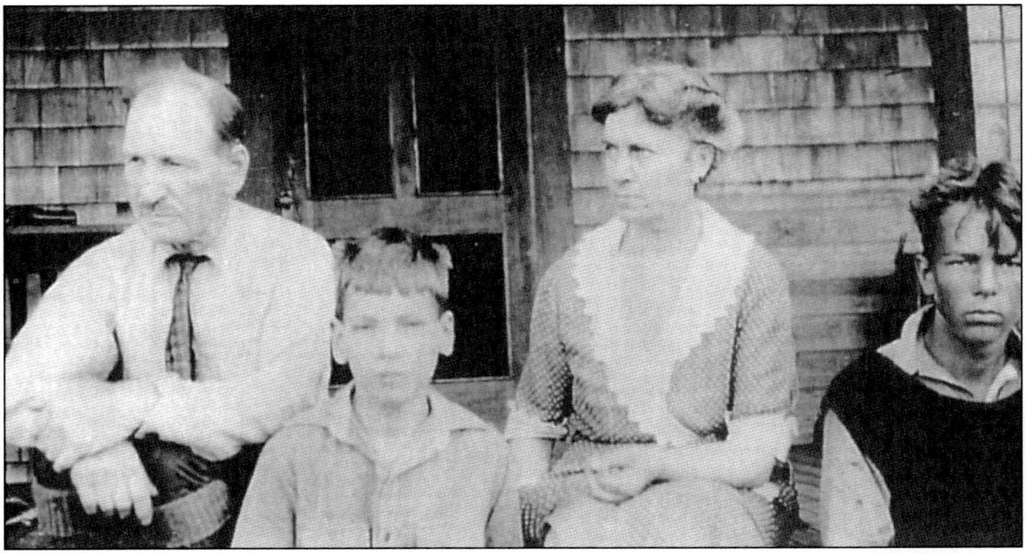

PROGRESSIVE EDUCATOR. Edward "Ned" Yeomans married Julia Day at Lake Forest, Illinois, in 1904. He and his wife adopted a baby, Andrew, in 1911, and three years later, another son, Edward Jr., was born. Desiring a better education for their boys, Yeomans became instrumental in promoting progressive education in the public schools of Winnetka, Illinois. His system encouraged students to progress at their own rates and to be responsible for their own learning. In 1919, the family returned to the Chicago area to give their boys a year in the Francis Parker School. While in Chicago, Yeomans published his progressive ideas on education in his book *Shackled Youth*. The 1922 photograph above includes, from left to right, Ned, Ed, Julia, and Andrew.

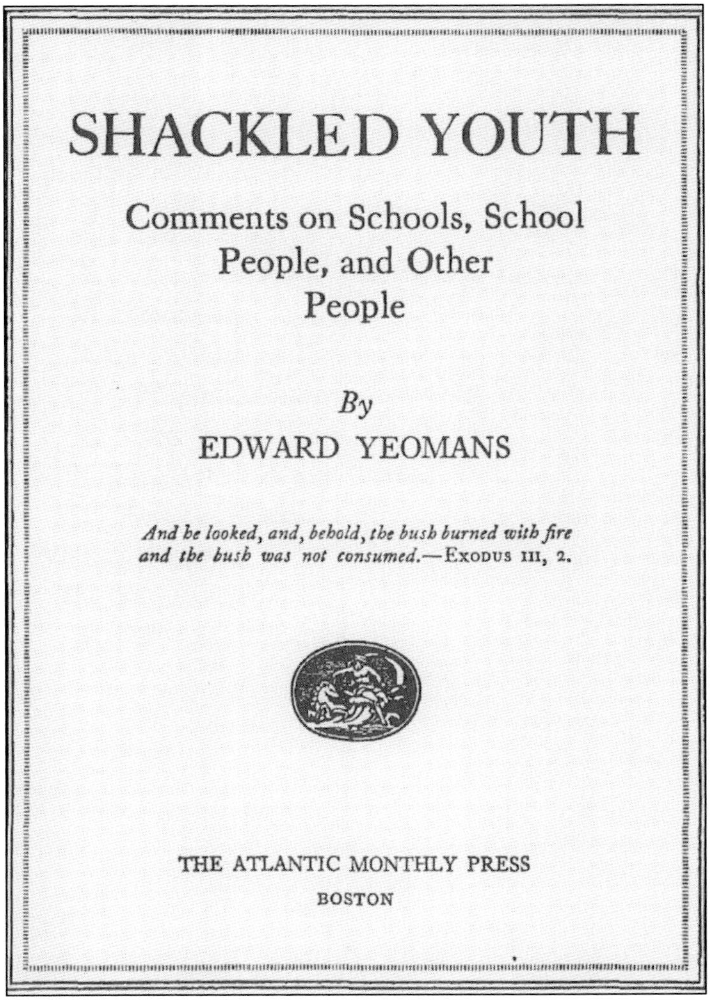

SHACKLED YOUTH

Comments on Schools, School People, and Other People

By

EDWARD YEOMANS

And he looked, and, behold, the bush burned with fire and the bush was not consumed.—EXODUS III, 2.

THE ATLANTIC MONTHLY PRESS

BOSTON

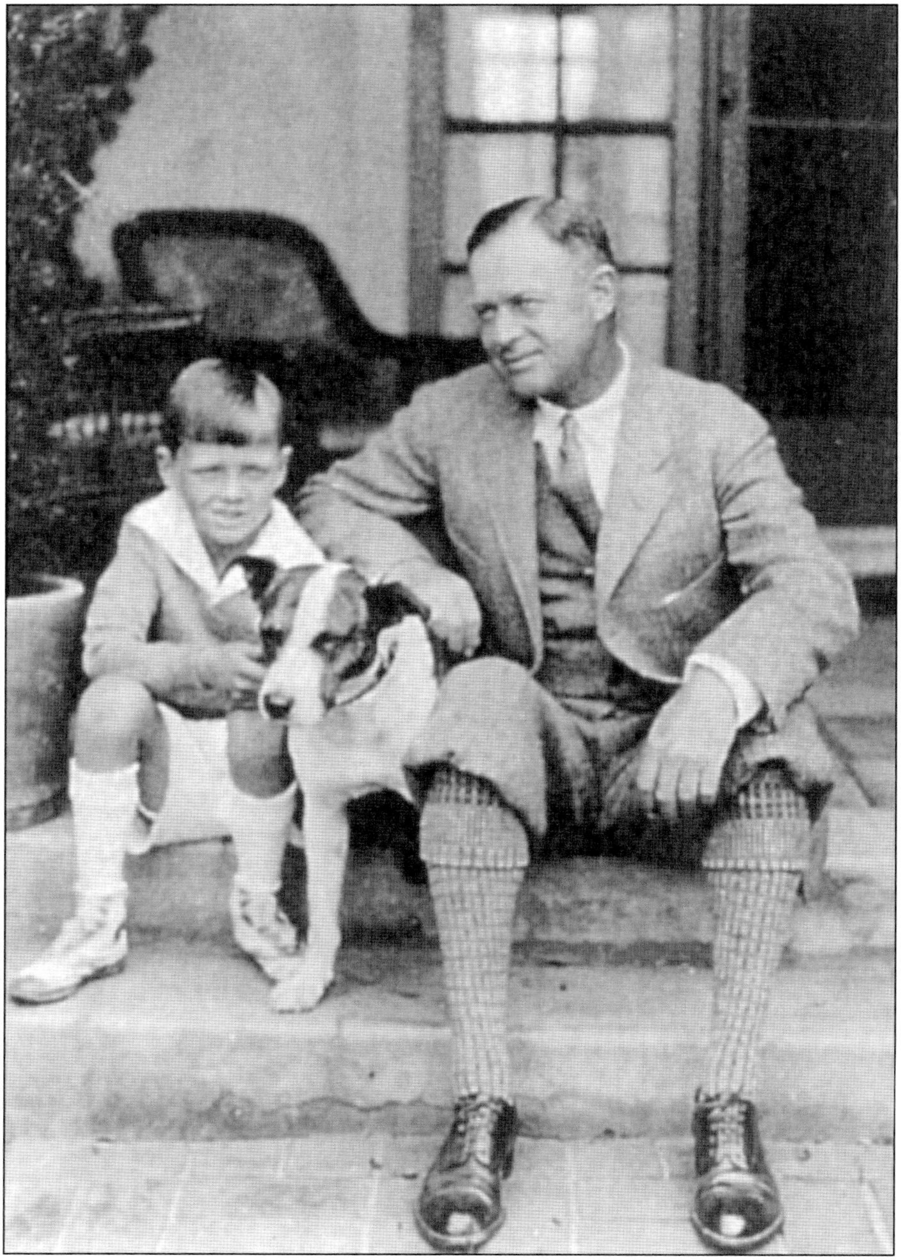

FRANK JEFFERSON FROST. Frank Frost was born in Missouri and earned an engineering degree from the University of Missouri. He had worked in a number of professions, most recently as the treasurer of the Standard Oil Company of New York. As a winter visitor to the Ojai Valley, Frost had read Yeomans's *Shackled Youth* and his pamphlets on progressive education with extreme interest. Frost wanted more for his only son, Morris, and had yet to find a suitable school. Encouraged by his wife, his mother, and Frost, Yeomans was persuaded to leave Illinois and set up residence in Ojai, where Morris Pratt Frost and the Yeomans' boys could experience the outdoor life of the West. In addition, Yeomans could create a school that would put into practice his unique perspective on childhood education. Frost approached Edward Libbey and asked him to donate a parcel of land from his Arbolada tract for this purpose.

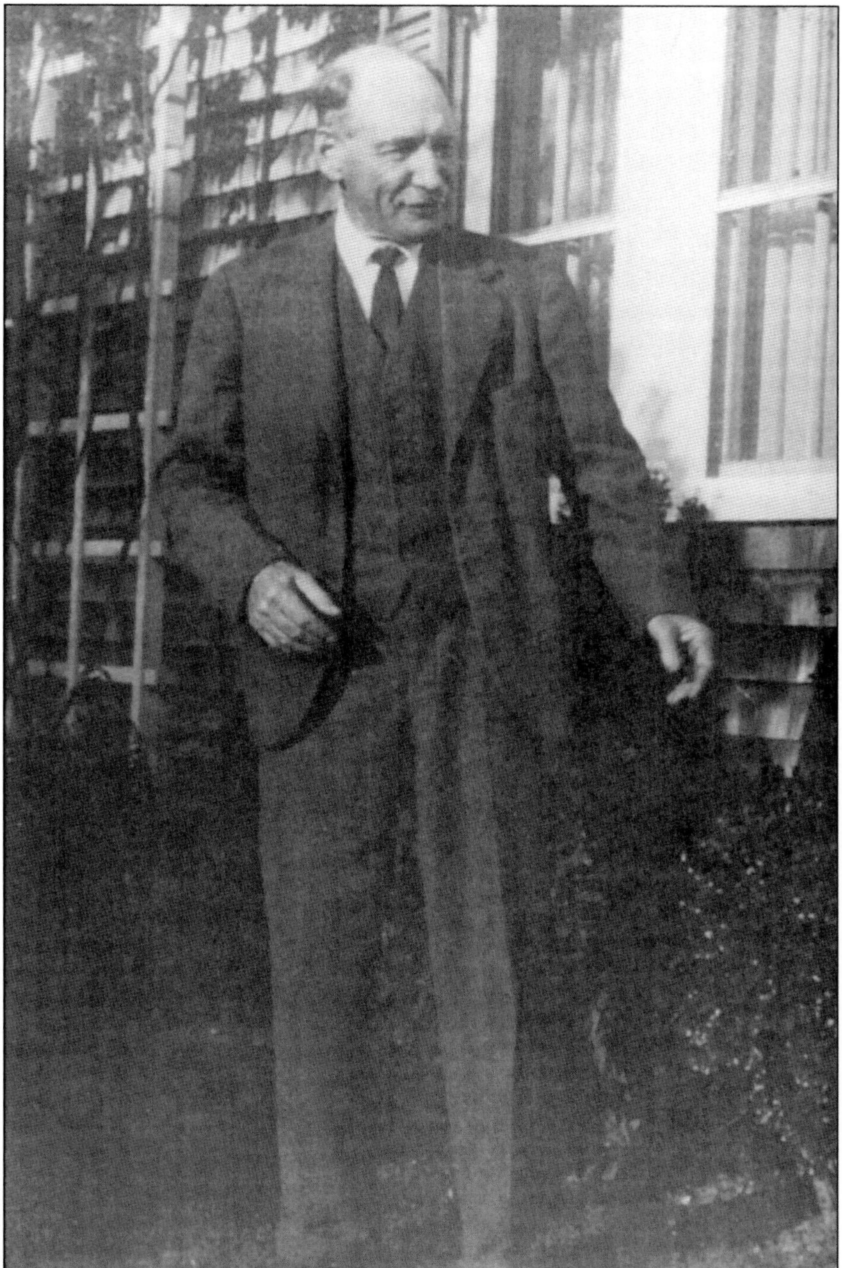

PHILOSOPHER. When Edward Yeomans, pictured here in 1941, first arrived in the Ojai Valley, he was awed by its simplicity and beauty. He was amazed by the orange groves and fruit orchards that ran from Ventura to Ojai. He saw the grandeur of the mountains and the stark beauty of the trees and shrubs on their slopes. Yeomans said, "It was the most beautiful spot on earth." In a sense, Yeomans's educational philosophy was fulfilled by the beauty of the Ojai Valley. Here, he could put the philosophy he had carefully crafted in *Shackled Youth* into practice. Here, he could create a school focused on experiential learning. In his words, "Unless a community is a good place for children, unless it can take care of their growth intelligently, it cannot stand the test of time."

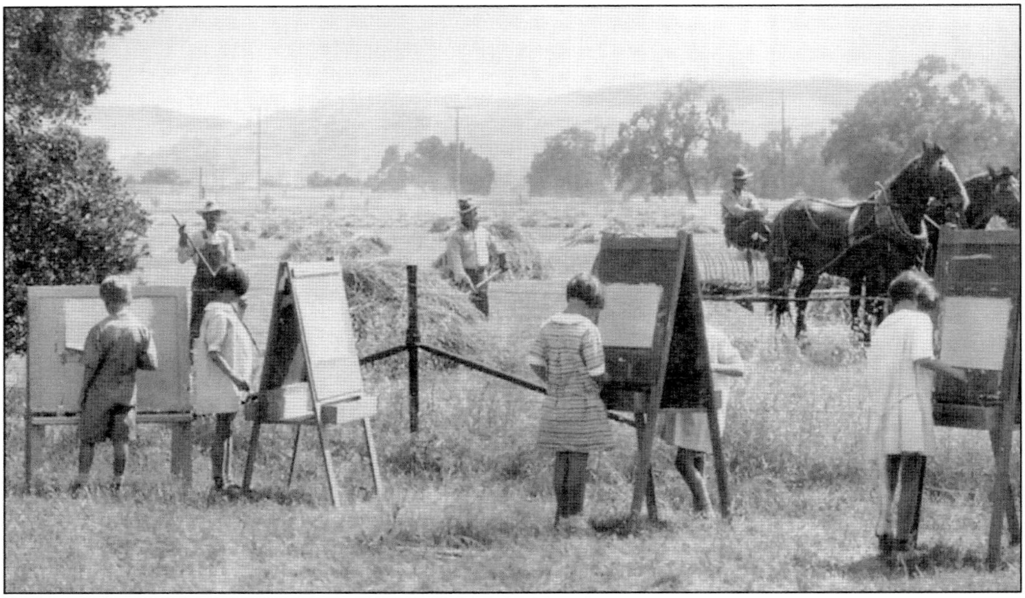

Basic Principles. Yeomans never compromised his educational ideals; educational reform was his dream and desire. He was motivated by the beauty of nature and intriguing conversation and was inspired by life outdoors. He felt compelled to speak on behalf of children across the country. Teaching was an art, and he felt that each teacher must be an artist. "Experiencing instead of telling" was one of his core principles. He envisioned a school where children could pursue artistic expression alongside mathematics, history, and science. Yeomans's precepts in action can be seen in this image, which shows children painting in the great outdoors.

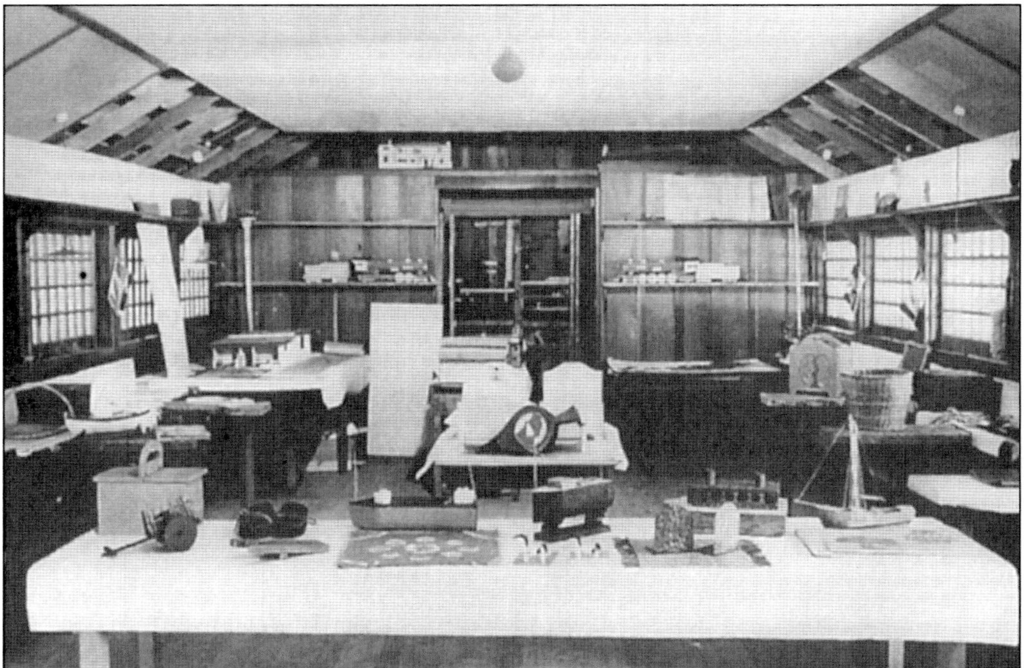

Ned's Shop. Written over the doorway of the OVS shop (this image shows the shop's interior) are the words of Horace, *Integer Vitae*, principles upon which Yeomans based his school.

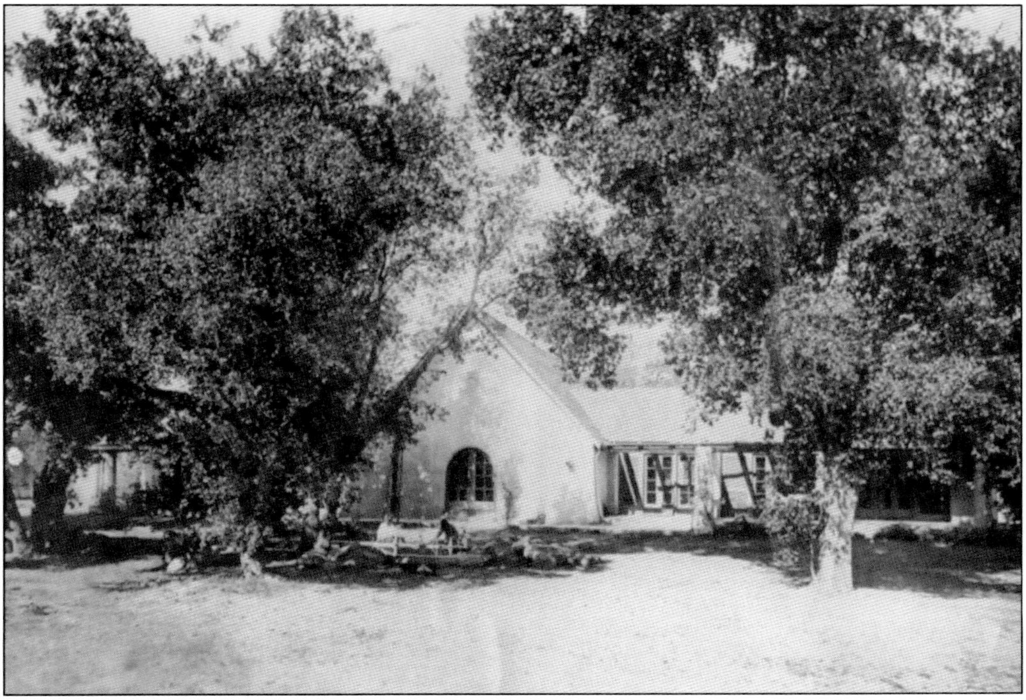

Early Donors. In 1923, Katharine Twichell, one of the founding members of the holding company that owned the school prior to incorporation in 1925, donated money for the first primary classroom building at OVS (above). While construction on new classrooms and the Frost Hall dormitory (below) was being completed, students continued their studies and residence at the Bristol cottages. Mary Bard, a charter member of the board of trustees, donated funds for additional classrooms, an assembly hall, and offices. In 1926, all OVS activities were moved to its present Lower Campus location.

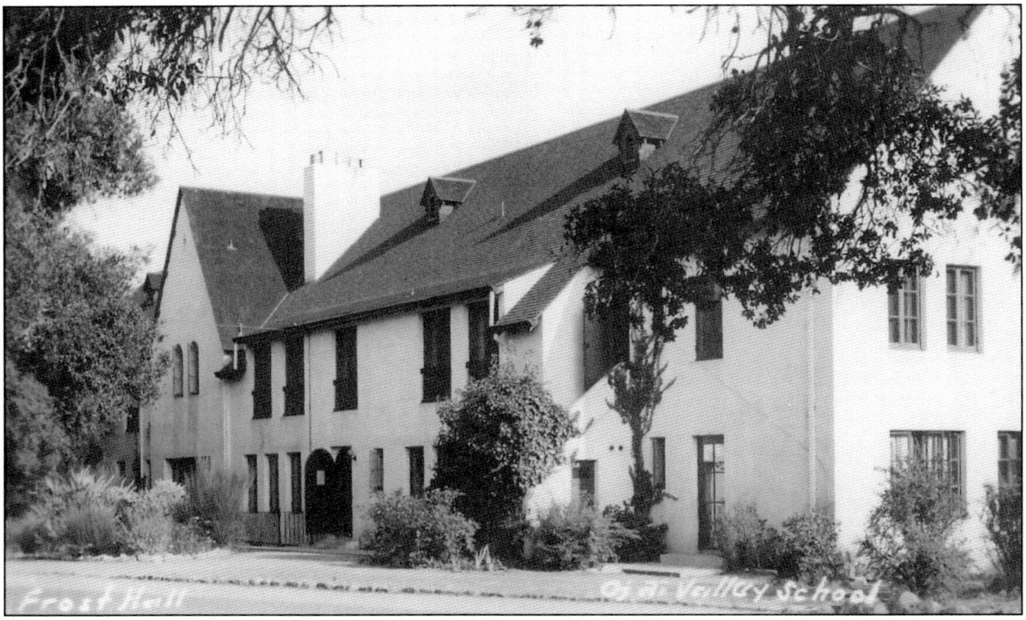

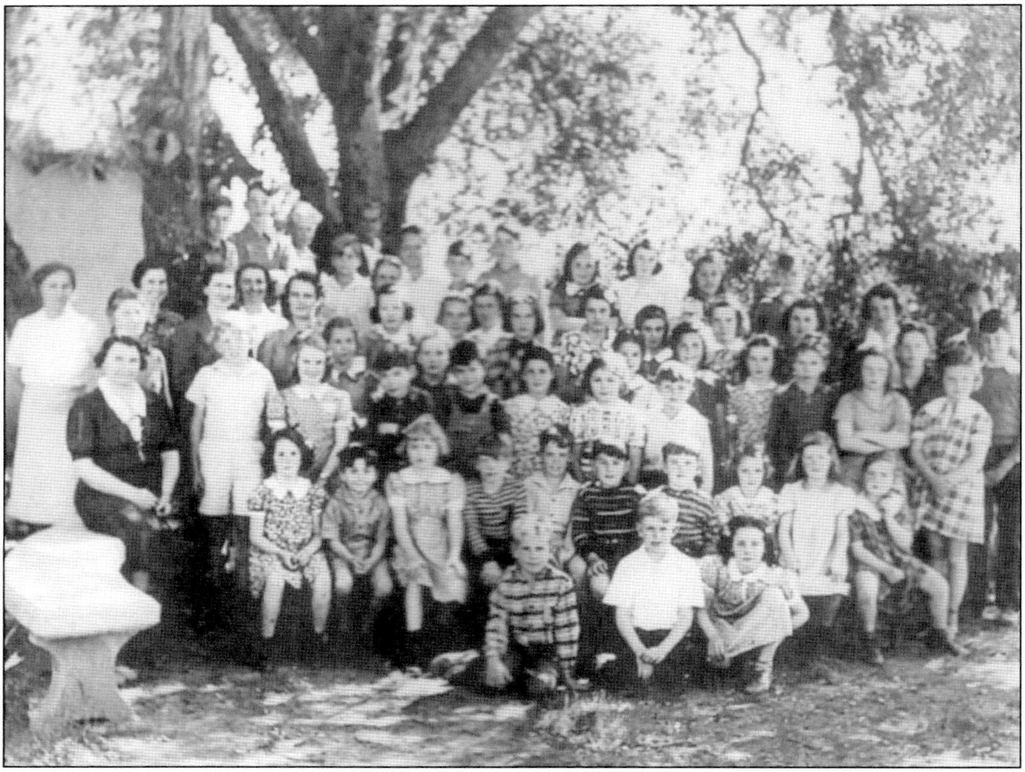

All-School Photographs. From its beginning, the school established a tradition of taking all-school photographs. This tradition has continued as the school has grown. This 1938 picture shows the 45 students enrolled that year.

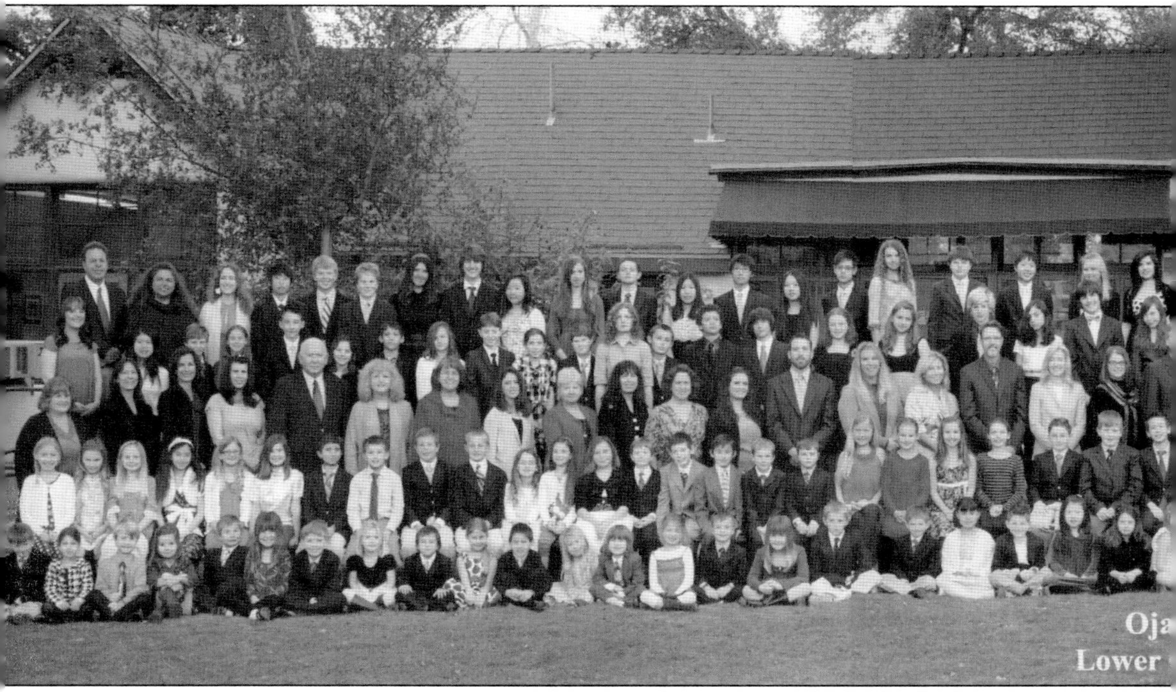

Boarding Student. In 1923, at age seven, Morris Frost was among the first boarders to attend OVS. He took up residence in the Bristol School cottages until the completion of Frost Hall in 1924. Morris's father, Frank, was more than willing to donate anything the school needed to give his son the education that followed Yeomans's beliefs. This image shows Morris at age 10 or 11.

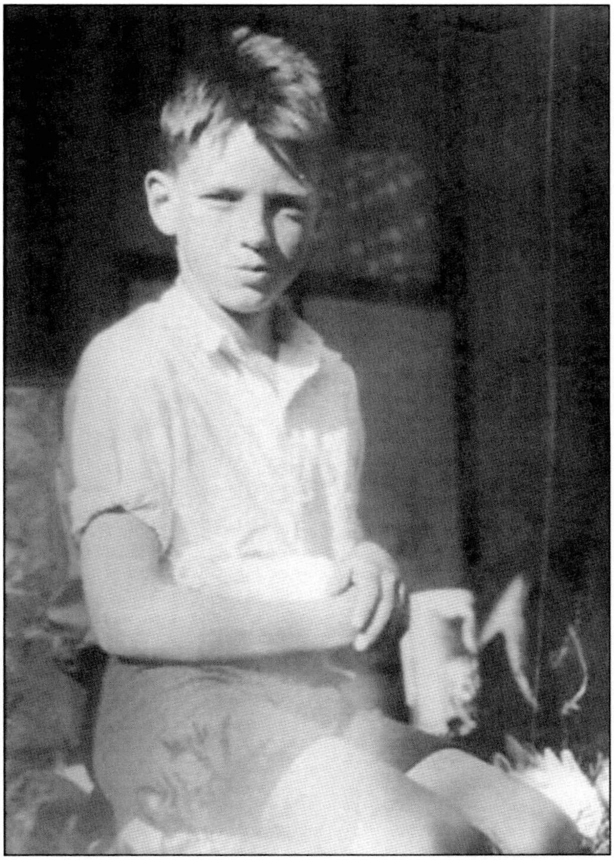

The School Has Grown. This image shows the Lower Campus in 2011. There are nearly five times as many students as in the 1938 image. Note that the dress code has changed but the venerable oak trees remain.

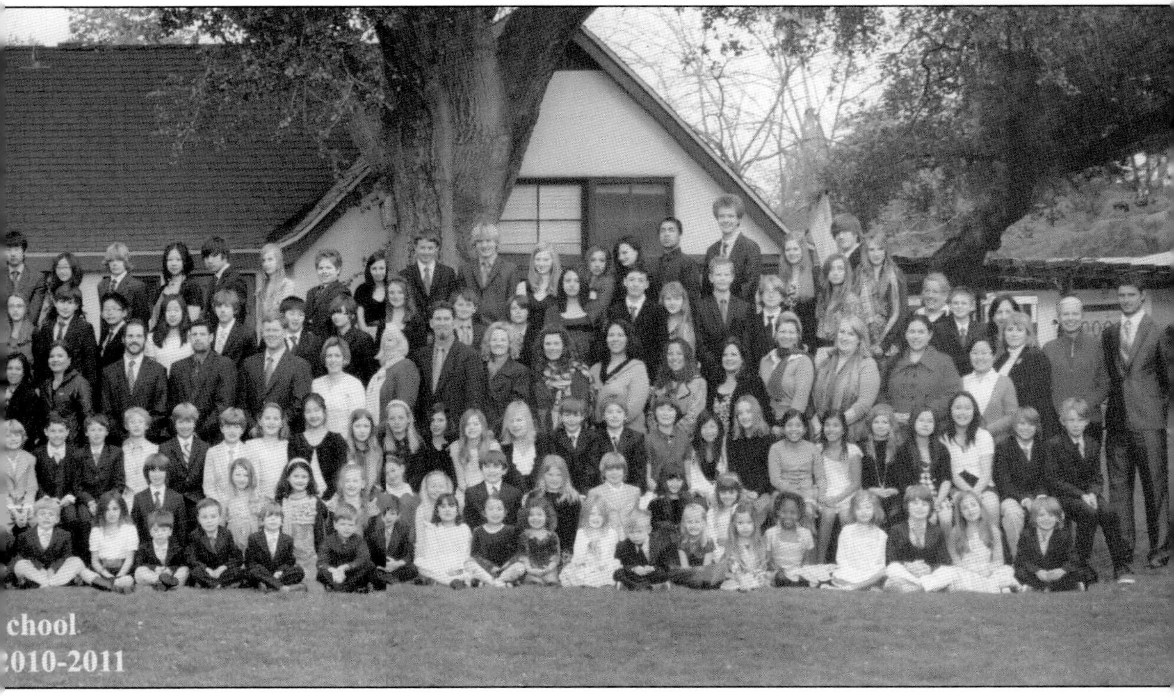

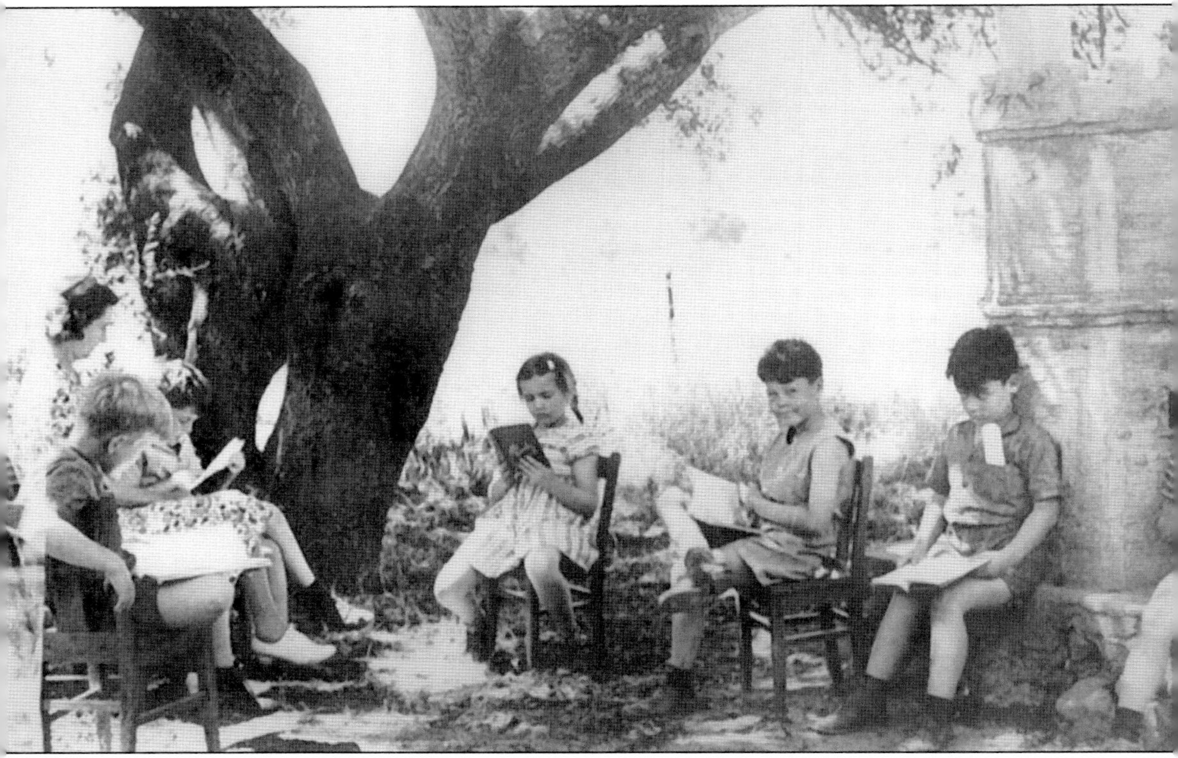

READING. One of Edward Yeomans's legacies is the belief that reading is the foundation of lifelong learning. Even before a student arrived on campus, he or she was expected to prepare for the upcoming year by reading five or six books over the summer and being prepared for an in-depth discussion during the first week of the fall term. Here, Kitty Bragg manages her reading class with quiet firmness. All the children loved and respected her.

Three

The Campus Grows

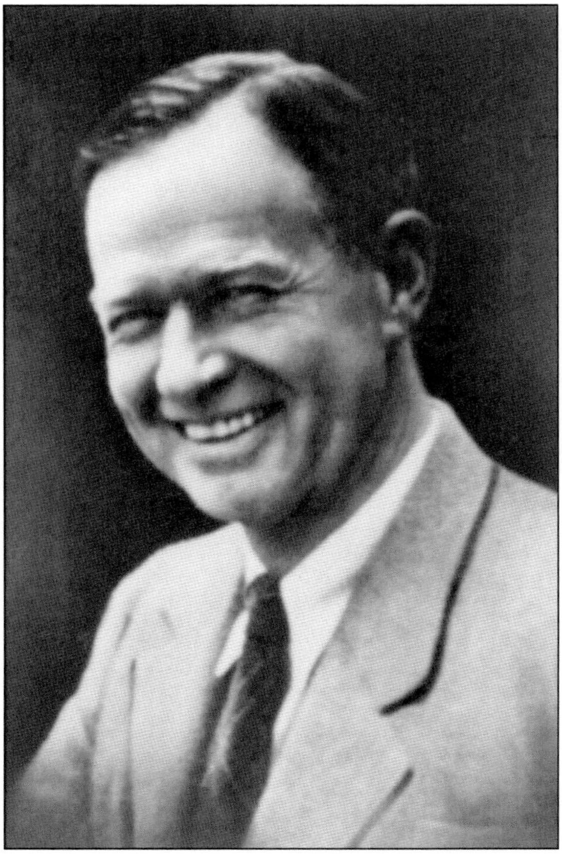

Early Growth. Frank Frost was a widower when he and his son Morris moved to Ojai. Morris attended the Bristol School until the opening of Ojai Valley School in October 1923. As he had promised, Frost supplied the funds to build a shop and a dormitory to hold 30 boarding children. By the fall of 1924, the dorm was filled to capacity. Almost 100 years later, this little school has grown to two campuses, accommodating more than 300 boarders and day students from prekindergarten to 12th grade.

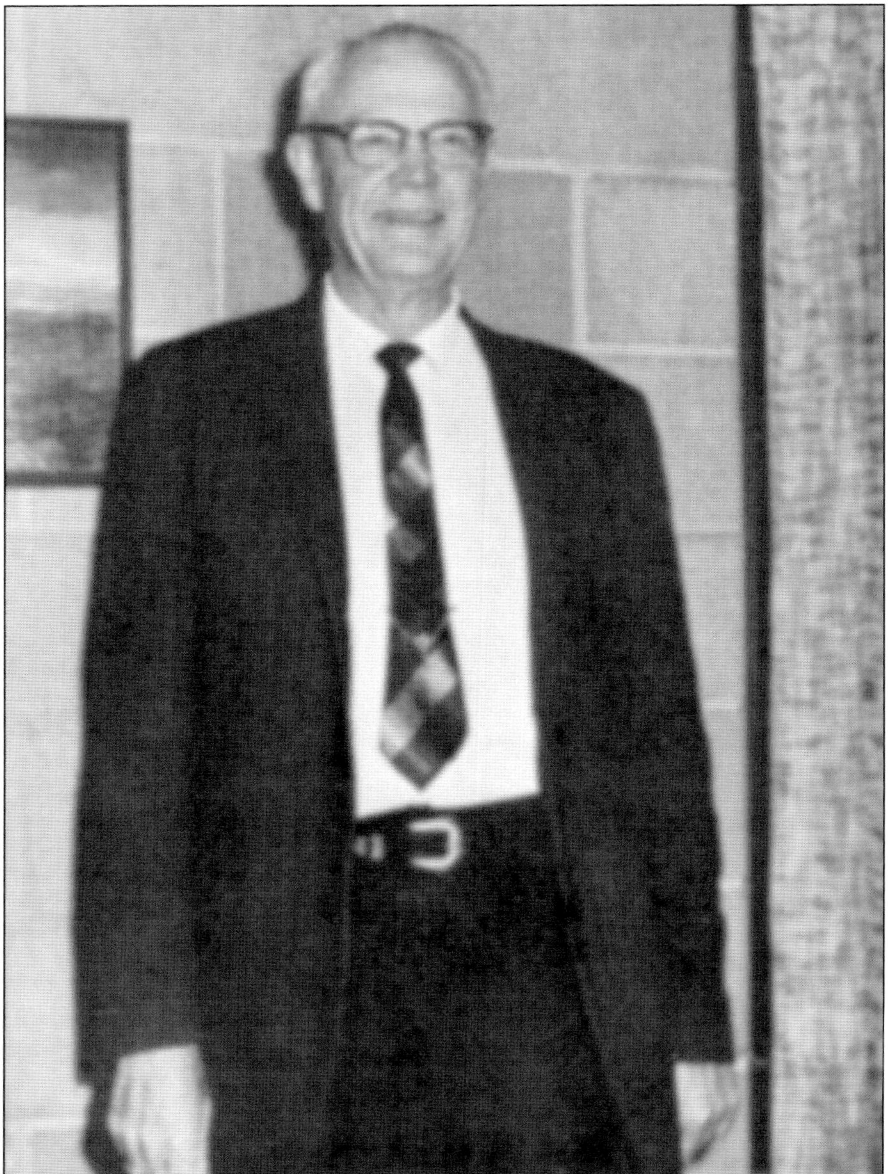

Pioneers. Ojai Valley School began as a tutoring program in the home of Phillip and Emily Van Patten. It grew under the guidance of Olive Bristol and flourished under the vision and philosophy of Edward Yeomans. Although Yeomans's view remained important to the ethos of Ojai Valley School, the "real world" of education inevitably intervened. Issues of funding and concerns that students were not receiving a conventional education were raised by parents and faculty. This eventually led to a restructuring of the school's daily schedule and curriculum. Classes were set up to be better aligned with standard subject matter, all the while retaining an emphasis on creativity, experiential learning, and individuality. This transition was orchestrated by a series of exceptional individuals, beginning with Gudrun Thorne-Thomsen and continuing with Wallace Burr (pictured). Teachers often worked without pay for long periods because they believed in the education of children and the values of the school's founders.

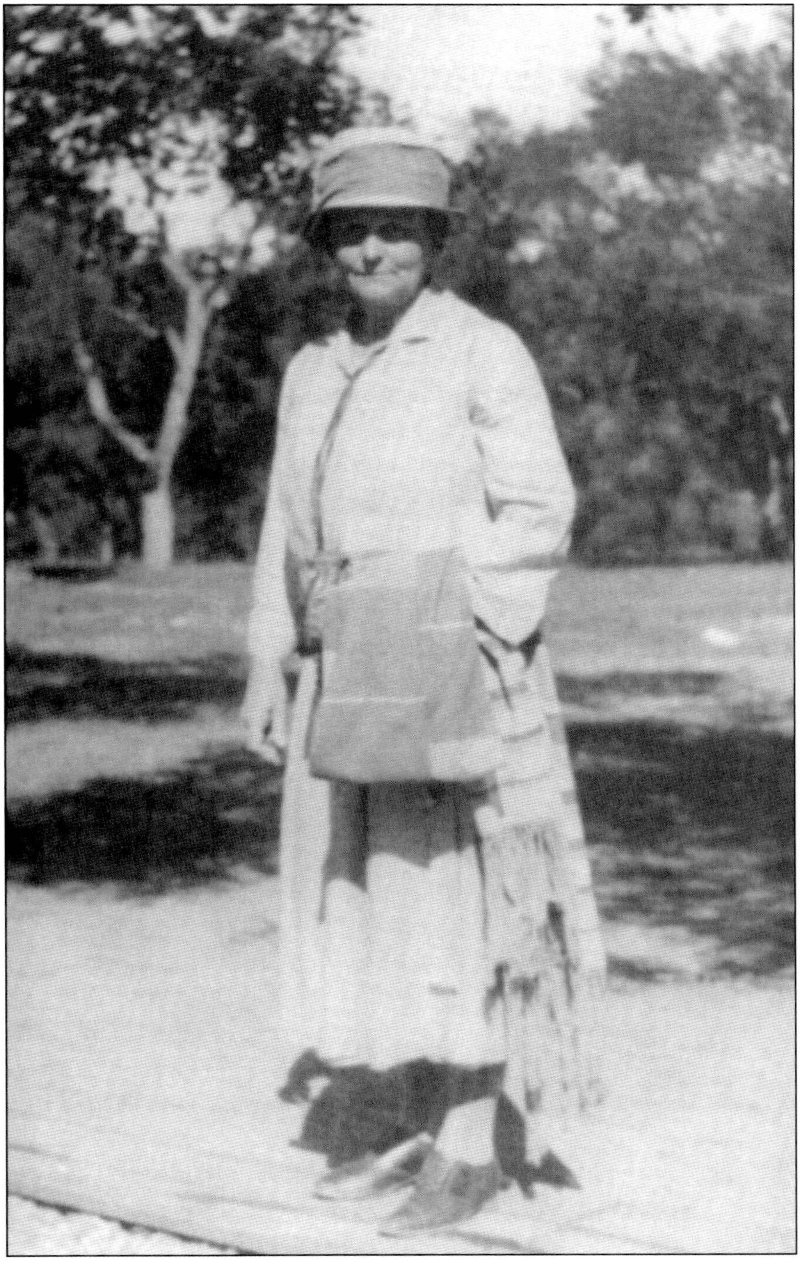

First Lady in Charge. Olive Bristol was contemplating retirement in 1921, and Yeomans saw an opportunity to open his own school with the existing Bristol enrollment. He agreed to purchase the school from the Bristols in 1922. The transfer took place on March 15, 1923, when the Bristol School became Ojai Valley School, continuing to operate on the Bristol property while the new campus was being completed. Then, tuition was $200 a year. Yeomans selected Gudrun Thorne-Thomsen (pictured), an advocate of progressive education and a Norse mythology teacher whom he had met in Chicago in 1919, as the first headmistress. One of her teachers, Kitty Bragg, admired her administrative abilities: "Mrs. Thorne-Thomsen was an exacting headmistress, but supported and defended her teachers, if necessary, until they proved inadequate or unworthy, in which latter case they didn't stay long at the school."

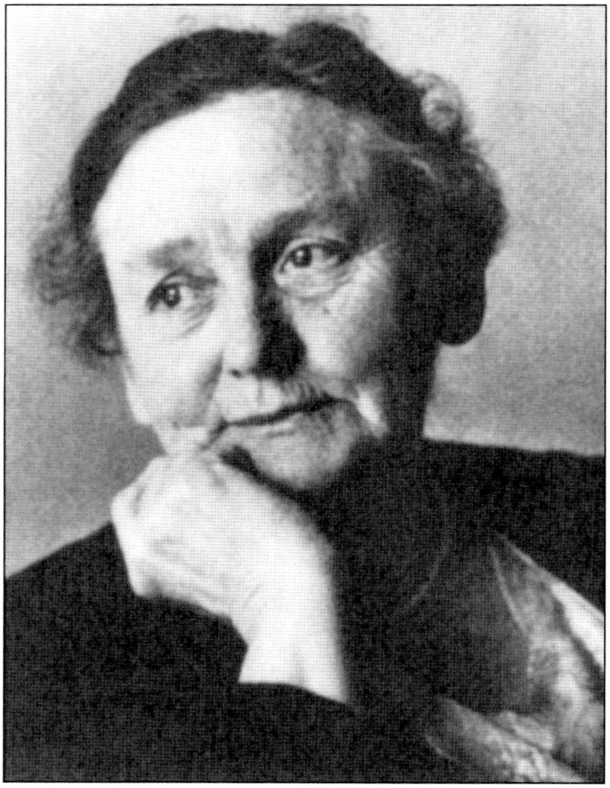

A Woman of Many Talents. When the Bristol School became Ojai Valley School in 1923, it was agreed that Thorne-Thomsen would make decisions regarding educational and disciplinary matters as the new headmistress. She was known for her lectures on children's literature and on improving the standards of education. She authored several children's books and was a much-loved storyteller. Thorne-Thomsen was a stern disciplinarian and served as headmistress from 1923 to 1936. In 1925, during her term, the first board of trustees was appointed. Those selected to serve on the board were Morgan Barnes, Frank Frost, Georg Thorne-Thompson, Carl Lindin, Mary Bard, and Edward Yeomans. When the school and its students moved to the new campus, there were 48 day students and 17 boarders.

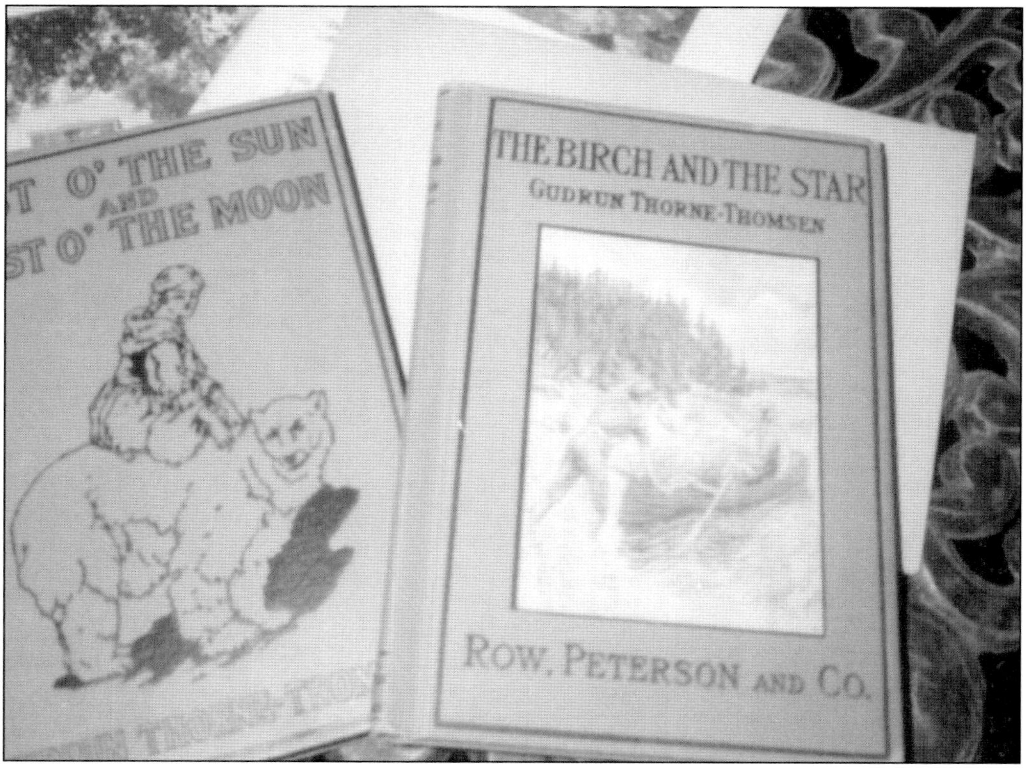

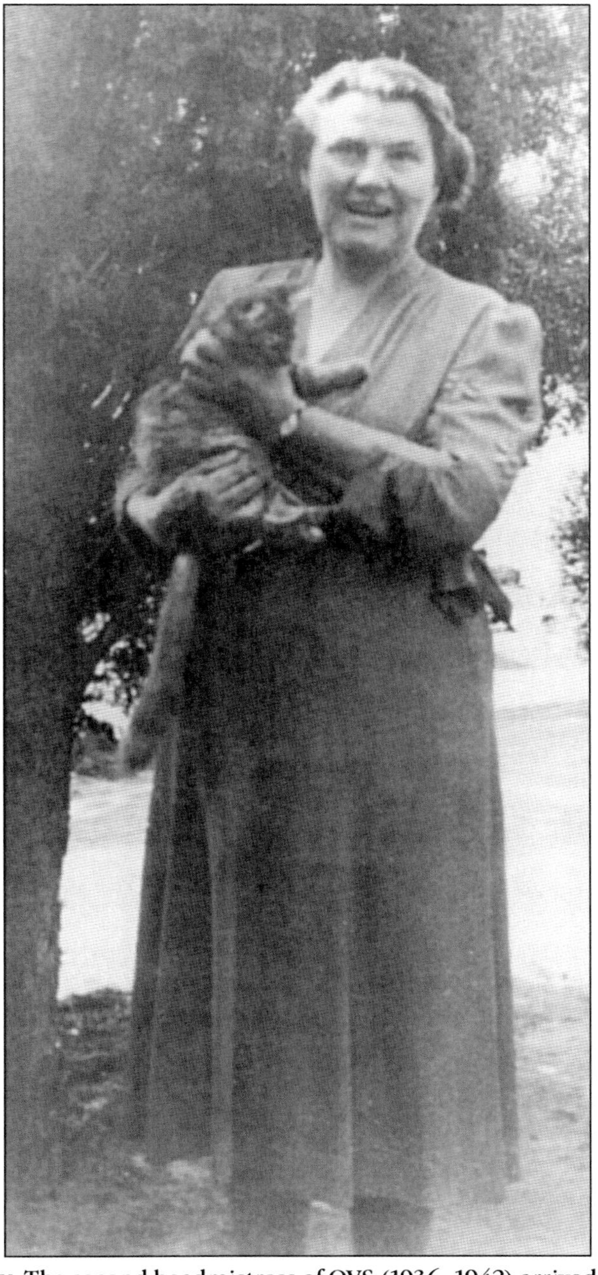

Myra Reynolds Linn. The second headmistress of OVS (1936–1942) arrived during the school's 14th year. She was trained in the Montessori method and married a young citrus rancher, Stanley Linn, in 1915. Together, they raised three daughters. Myra met Edward Yeomans in 1936 and discovered that his philosophy was very much like her own. According to John Herbold, "Mrs. Linn was a great soul who fought to hold the school together." She also served as teacher, housemother, and curriculum developer. She was a strong but kind disciplinarian. Promoting progressive education in the 1930s, when the economy was struggling, made it difficult for OVS to survive. Myra Linn helped to ease the burden by introducing the concept of faculty residents. This gave the children role models inside and outside the classroom and a true "sense of family."

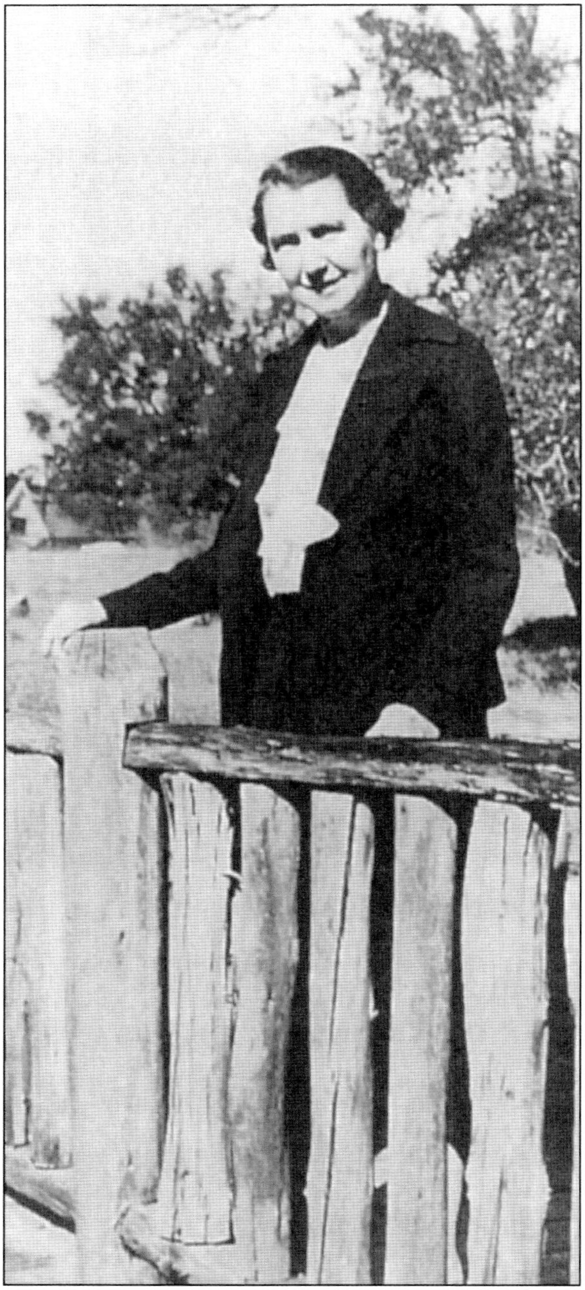

An Expectation of Greatness. Kitty Bragg, who came to OVS in 1931, was known for generating excitement in the elementary classroom. During her 26-year career at OVS, she inspired her children through kindness, consistency, and magnetism. It has been said that if one expects greatness, one will achieve it. Bragg expected greatness from her students, and they did not disappoint her. She was loyal to her children even through the school's lean financial years. Bragg was willing to take a cut in pay and also serve as a dorm parent in order to help keep the school on its feet. She was an exceptional teacher and leader. Both the head of teacher training at Santa Barbara State College and Wallace Burr, her principal for much of her career, called her one of the finest primary school teachers in California.

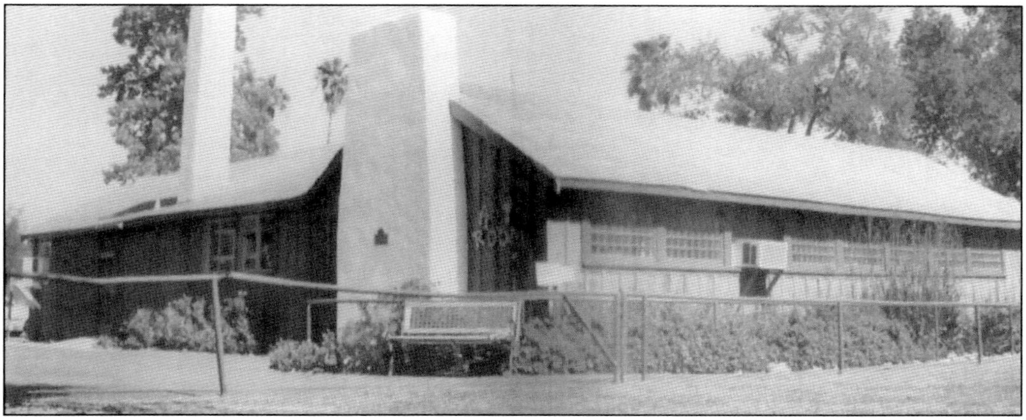

THE HUB. Yeomans's belief in hands-on education meant that the shop was the hub of the school. Yeomans would read aloud the works of William Shakespeare, Walt Whitman, and Emily Dickinson while children worked on both art and craft projects by the warmth of the fire. The students took great pride in their own creations and were inspired by Yeomans to pay particular attention to detail. Yeomans was not concerned with the management of the school; he was confident that Thorne-Thomsen and her teachers were capable of running the instructional aspects of the institution while he supervised creative activities from his beloved shop.

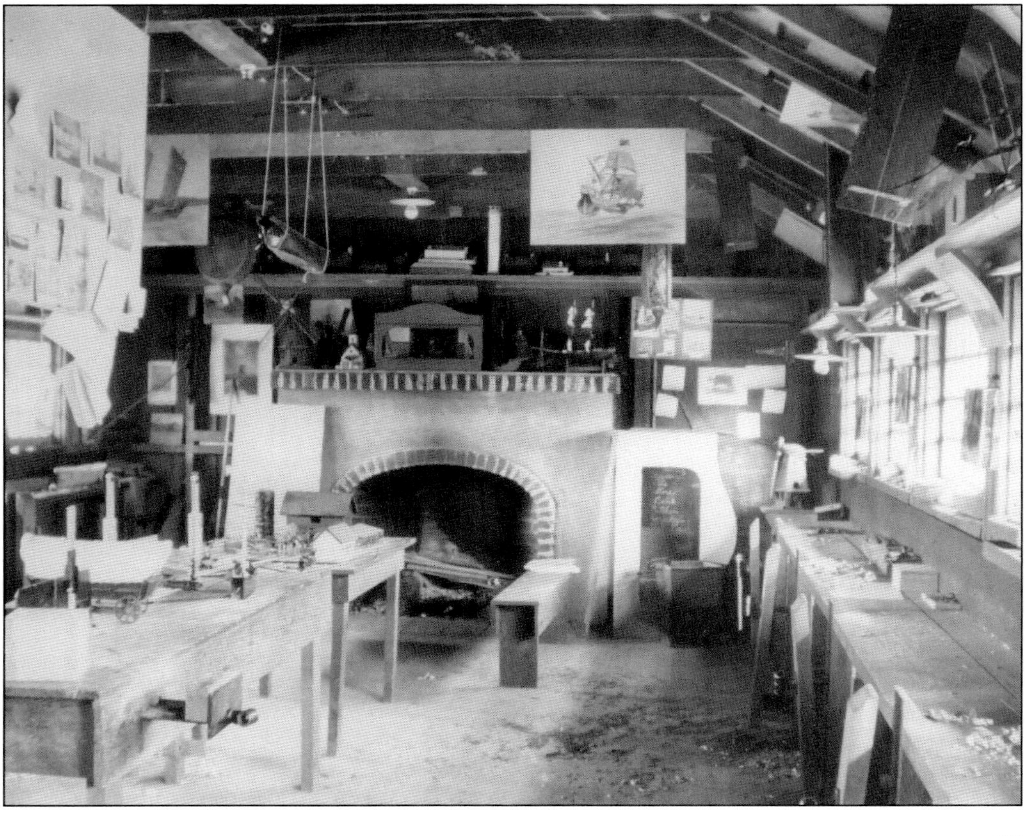

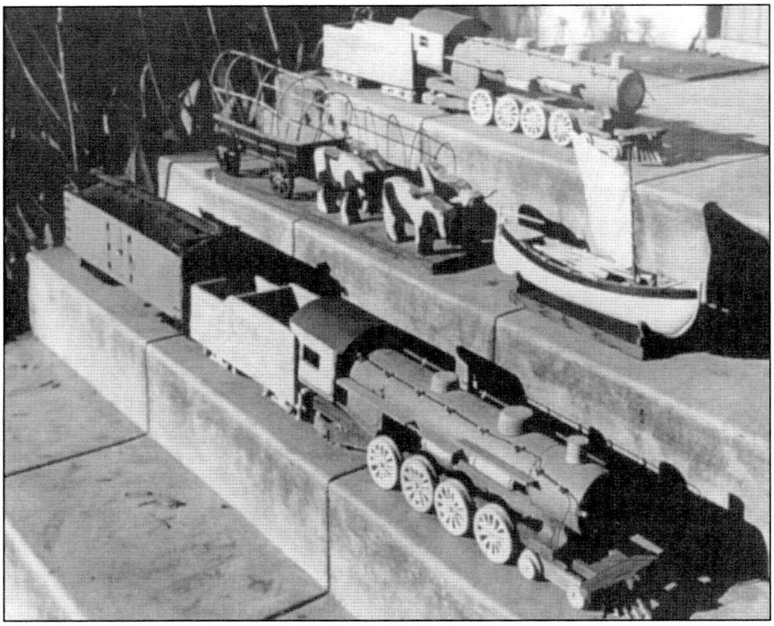

Hands-On Education. Anne Wilkinson recalled, "No one can be happy unless a part of each day is spent creating with the hands; this is the very core of Mr. Yeomans's creed." Indeed, Yeomans seemed happiest and most at home when creating in his shop. This image shows models fashioned from wood by Yeomans.

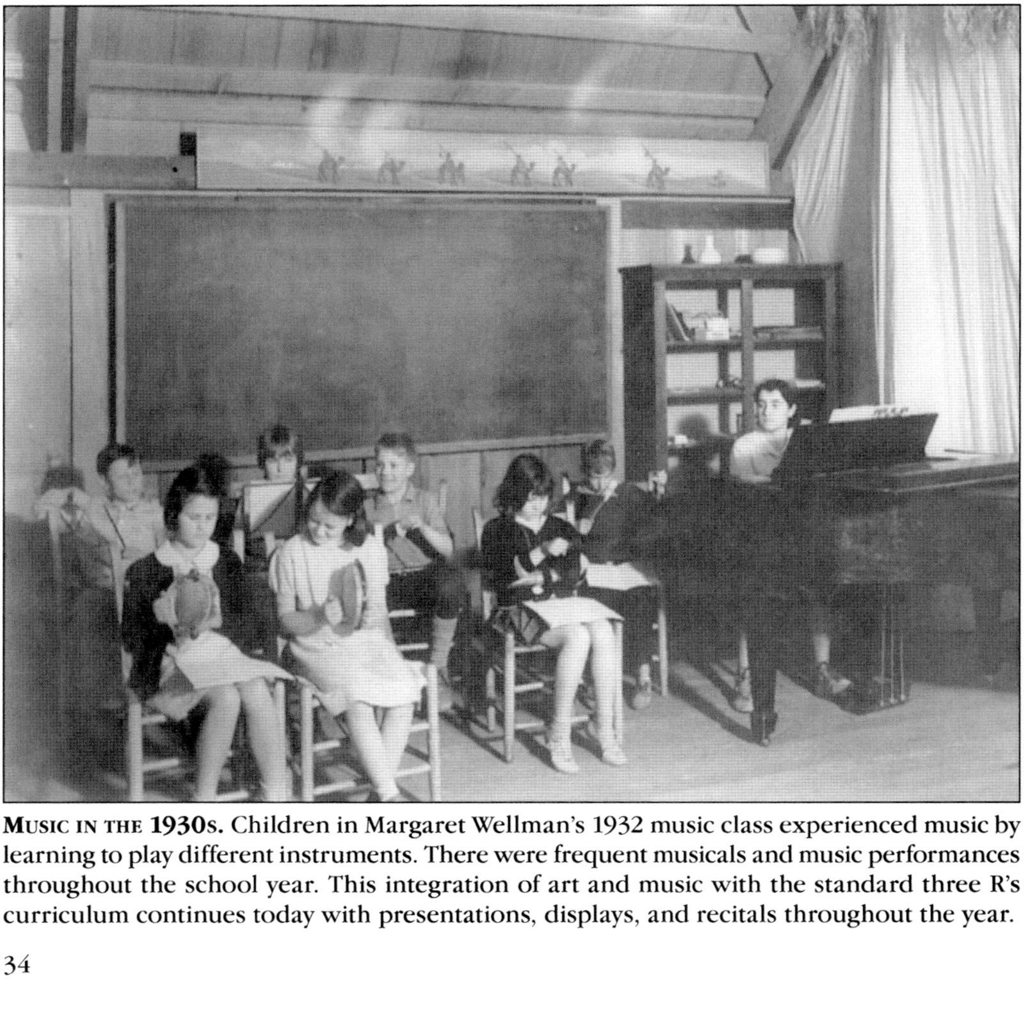

Music in the 1930s. Children in Margaret Wellman's 1932 music class experienced music by learning to play different instruments. There were frequent musicals and music performances throughout the school year. This integration of art and music with the standard three R's curriculum continues today with presentations, displays, and recitals throughout the year.

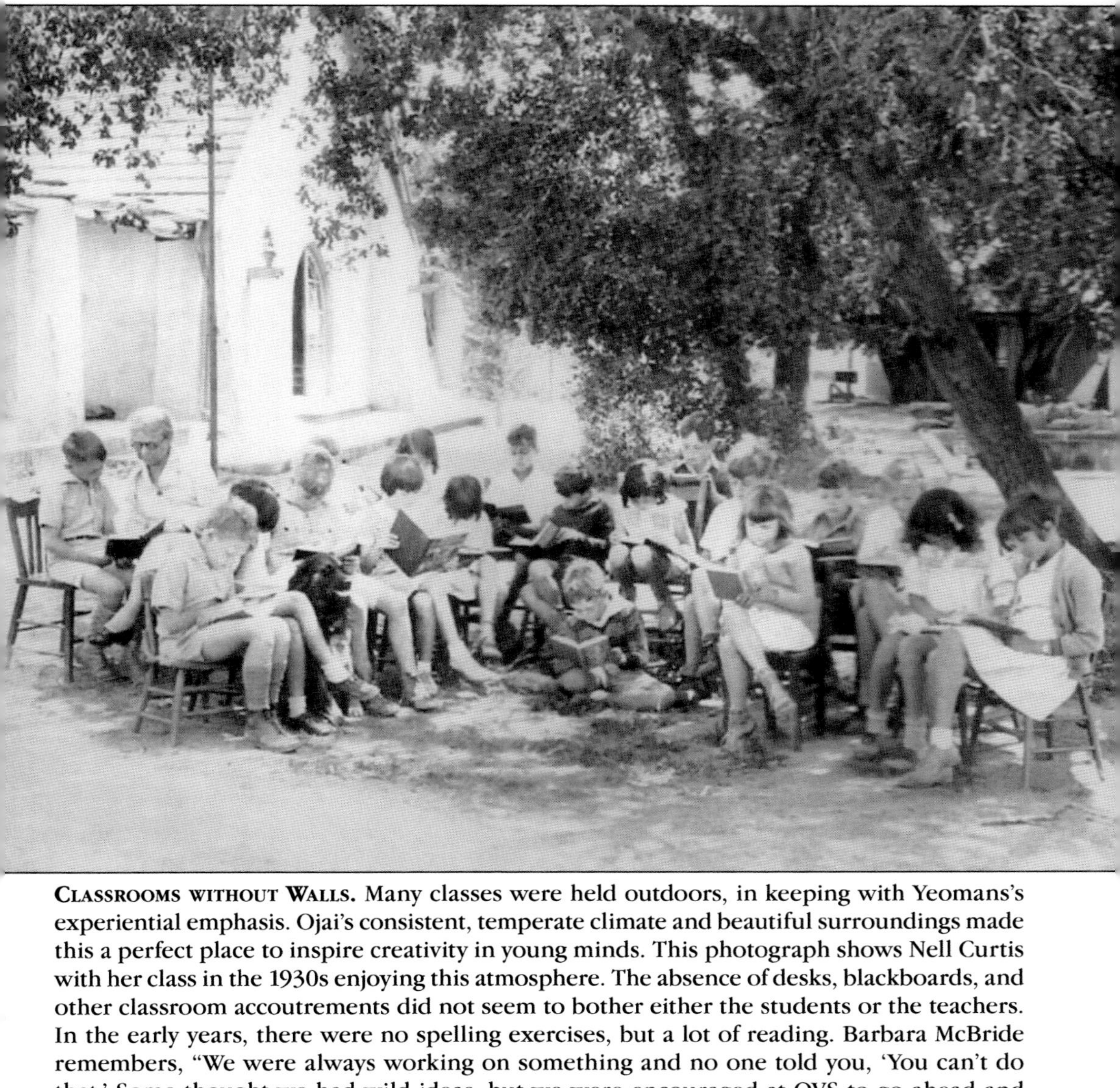

Classrooms without Walls. Many classes were held outdoors, in keeping with Yeomans's experiential emphasis. Ojai's consistent, temperate climate and beautiful surroundings made this a perfect place to inspire creativity in young minds. This photograph shows Nell Curtis with her class in the 1930s enjoying this atmosphere. The absence of desks, blackboards, and other classroom accoutrements did not seem to bother either the students or the teachers. In the early years, there were no spelling exercises, but a lot of reading. Barbara McBride remembers, "We were always working on something and no one told you, 'You can't do that.' Some thought we had wild ideas, but we were encouraged at OVS to go ahead and try them."

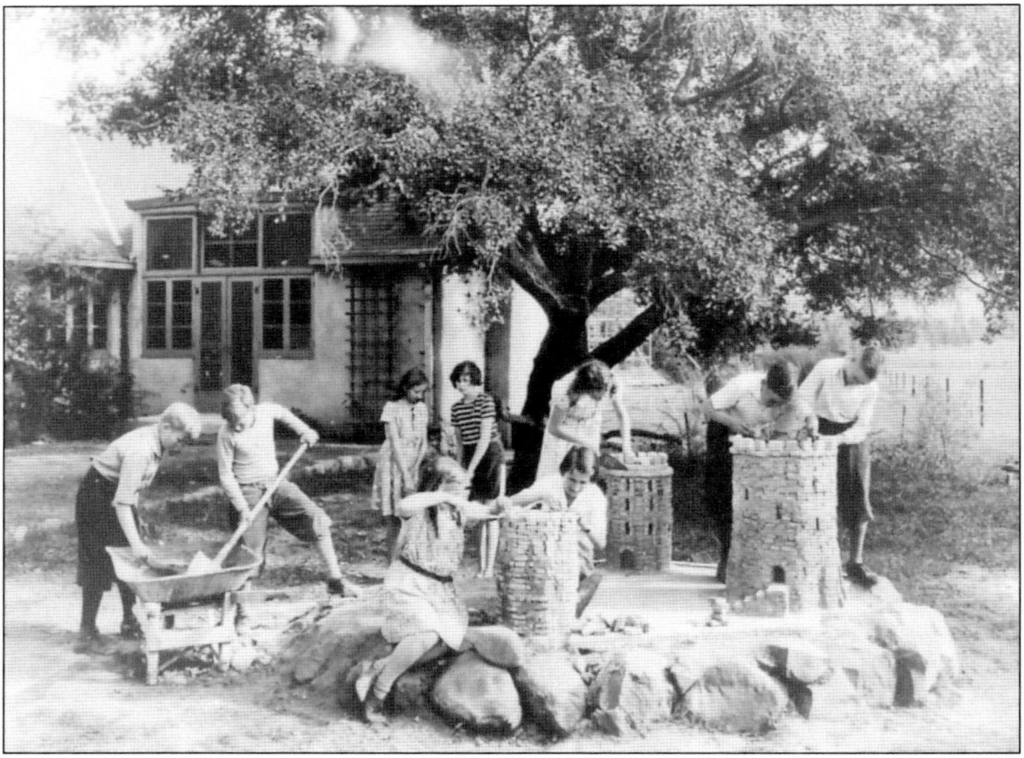

Building the Castle. In the 1930s, there were many unusual projects designed to stimulate children's interest. Children took apart and reassembled an automobile motor, made paper, and built a replica of Caernarvon Castle as an English project. The castle was designed by art and shop teacher John Phillip Ascott. The children made small cement blocks proportioned on a scale of a half inch to a foot for the castle's construction. A realistic moat was built around the castle, and a dungeon was later added (below). Part of this castle still stands today just outside the Lower Campus girls' dorm, a testament to its excellent workmanship.

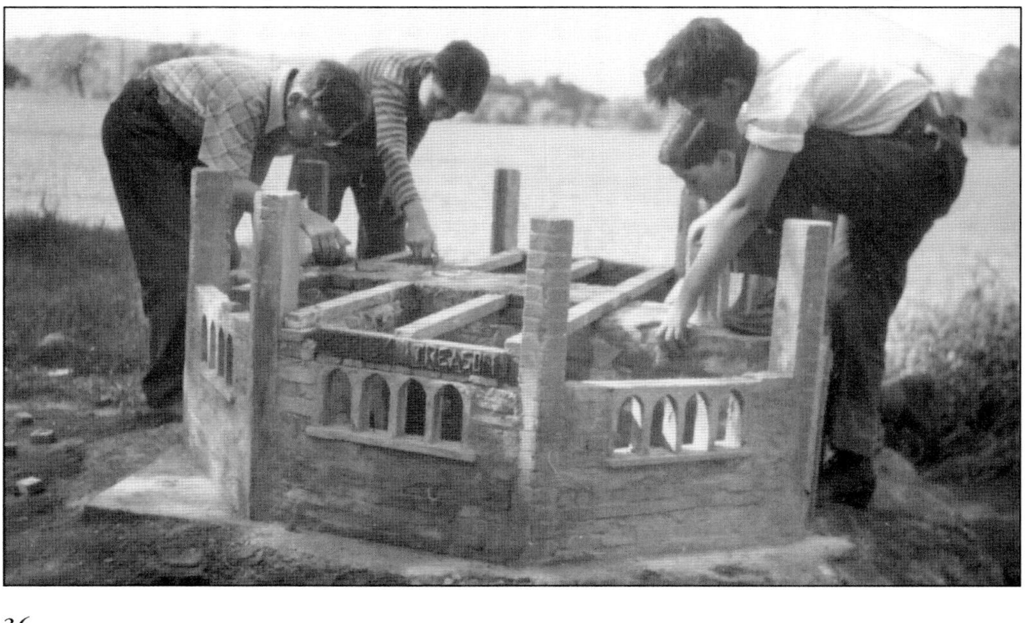

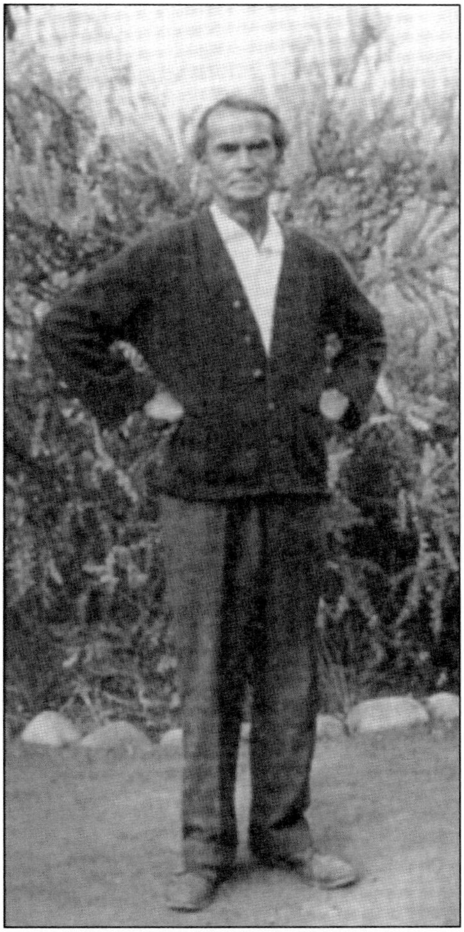

John Phillip Ascott. Hired in the late 1920s for duties ranging from custodian to shop master, Ascott was known as a jack of all trades. He supervised the animals (including the horses), planted trees, and tended to the gardens and landscaping. He inspired children to create things with their hands. The replica of Caernarvon Castle, which Ascott helped the children to design and build, remains today as a symbol of Yeomans's basic principles. Ascott's classic 1927 woody station wagon, shown below, was always shined and polished. A highlight for the children was a spin in his car.

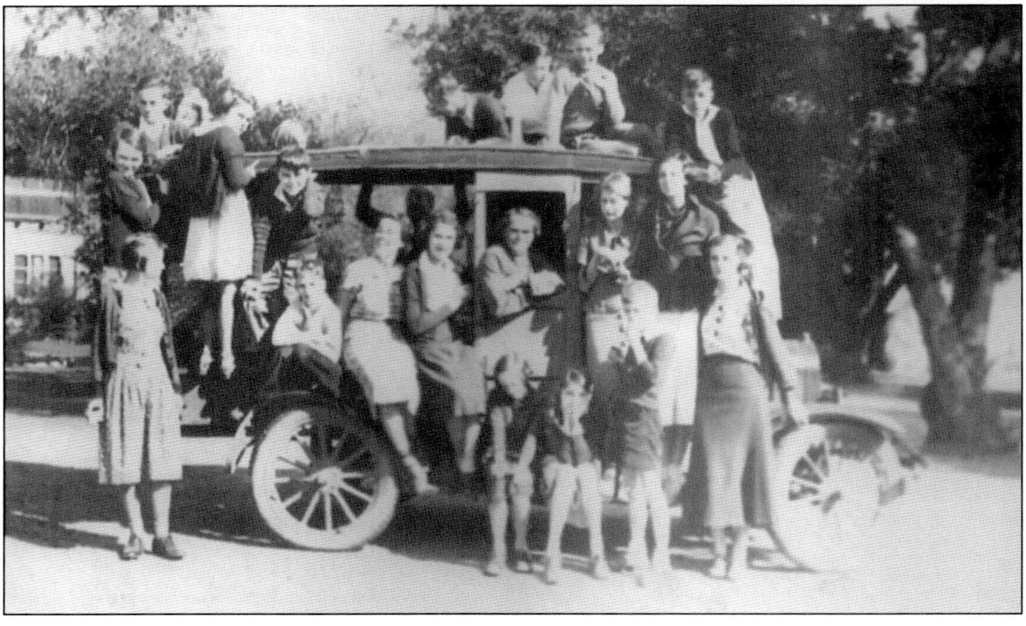

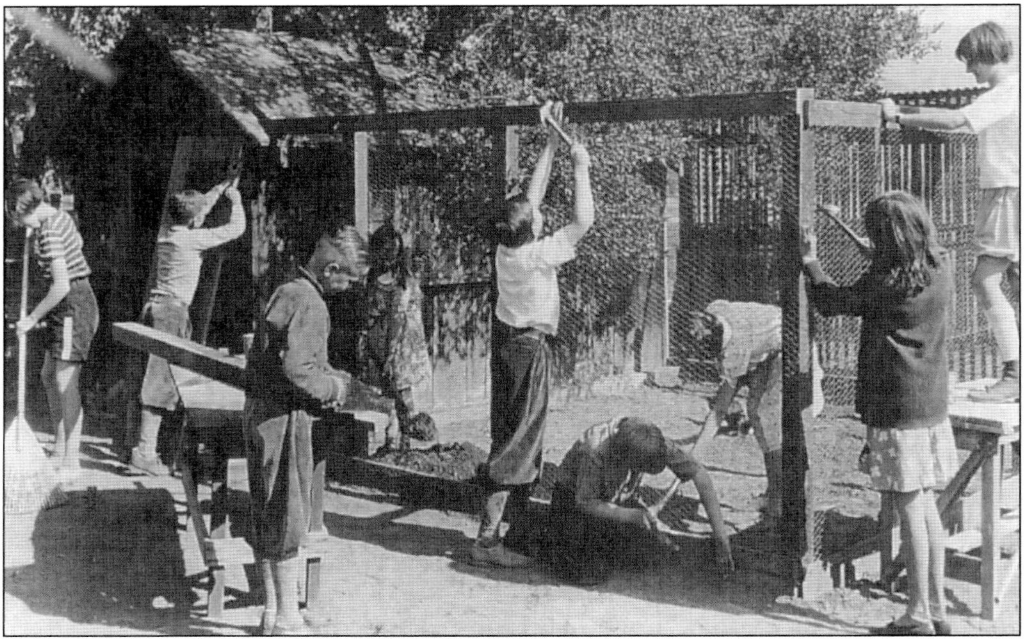

CHILDREN AT WORK. Saturday mornings were spent in a unified effort of sweeping, raking leaves, picking up trash, and caring for animals. It was school policy that everyone pitch in and do his or her share. In this way, the children felt some ownership in the school. After lunch, they had free time for playing games, riding horses, going on excursions, and creating art projects. Students even constructed animal pens, as shown in this 1932 photograph. Pictured here are, from left to right, Carmen Revnes, Herb Lyttle, Jim Drace, Peggy Smith, Richard Bard, McKee Mhoon, Louise Butler, Helene Myers, and Laura Gardner.

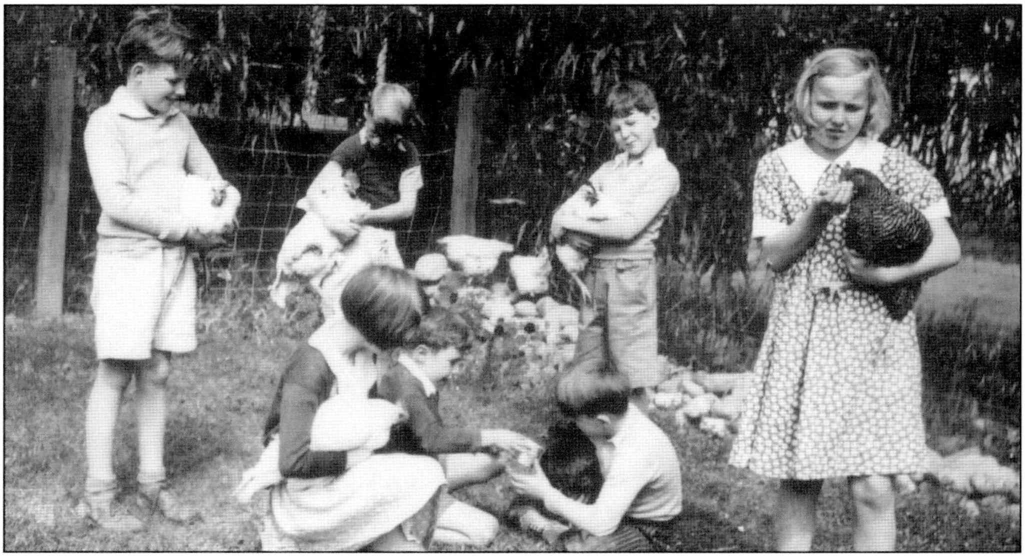

THE WORK ETHIC. The school reinforced each student's self-worth. Children learned to demand high standards in their own work and behavior, validating the philosophy of "experiencing instead of telling." Children raised chickens to produce eggs to take to market. Chickens were used to teach us the concept of price and cost. The children bought the feed and sold the eggs. They oversaw the process from beginning to end.

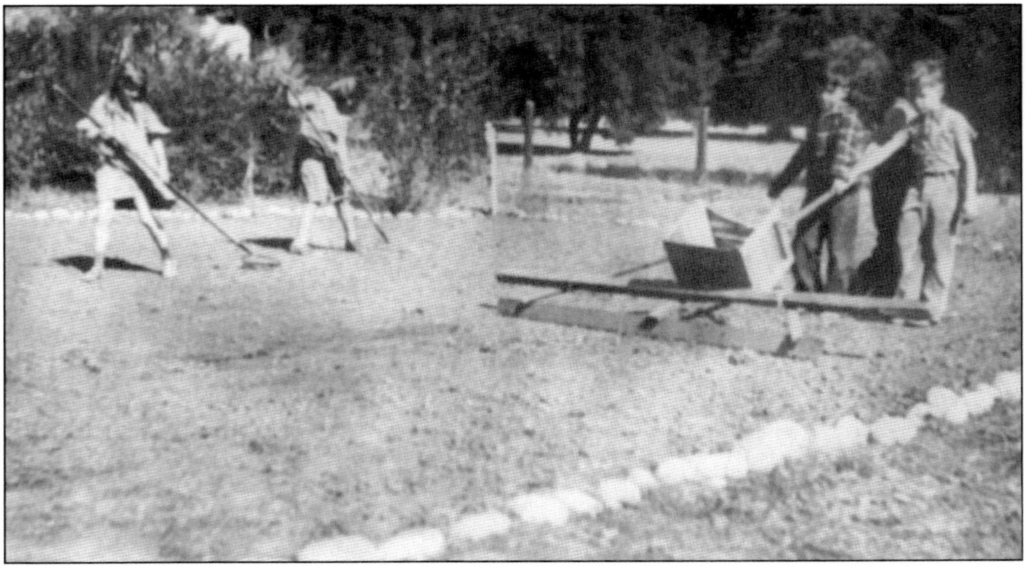

Self-Worth. Pictured above are second- and third-grade children working together to build a croquet field in the 1930s. Students were encouraged to participate in most of the school functions as well as construction. These projects reflected some of the key aspects of Yeomans's educational philosophy. First among these was the idea of creative and experiential work with an end product in mind—a playing field, a model castle, or a replica of a California mission. The second concept was teamwork. Each of the projects required participation and cooperation among the students. While this may not seem so unusual today, it was truly innovative in the 1930s, especially at the elementary level. John Phillip Ascott supervised the construction of the 1930s cabin, seen below, which gave children a feeling of accomplishment.

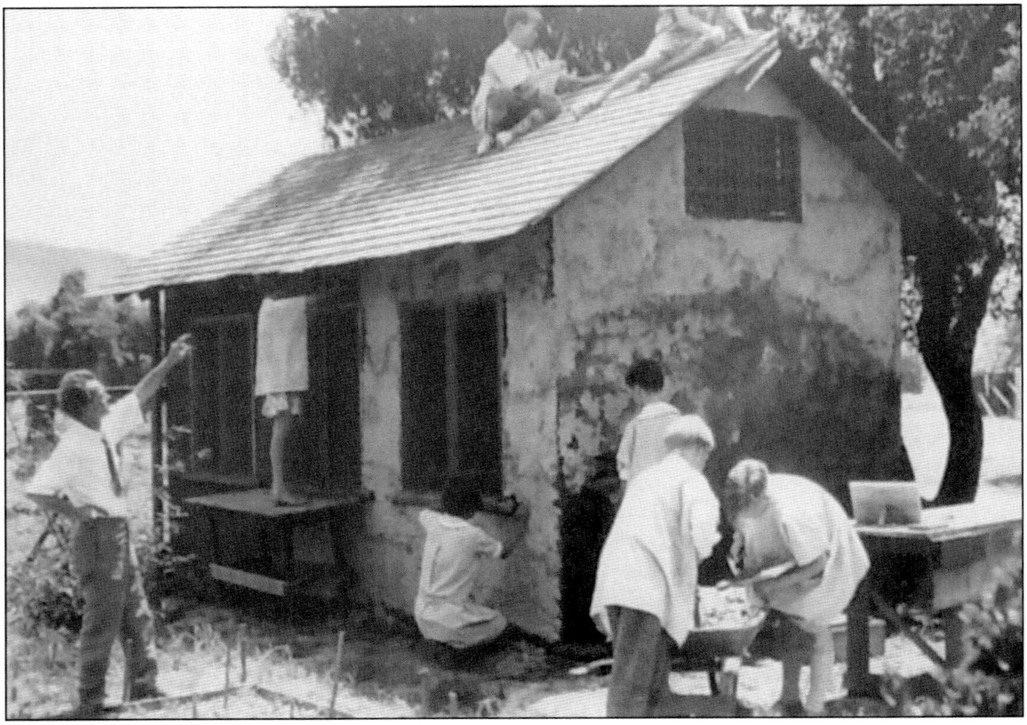

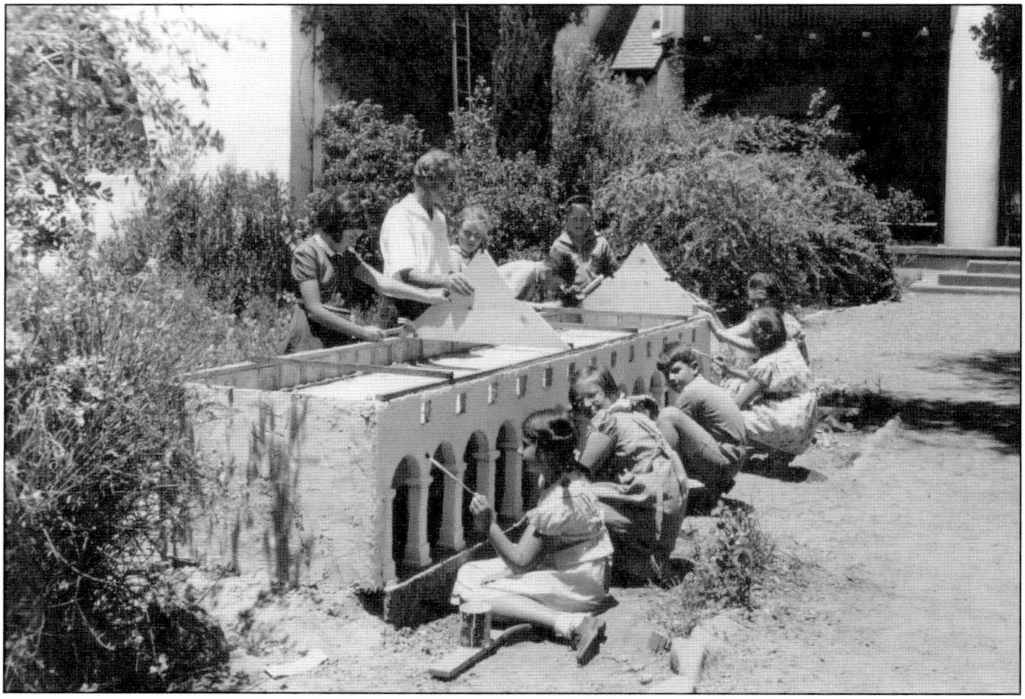

Creativity. Children work together during the 1937–1938 school year to complete a replica of the Santa Barbara Mission (above) under the direction of Laura Ingram. Every child is different, and it is up to the teacher to discover what techniques might encourage a student to be productive. For the fearful or recalcitrant child, working with his or her hands might be a way of expressing or controlling emotions. Young children do not realize the impact creative teachers have on their formative years. However, years later, as adults, they will see these influences emerge and will surely remember whom to credit. Below, children learn about gardening in Betty Marsh's 1935 class.

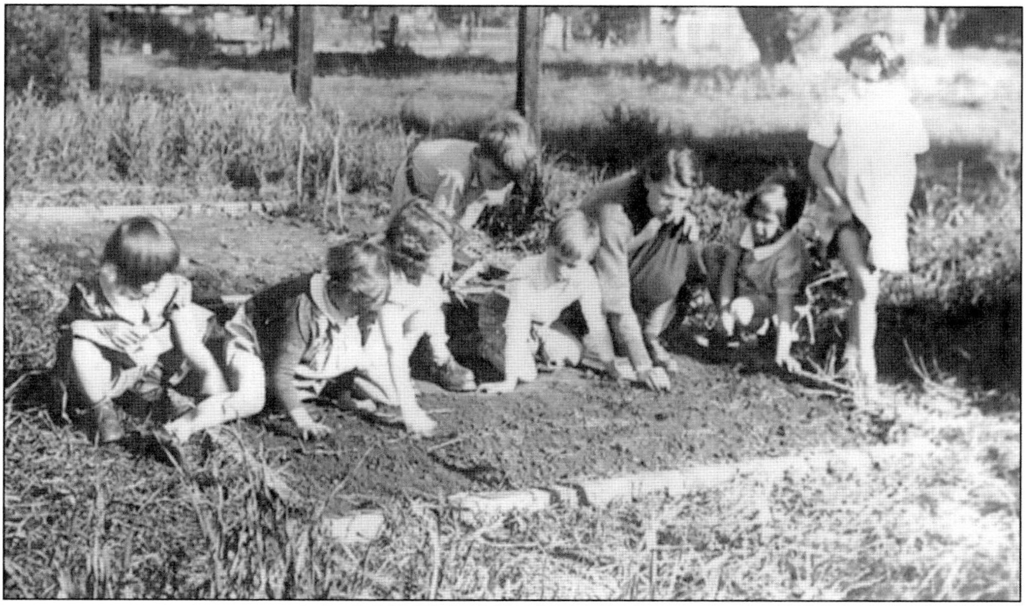

Four

Wallace Burr Arrives

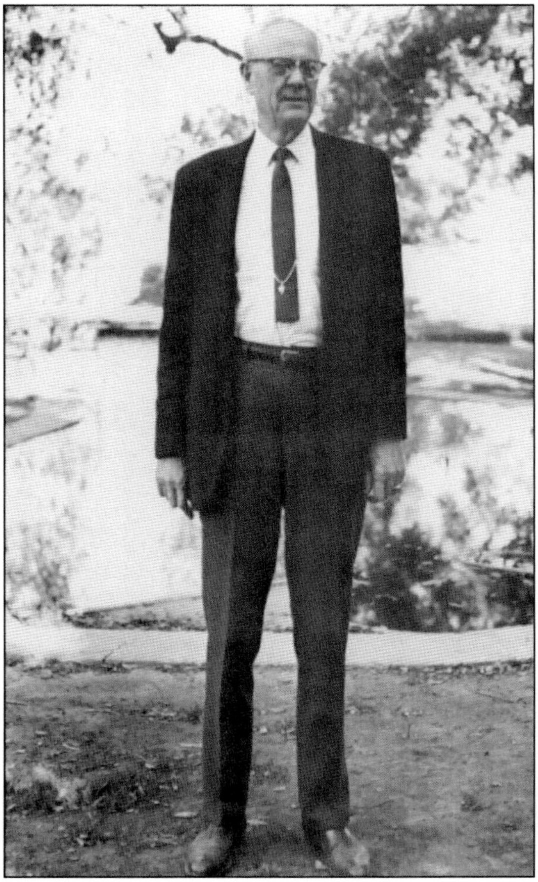

Wallace Burr. In 1943, OVS enrollment had dropped to 22 students, and there was talk of closing the school. The chairman of the Ojai Valley School Board of Trustees, Dr. Murray Peabody Brush, recommended that Wallace Burr be hired to nurse OVS back to health. Burr had been a teacher, administrator, and financial manager at California Preparatory School in Covina for nine years. As the clientele at OVS changed, there was a need for more structure, so a more traditional grade-level approach was adopted. Grades and six-week written reports were sent to parents, while the school maintained elements of a progressive education, promoting art, music, and love of nature. Two-hour, supervised evening study halls were started for children between the fifth and ninth grades. Burr served the school as headmaster from 1943 to 1972. "Nothing less than your best" was the motto first put forth by Burr in the 1940s. Another favorite Burr quote came from the Chinese philosopher Confucius: "Consider that I labored not for myself alone but for all of them that seek learning."

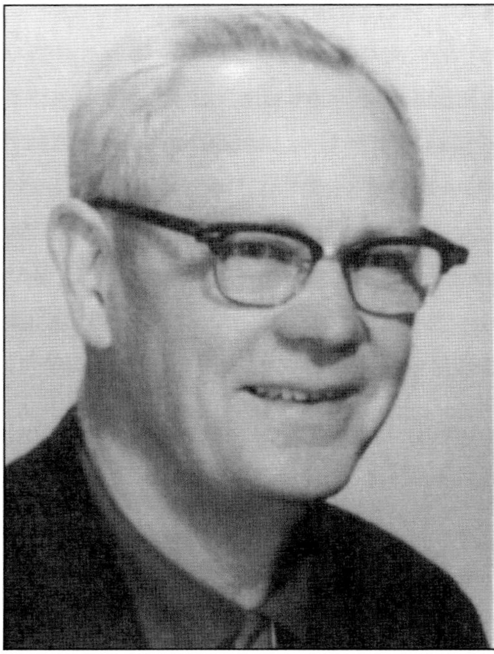

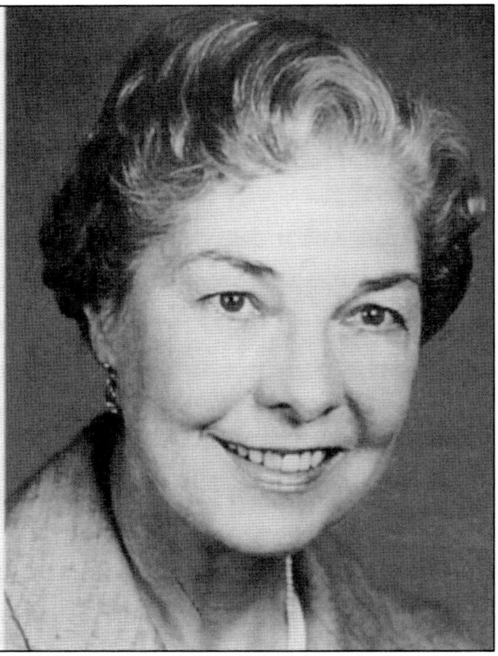

A Team Effort. Wallace Burr brought to OVS expertise in increasing enrollment and financing a school. With no money in the bank, he decided to generate funds by offering a summer program. This was a success, taking in $5,000. His wife, Dorothy Burr, managed the kitchen and created recipes and menus. Wallace, Dorothy, and their two young sons lived on campus for two years so they could be close to day-to-day activities. Since no faculty residences were available, the Burrs turned two classrooms into their home. The castle stood right outside. In 1945, in order to encourage the further development of Libbey's Arbolada, a lot was offered to the Burrs for $800. They built a home right across the street from the school, on El Paseo Road, and it is still maintained as faculty housing today. Their previous home became the home economics and sewing rooms.

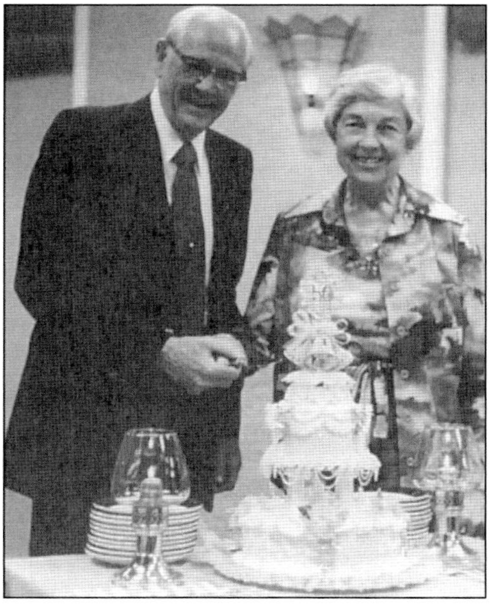

Burr Anniversary. Wallace and Dorothy are pictured here on their 50th wedding anniversary, January 1, 1978.

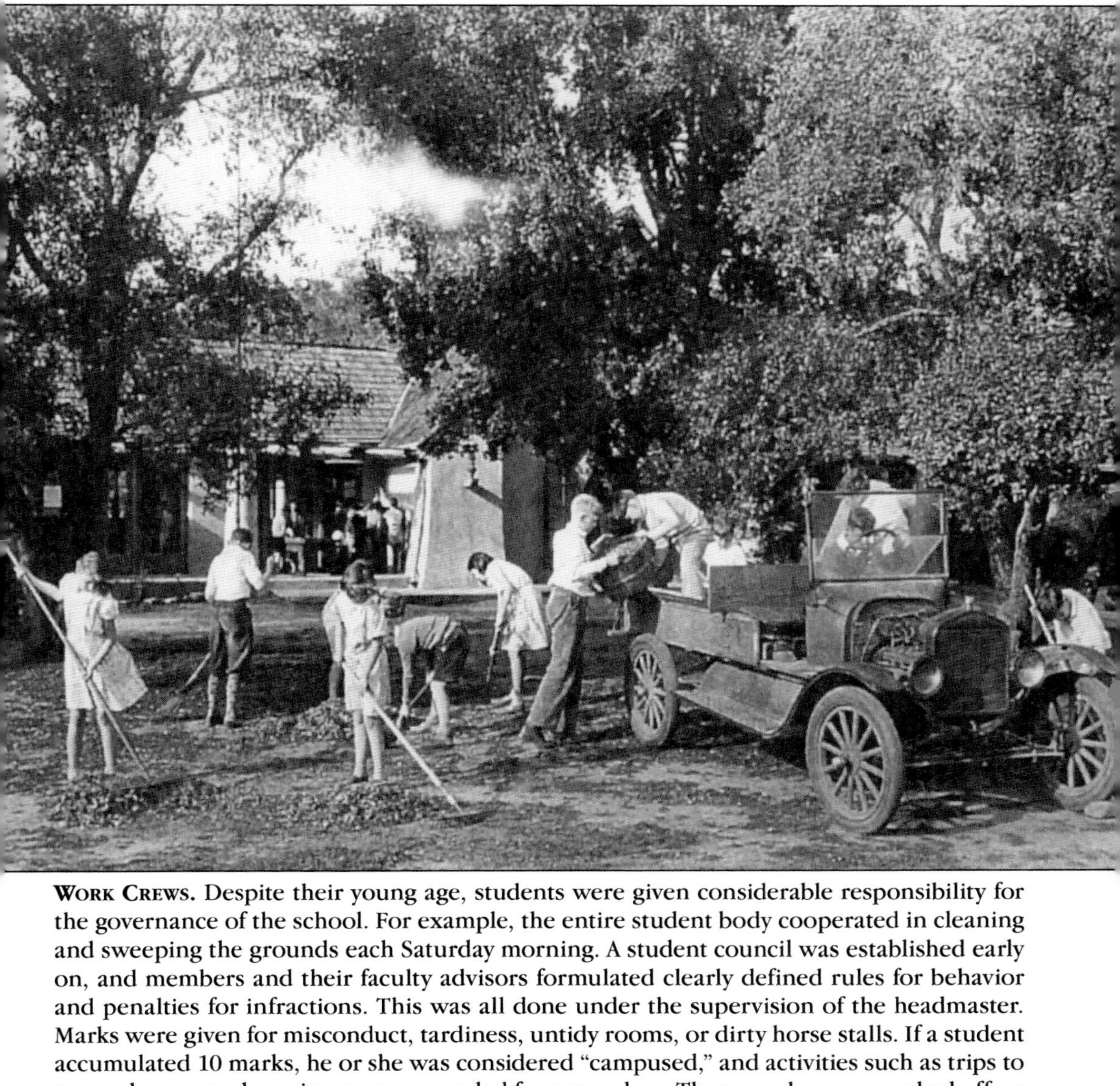

Work Crews. Despite their young age, students were given considerable responsibility for the governance of the school. For example, the entire student body cooperated in cleaning and sweeping the grounds each Saturday morning. A student council was established early on, and members and their faculty advisors formulated clearly defined rules for behavior and penalties for infractions. This was all done under the supervision of the headmaster. Marks were given for misconduct, tardiness, untidy rooms, or dirty horse stalls. If a student accumulated 10 marks, he or she was considered "campused," and activities such as trips to town, dances, and movies were suspended for seven days. These marks were worked off on weekends by performing tasks like digging in the garden, painting fences, or maintaining trails. Eventually, marks could be eliminated by running one-mile laps.

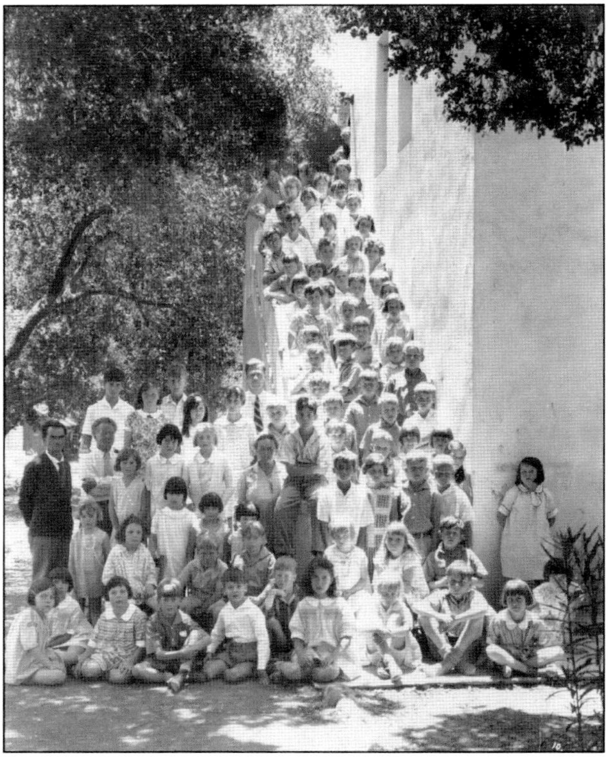

Physical Plant Improvements. When Wallace Burr arrived, Frost Hall, then 20 years old, was in dire need of renovation. Burr, with the support of his board of trustees, put plans into action for the addition of furnaces, rewiring, revamping of the plumbing, enlargement of the dining hall, and construction of fire escape steps by the dorm. Several new buildings and a horse stable were also added to the campus during this time. Edward Libbey donated seven more acres west of the campus in 1943, where newly constructed girls' dorms were completed in 1955. The image at left shows the steps from the dorm in 1930; in the image below, taken 84 years later, the 2014 elementary students pose on the same steps.

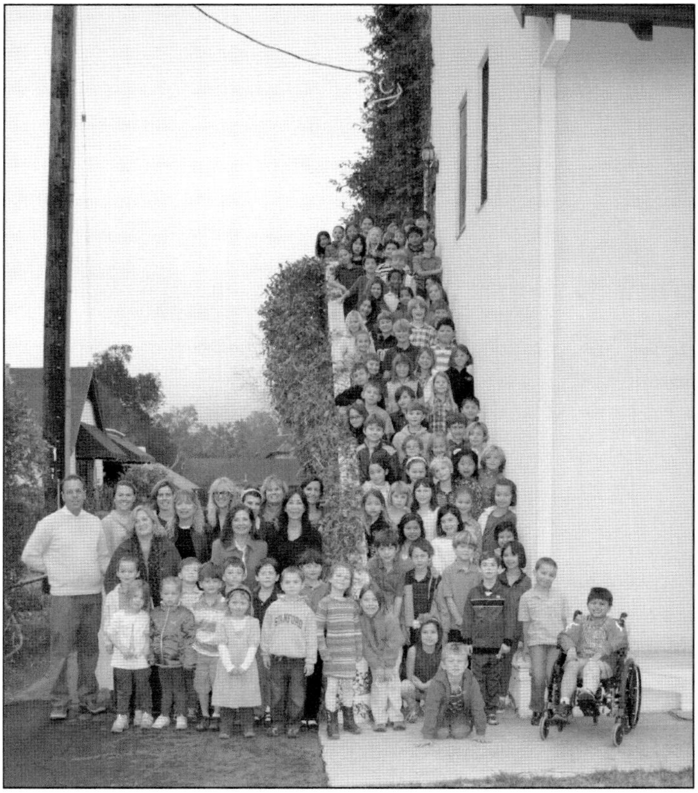

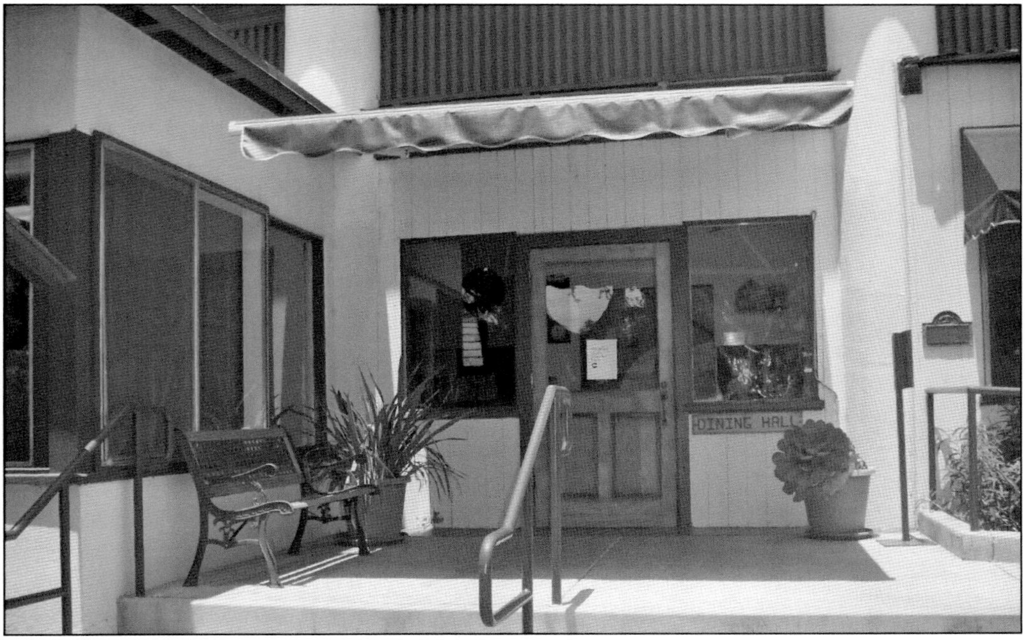

Family Meals. During meals, the whole "family" would gather. The dining room began in one room of Frost Hall, and by the 1960s, there were nine tables of eight with a faculty member at each table. Attendance at meals was mandatory and family-style seating encouraged proper etiquette. Grace was always recited before meals, and proper manners were required. One never sat down before the table head had taken his seat; nor did one ever reach across the table. Serving dishes were always offered to the faculty member first. When clearing the table, one dish was to be carried in each hand to the kitchen; no stacking was allowed. Since the enlargement and renovation in 1943, the layout of the dining room at the Lower Campus remains the same.

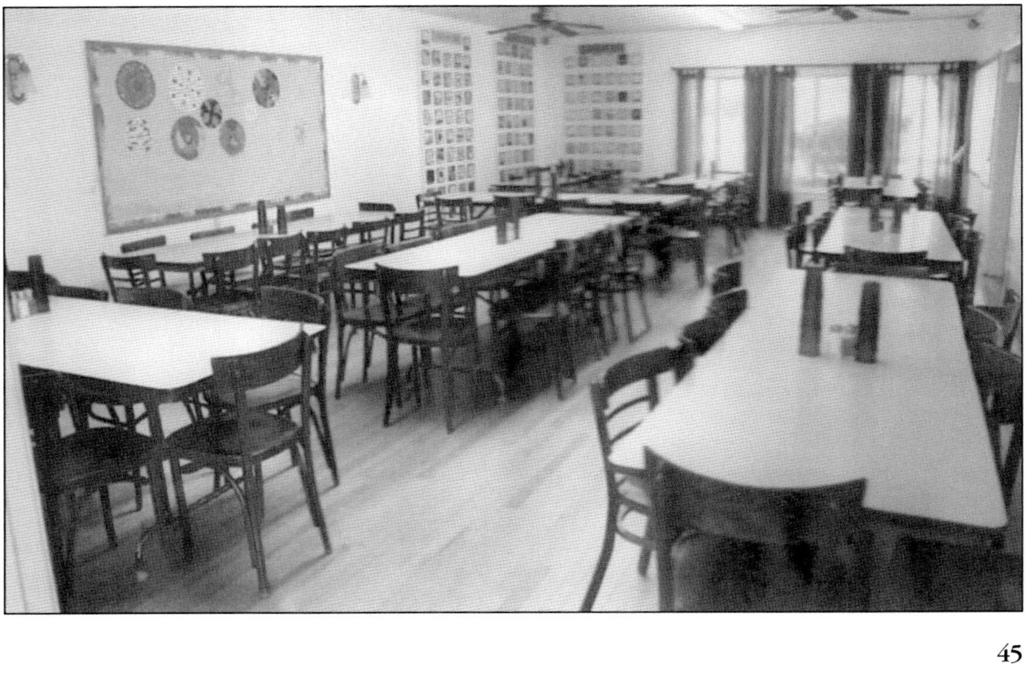

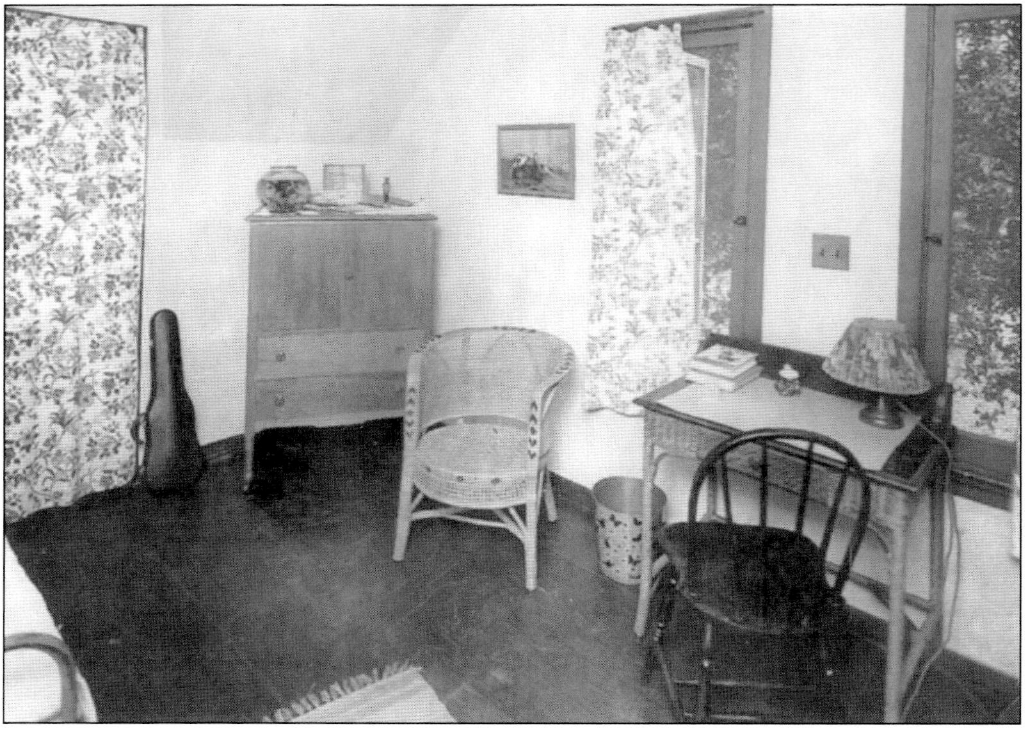

Dorm Rooms. The appearance of the campus was always important to the school community. Students were expected to maintain their rooms and the school grounds. A typical dorm room (seen above in the 1930s and below in 2014) housed one or two students. An extra bed was sometimes added for summer sessions. Each room was sparsely furnished with just a desk, chair, bed, and small closet. Dorm responsibilities were assigned weekly, and rooms were inspected daily by the dorm mother or student dorm captain. The rooms provided a sense of privacy and personal space. Although the rooms were small, students could decorate, within reason, to encourage a comfortable, homey atmosphere. The author remembers wallpapering her walls with photographs of the Beatles in the 1960s.

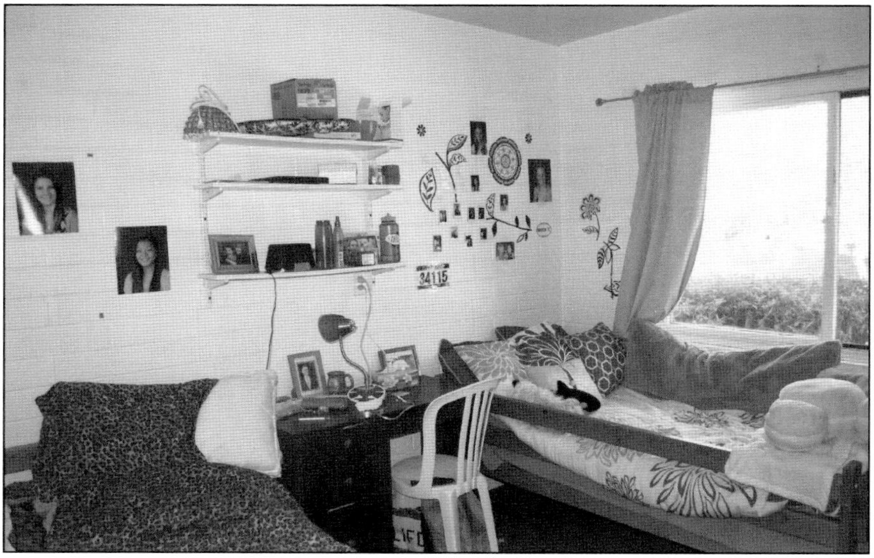

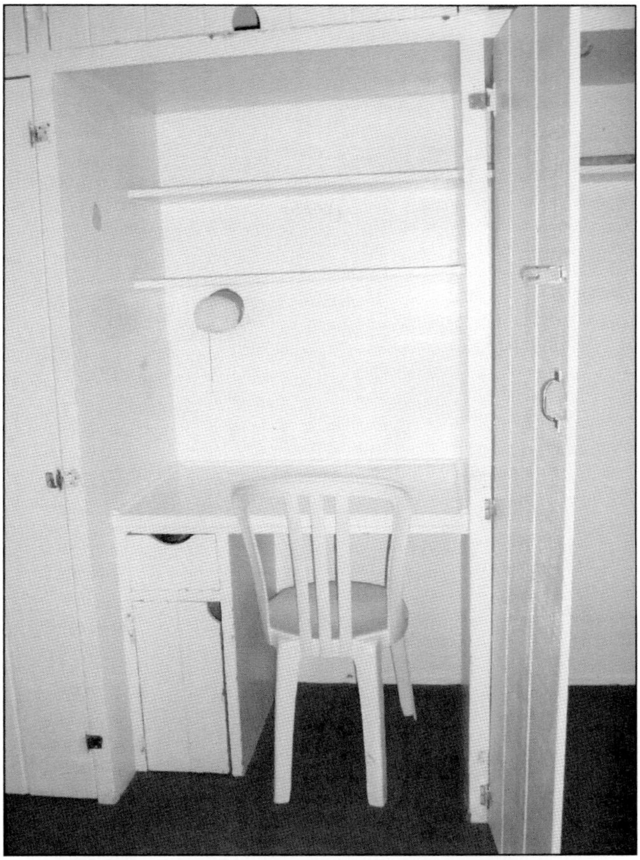

Simple Living. Dorms were occupied by 20 girls or boys and were always a bustle of activity, with music and laughter resonating through the halls. The absence of television, both in the days before it was widely available and later by design, promoted more creative thinking, reading, and socializing. Rooms were simple, and neatness was stressed. The school day was structured by a series of bells. Mornings came early with the 6:30 a.m. bell. Breakfast began at 7:00 a.m., rooms were cleaned and inspected after breakfast, and classes began at 8:30 a.m. Two-hour, supervised nightly study hall was required before students could enjoy an hour of free time. Lights went out promptly at 10:00 p.m.

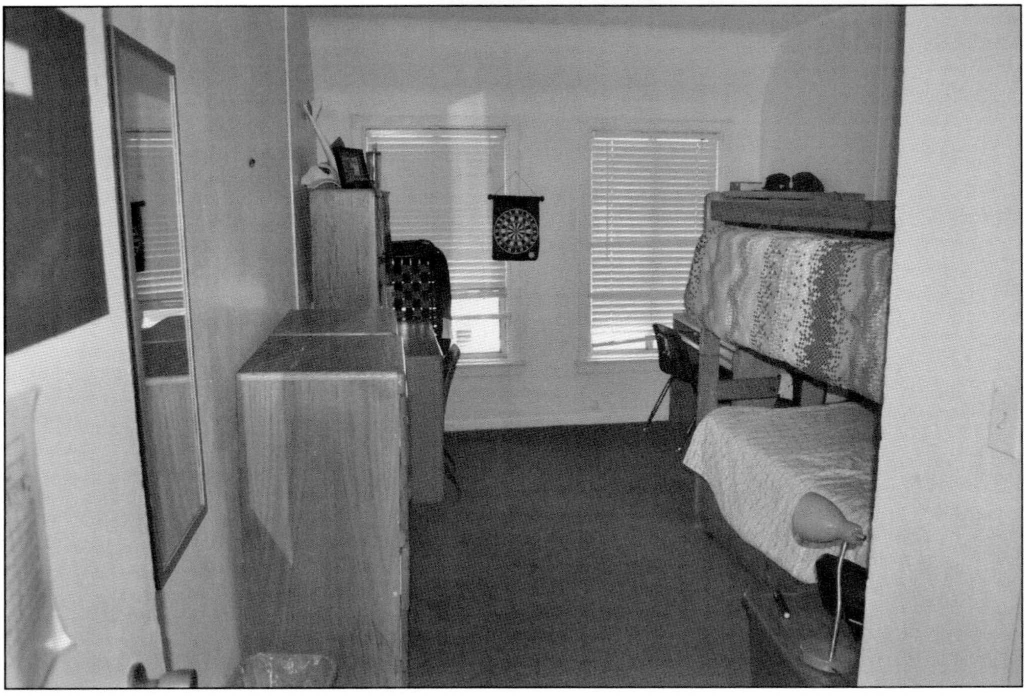

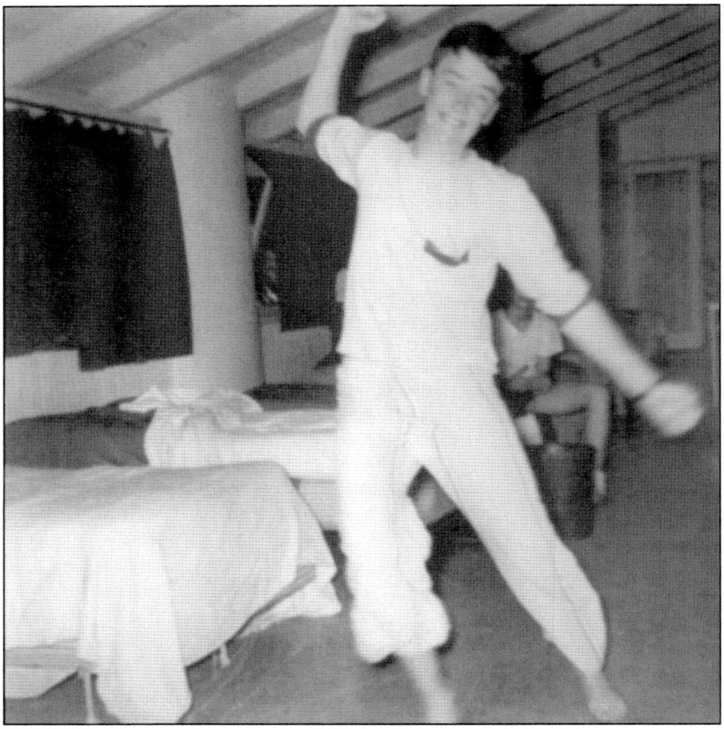

Sleeping Porch. In the early days of Frost Hall, OVS boys slept together on a sleeping porch (pictured at left). Roommates rotated weekly between the porch and a dorm room. About 15 girls shared rooms on the second floor. By the early 1960s, dorm rooms in Frost Hall were enlarged to accommodate two boys each, and the sleeping porch became a thing of the past. As before, the rooms were equipped with beds, study desks, closets, and shelves. Bathrooms and showers were down the hall.

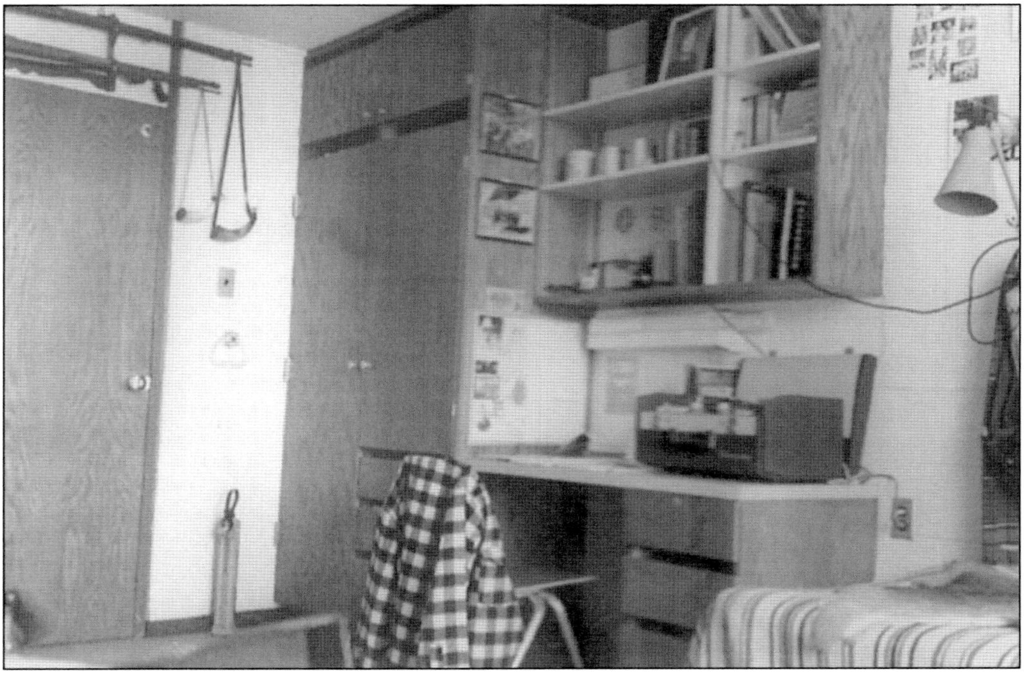

Rooms for Boys. Similarly, the double-occupancy rooms for boys at the new Upper Campus were simple. In 2013, more than 50 years after the first dorm's construction, remodeling was being planned. After a full day of academics, physical exertion, and daily responsibilities, sleep was a welcome respite. Lights-out was still 10:00 p.m., but occasionally, one would try to catch a few more minutes of study time by the dim light of a flashlight.

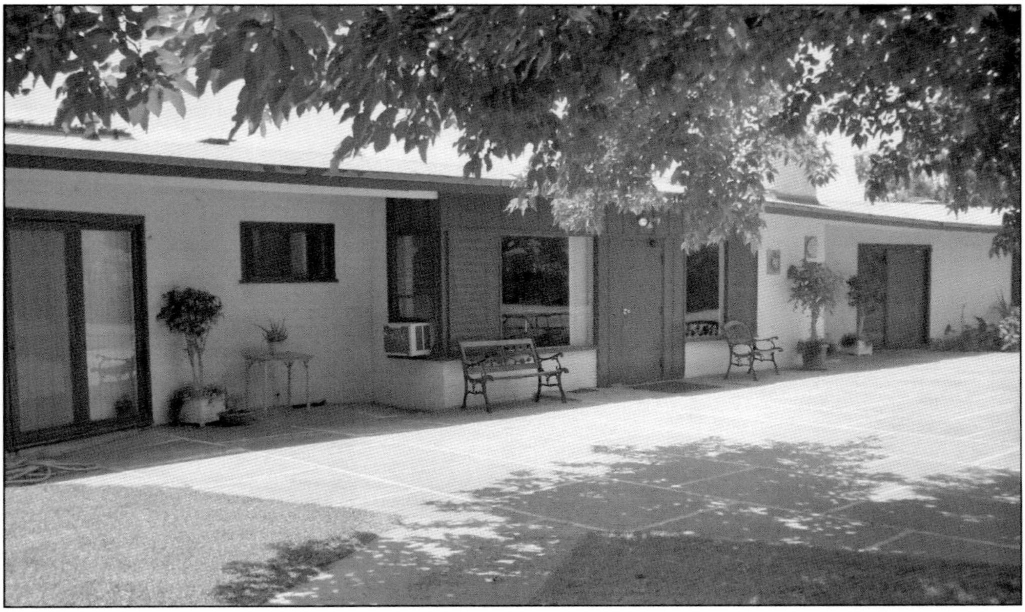

Lower Campus Girls' Dorm. The 1955 girls' dorm had two wings with a central common area. This common area was a place where meetings, games, and formal faculty-parent teas were held. Carpeted floors, kitchen facilities, and the fireplace made for a comfortable, homey atmosphere. After evening study hall, girls found the living room to be a restful gathering area before bed. Here, they could chat with each other or with the dorm parent about schoolwork, boys, or pertinent issues of the day. Occasionally, dances, talent shows, award ceremonies, and other forms of entertainment were held on the outdoor patio.

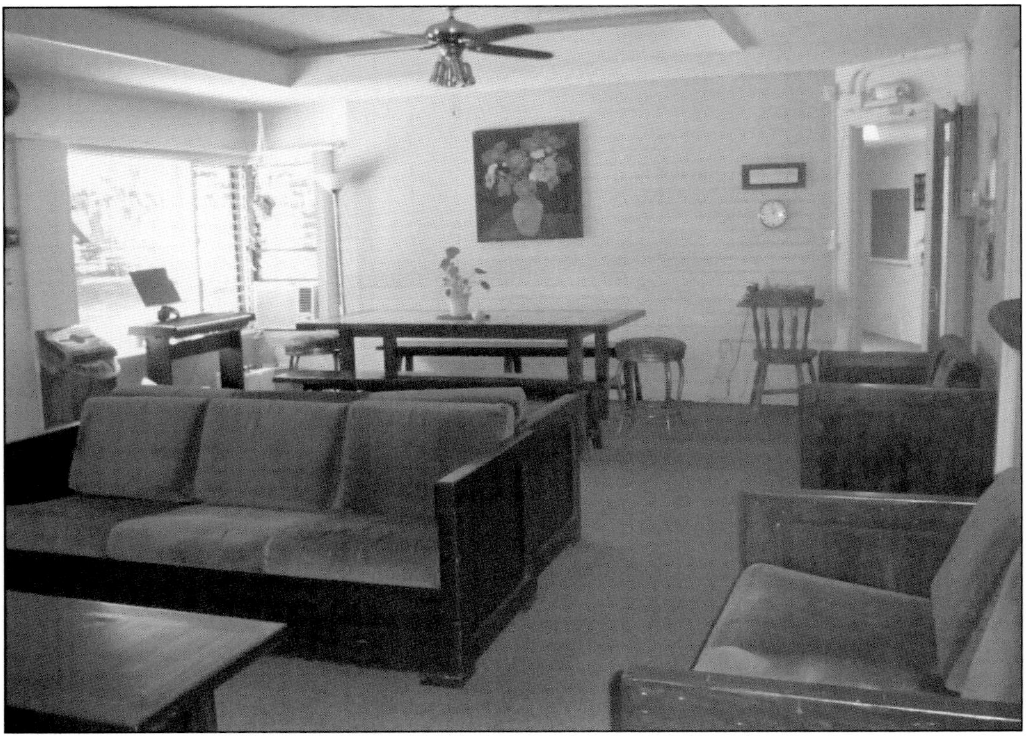

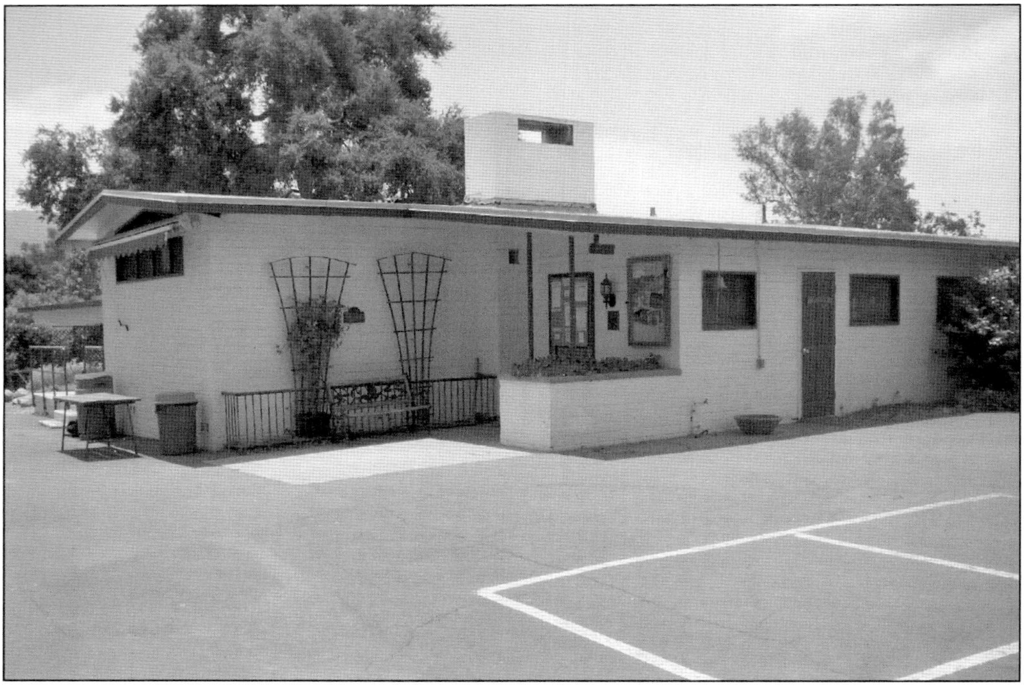

Rodney Hobson Smith Academic Center. In 1951, a multipurpose room was built near the stables. Assemblies were held here every morning for many years, and the site was also used as the music building, boasting three practice rooms, each with its own piano. These could be used for vocal, instrumental accompaniment, or piano lessons. In addition, there was a grand piano on the stage. Students enjoyed weekly dances and movies here in the 1950s and early 1960s. There was an attached outdoor stage where plays, dances, and graduation ceremonies were held until ninth graders moved to the Upper Campus in 1973. Today, eighth graders continue to celebrate their rite of passage here.

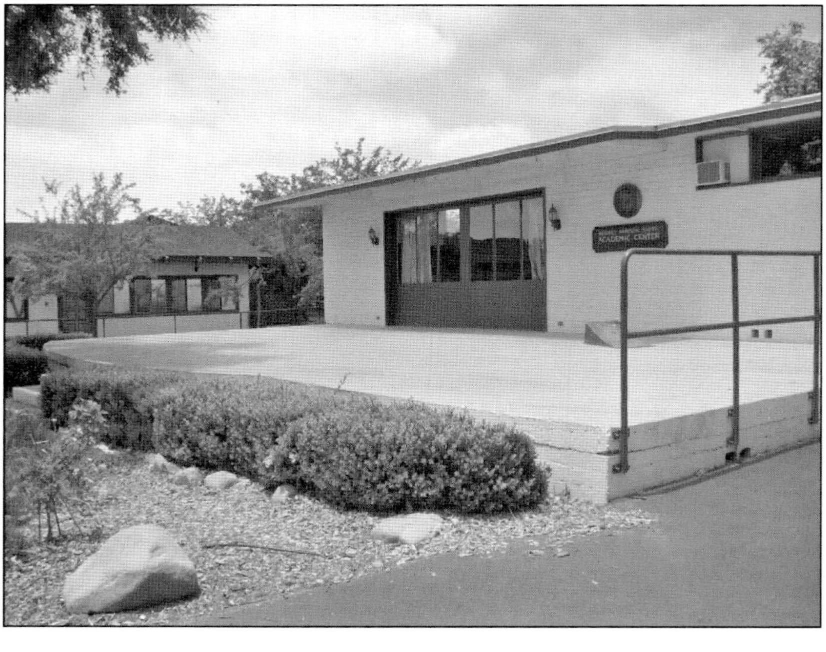

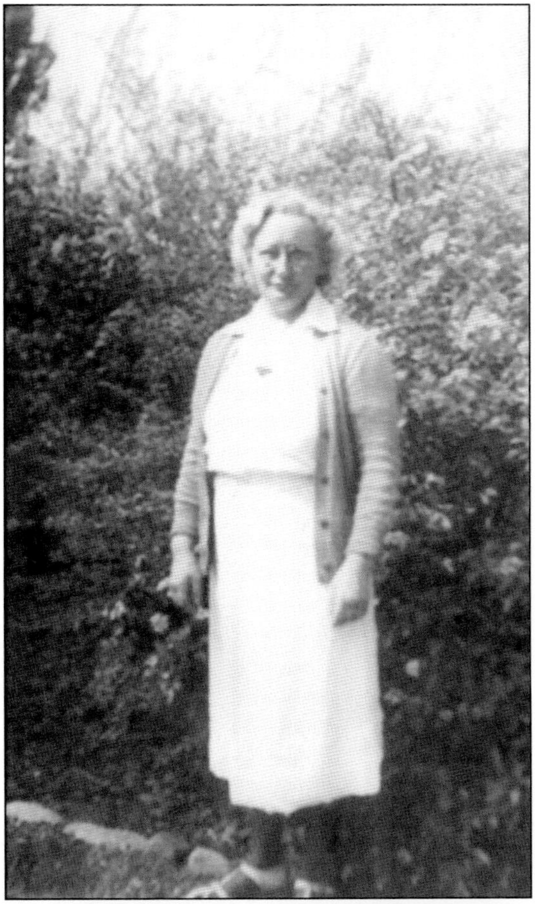

The First Infirmary. When Laura "Sally" Lund came to OVS in 1928, she was put in charge of the first infirmary. She remained until 1943. Lund was also in charge of the younger children in the dorm. A native of Sweden, with a strong accent, she was famous for giving her charges cod liver oil. In 1959, a new infirmary (below) was completed, with fourteen beds and two quarantine rooms. This facility could house boys and girls, as needed, with a full-time nurse on duty. In the mid-1960s, while awaiting the completion of the first Upper Campus boys' dorm, the infirmary housed 10 boys and, later, 14 girls.

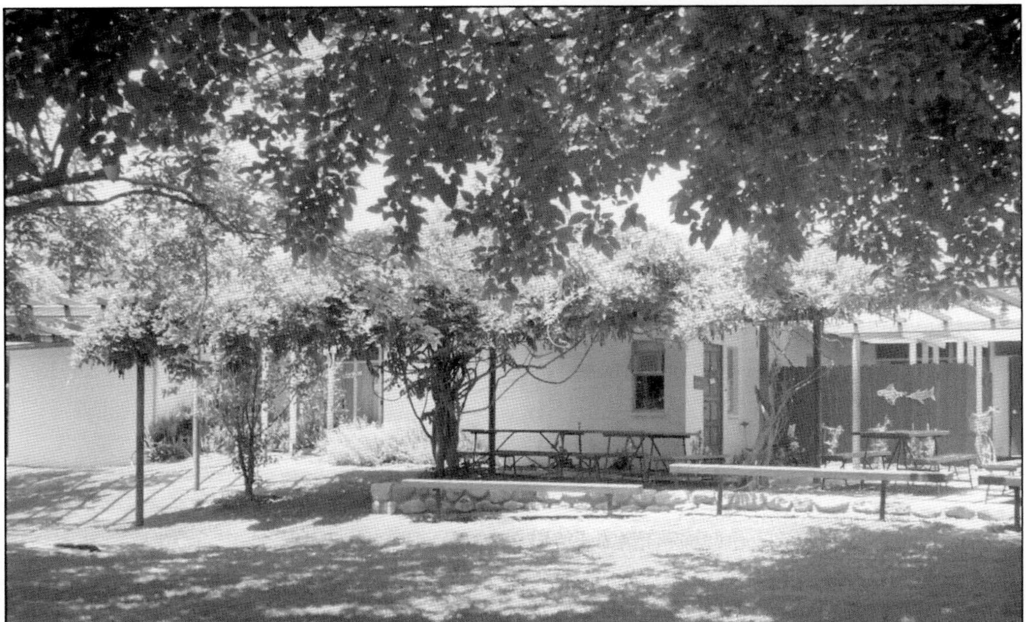

The OVS alma mater

In a valley surrounded by mountains
Lies a school we shall all recall.
Where the citrus grows and prospers,
And the oak stands stately and tall.
In California's sunshine
We too like the oak will grow.
Ever reaching skyward
The upper air to know.
As the years add understanding
To ideals implanted here.
Loyal sons and loyal daughters
Will sing your praises clear.
OVS in the valley of sunshine,
OVS in nature's nest,
Ever reaching skyward,
We pledge to you our best! (86)

ALMA MATER. As OVS emerged from the challenging years, Wallace Burr asked music teacher Elizabeth Wittausch to write an alma mater for the school. The song she composed captures Yeomans's early visions of groves of citrus trees ringed by stately mountains located in a "valley of sunshine." It also uses imagery that echoes Yeomans's nature-touched educational philosophy and the ever-present oak tree symbol that has become a central icon for the school.

Five

THE BURR YEARS

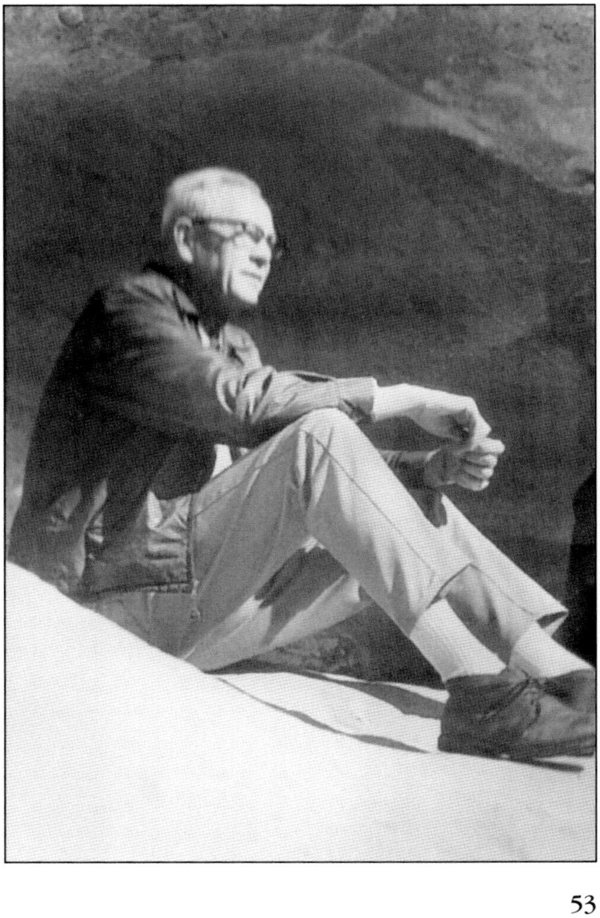

THE DREAMER. Almost from his earliest days at the school, Wallace Burr dreamed of adding grades 10 through 12. In the early 1960s, with more than 100 students enrolled in grades three through nine, there was more and more pressure from parents, alumni, friends, and benefactors to enlarge the school so that children could finally graduate from OVS. Burr tapped charitable foundations and lending institutions but quickly saw the need to ask for the support of OVS alumni. On May 8, 1961, he was able to purchase the 195-acre Alves Ranch in the foothills at the east end of the Ojai Valley for $30,000. This would soon become Ojai Valley School Upper Campus. By 1964, there were 219 students enrolled in grades three through twelve. Burr, the longest-serving headmaster at OVS (1943–1972), wanted open space where students would have access to trails for hiking and riding.

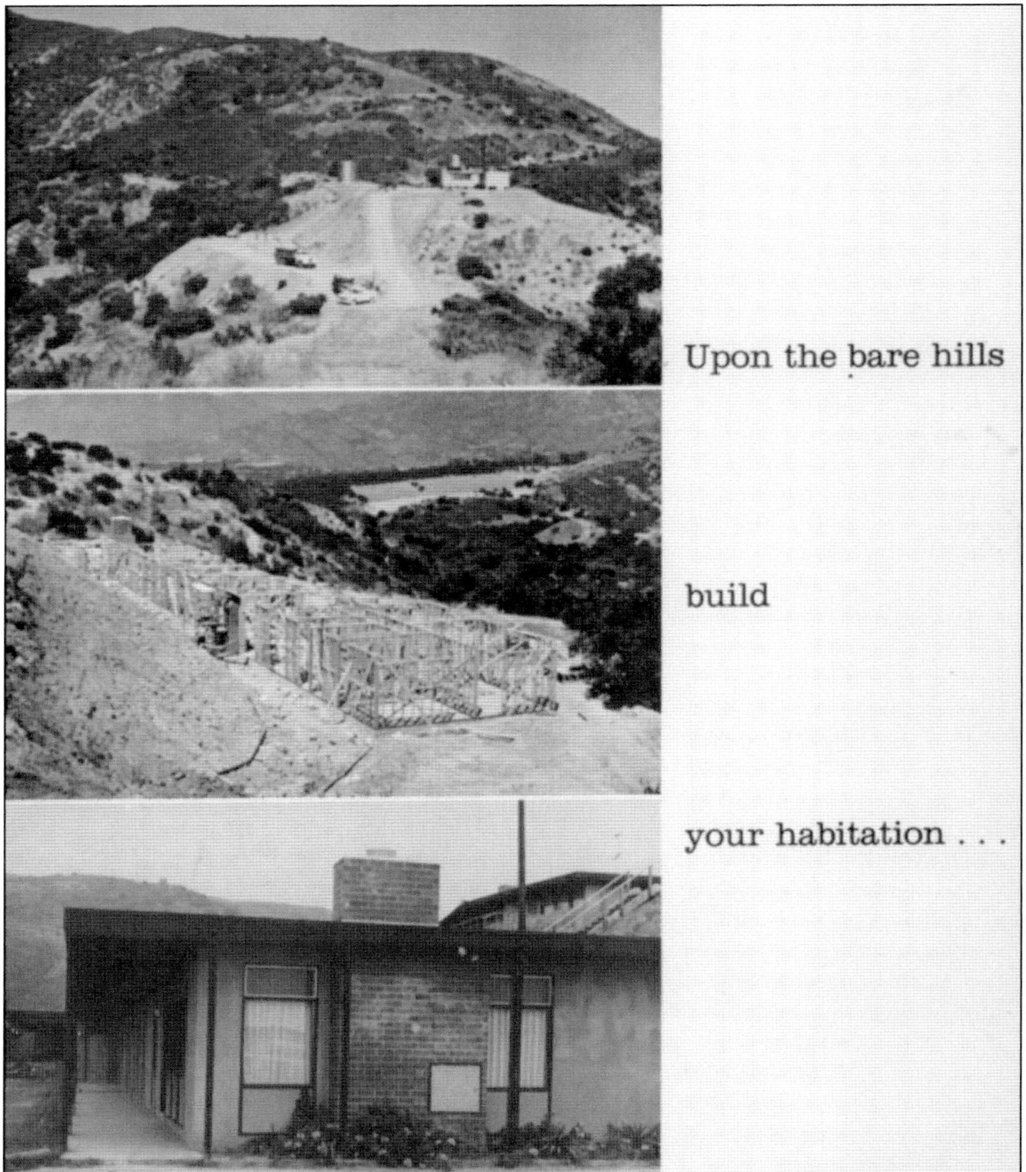

Upon the Bare Hills Build Your Habitation. The first boys' dorm at the Upper Campus, built in 1962, was named Bristol Dorm after the original Bristol School. It became the home of 16 rowdy 10th-grade boys. In the early 1960s, Mike Hermes, an alumnus of the OVS Lower Campus, was hired as an athletic coach and the first dorm parent at the Upper Campus. Mike lived in the boys' dorm with his wife and their three daughters. Before classrooms were completed, the boys were bussed down the hill to the Lower Campus for meals, classes, and other activities. In 2009, this dorm was renamed Hermes Hall.

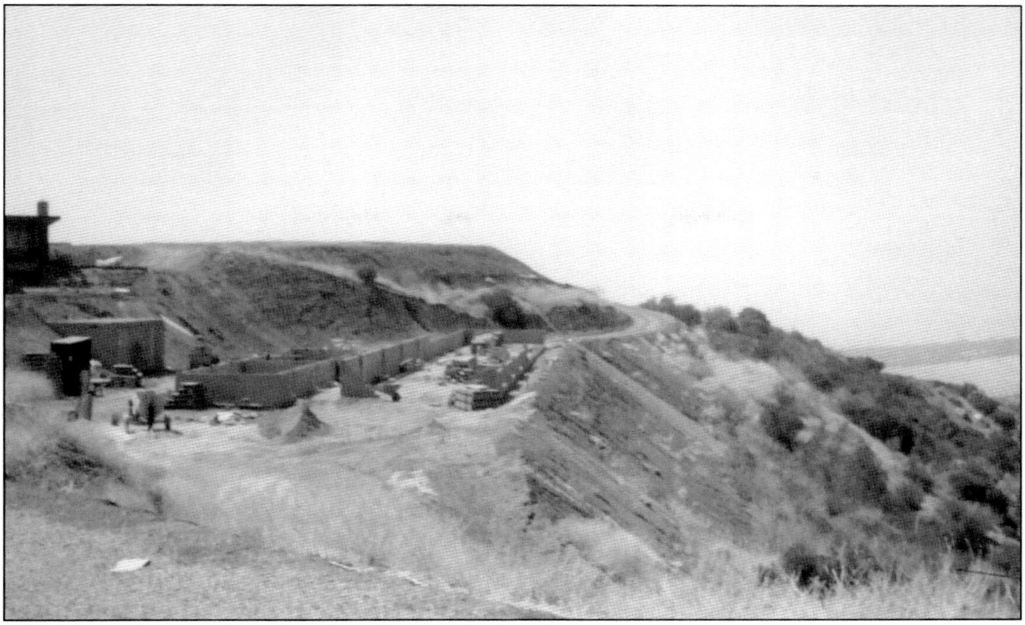

Classroom Construction. In the beginning, boys lived at the Upper Campus and were bussed to the Lower Campus for classes in a 1946 yellow bus affectionately known as Petunia Rollingstone (below). The road up and down the hill was not much more than a twisted cow path through a canyon. These daily trips were remembered as bone-shaking rides full of laughter and singing. January 4, 1965, marked the beginning of classes at the Upper Campus. The newly constructed Wallace Burr Hall included eight classrooms, a library, a science lab, and offices. High school girls were now bussed to the Upper Campus in the same small, 1946 yellow bus. Sometimes, a few boys would challenge the bus, driven by Mike Hermes, to a race up the hill with only a five-minute head start. The boys would often block the road with boulders to increase their chances. This was all great fun and filled with camaraderie.

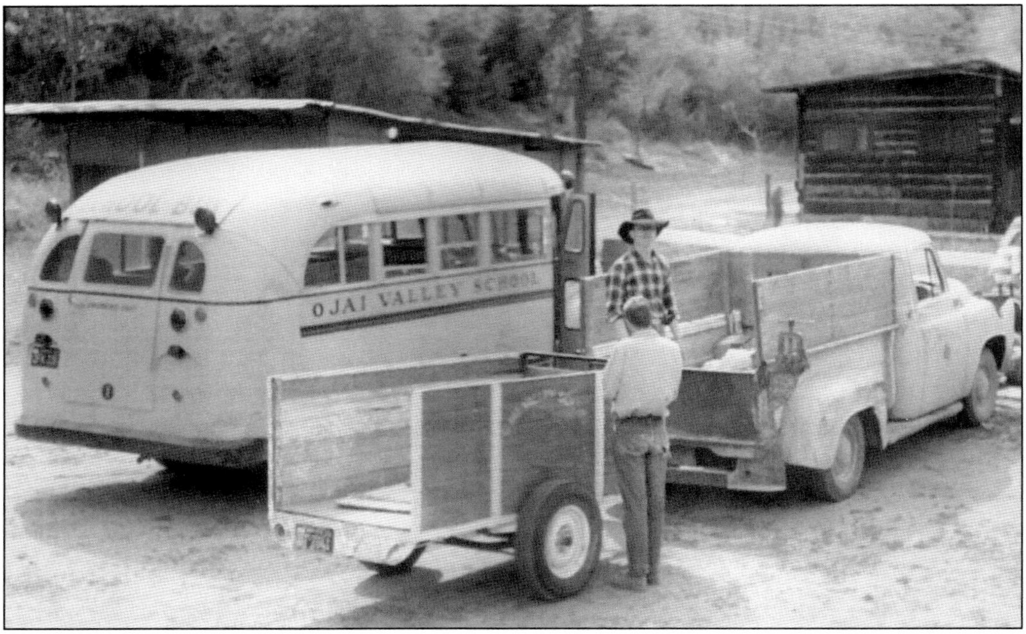

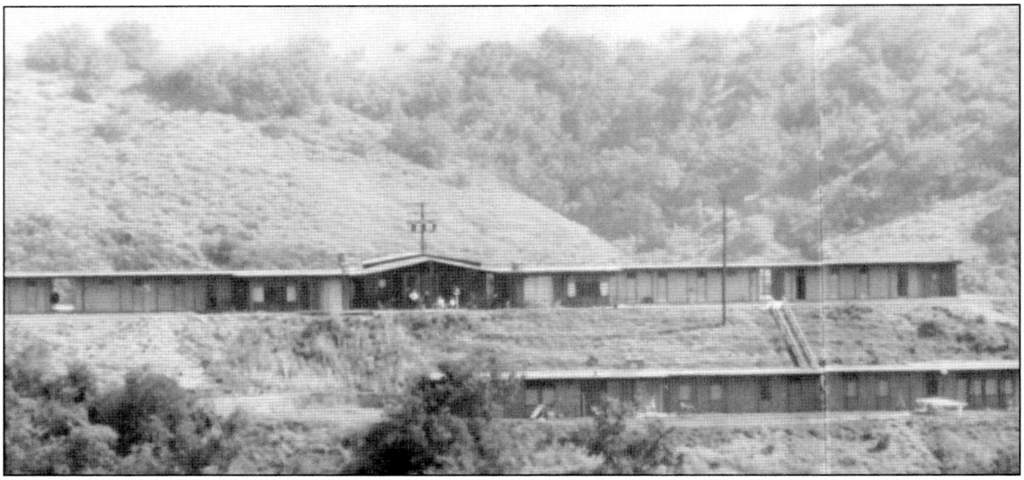

Home in the Hills. Each year, another grade was added, so two new boys' dorms were needed in 1963. This panoramic view shows all three dorms. The dorms were named Boney Bean, (top right), named after a fictional Chumash clan imagined by Wallace Burr, Tower House (top left), so called because of the nearby water tower, and Bristol Dorm (lower right). A dining hall built between Boney Bean and Tower House also served as a meeting room, lecture hall, theater, and site for weekly dances and movies. The plaque below was dedicated in 2009 when Bristol Dorm was renamed Hermes Hall. Spencer Garrett (U65), the first Upper Campus student council president and today a member of the OVS Board of Trustees, remembers the beginnings of the Upper Campus and recalls "the spirit of being in on something new," noting, "We recognized our role as pioneers."

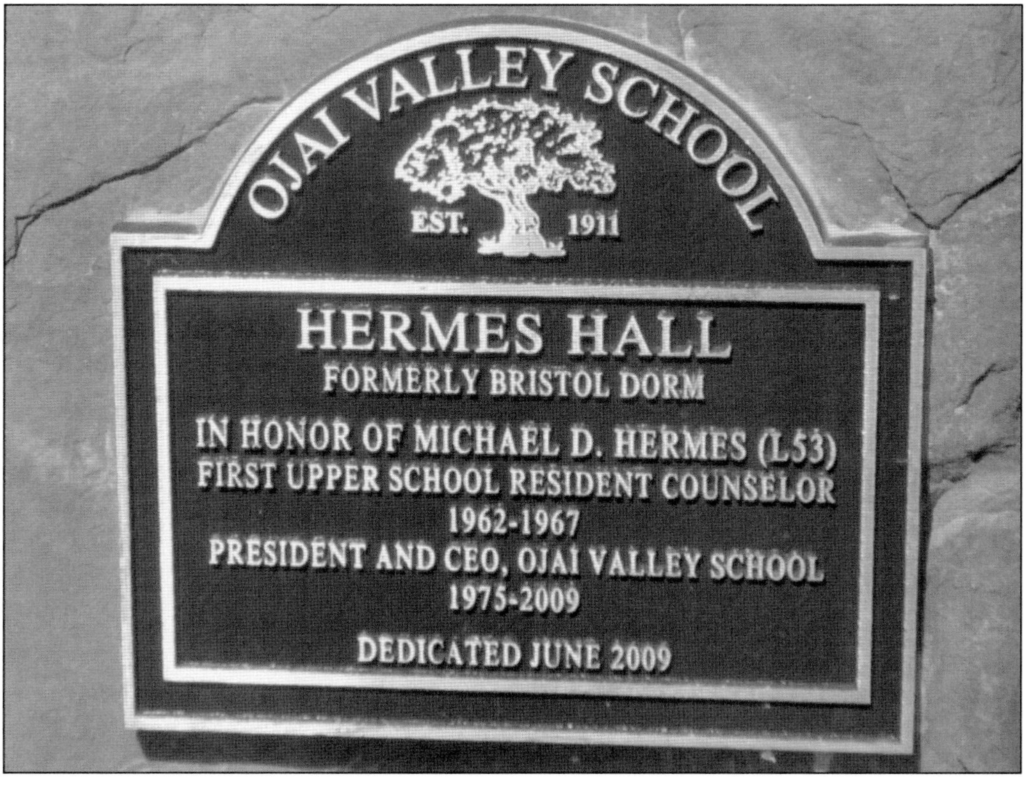

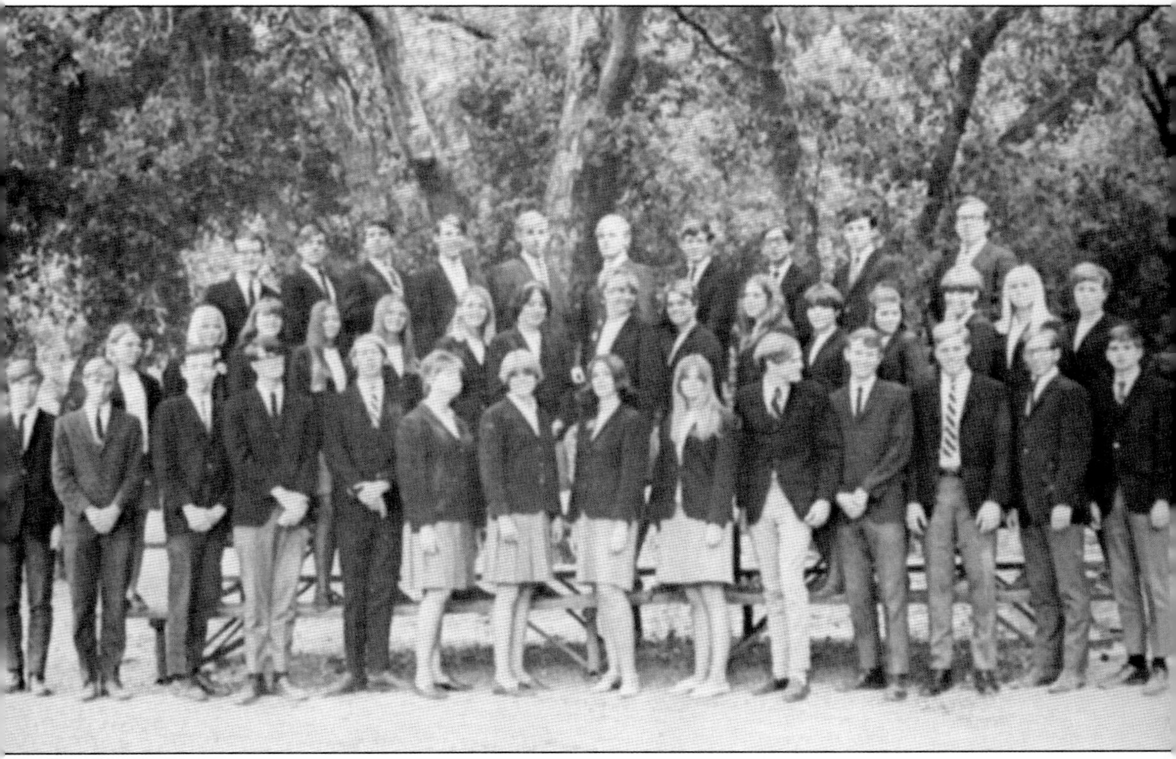

Uniforms. Growth brought many changes as the campus expanded and grades were added. There had not been this many drastic developments since Yeomans first opened the doors of Frost Hall. The introduction of uniforms was looked upon with mixed feelings by the students in the mid-1960s. The winter uniform, also worn for evening and Sunday vesper services, was a knee-length, grey wool skirt with navy blazer for girls, and dark pants with white shirt, tie, and navy blazer for boys. Girls were allowed to wear a variety of mix-and-match uniforms that came in red, white, or blue. Boys wore sports shirts, dark pants, and dress shoes. If shirts were not tucked in, or if clothes were dirty or unkempt, marks were awarded. The 1967 junior class is seen here in full dress uniforms, posing beneath some of the beautiful oaks at the Upper Campus.

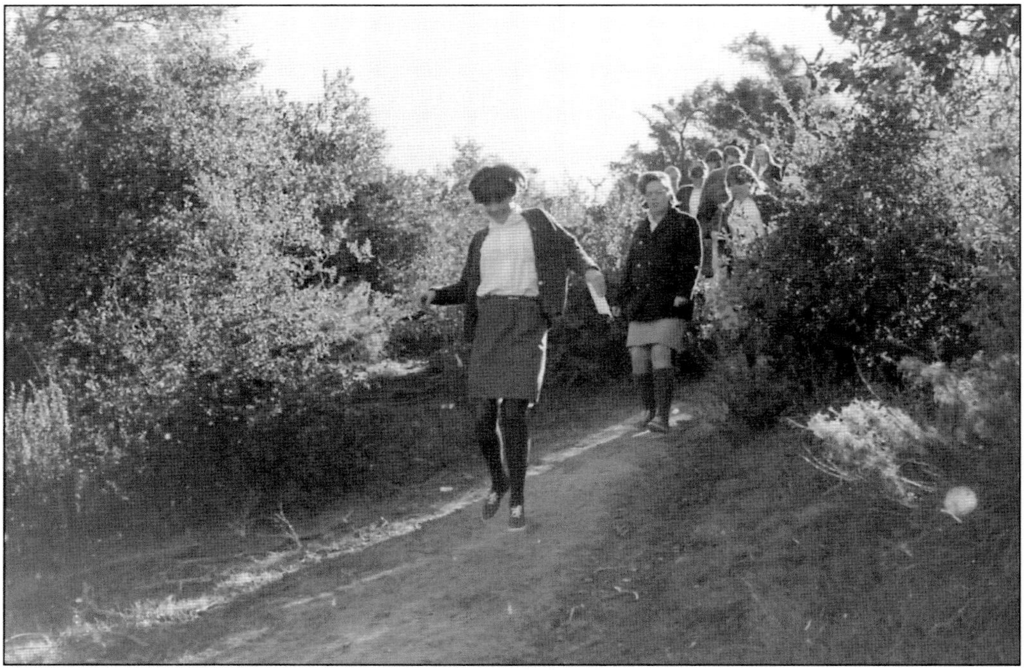

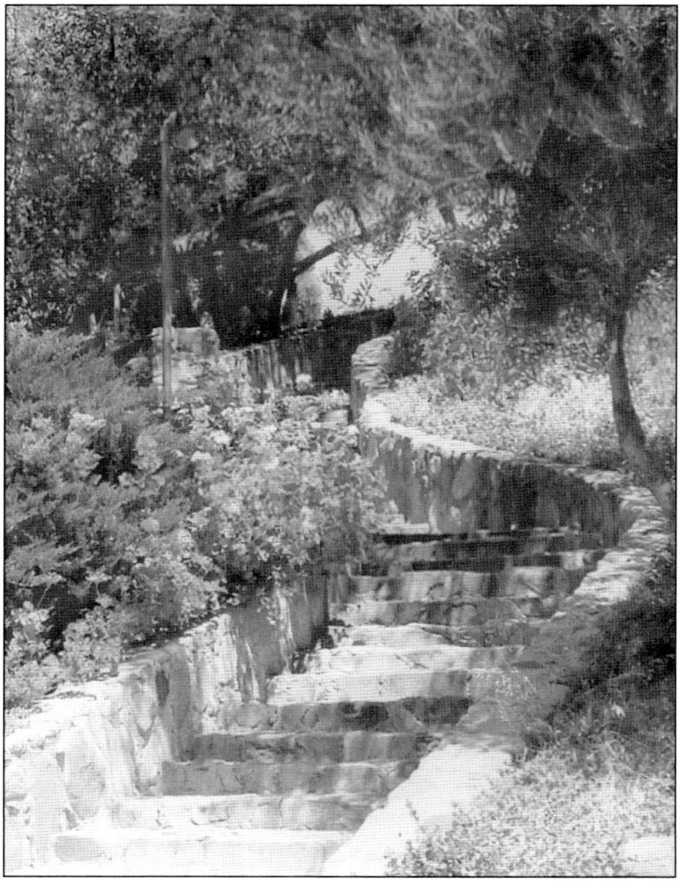

A SHORTCUT. Traditionally, in order to get from the Upper Campus dorms and classrooms to the playing fields, one would have to walk down the lengthy, winding road that circled east through the woods, then back west past the amphitheater. By 1966, the trek from the classrooms to the fields and amphitheater had grown tedious, so the students created a shortcut through the brush and trees. Shown above, Mary Ann Mordock (U68) leads the pack down the shortcut. This blazed trail, now known as Chicken Head Trail, remains the same. The Boney Bean Stairs (left) connect Boney Bean Dorm to the classrooms.

PREPARATION FOR THE FIRST GRADUATION. The Upper Campus's outdoor amphitheater was completed toward the end of the 1964–1965 school year. With graduation looming and construction of the venue still incomplete, school was let out for a few days so that Upper Campus students could help with finishing touches. These included pouring the last layers of concrete and constructing wooden benches. The outdoor setting, in the midst of oaks and hedges, was spectacular. Between 1965 (with its first graduating class of 28) and 2014, a total of 1,145 students—filled with pride, life skills, and friendships—have crossed this stage to receive that coveted OVS diploma.

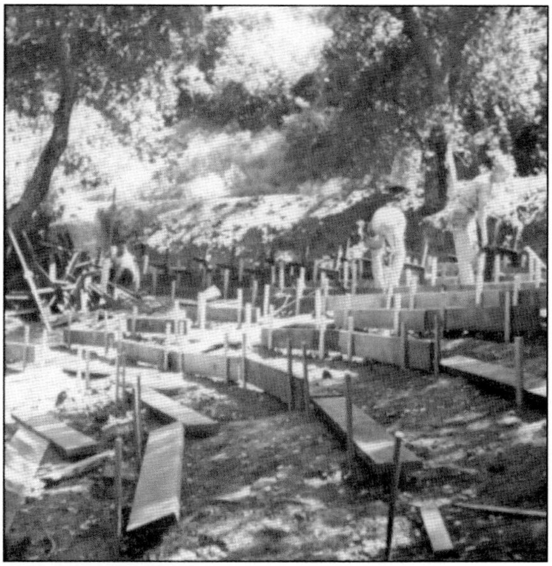

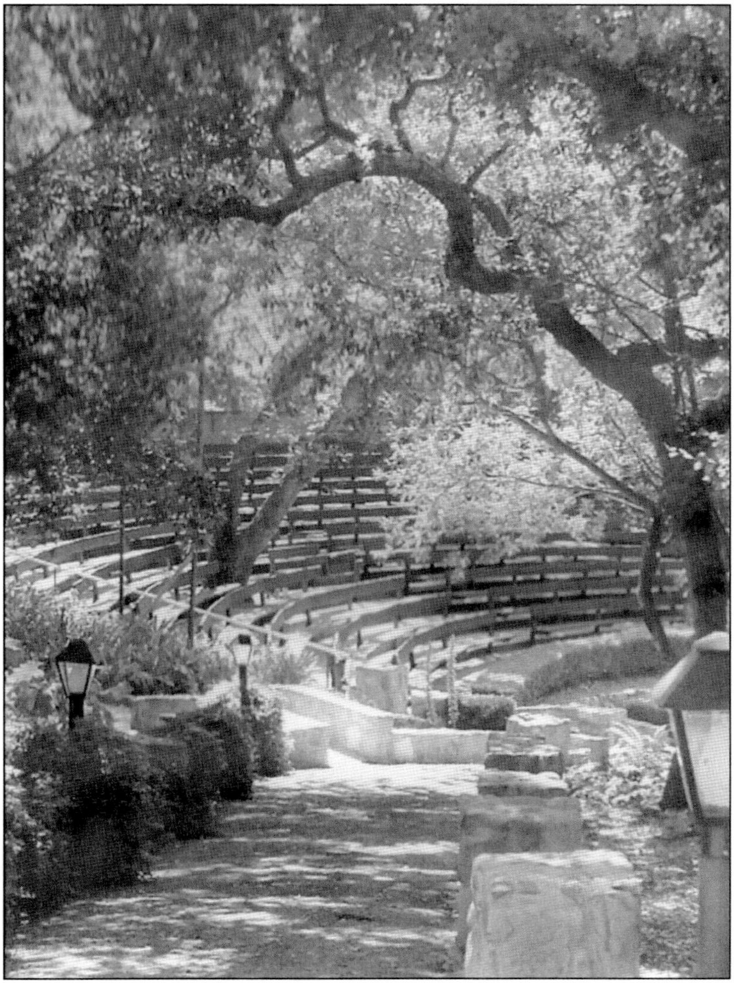

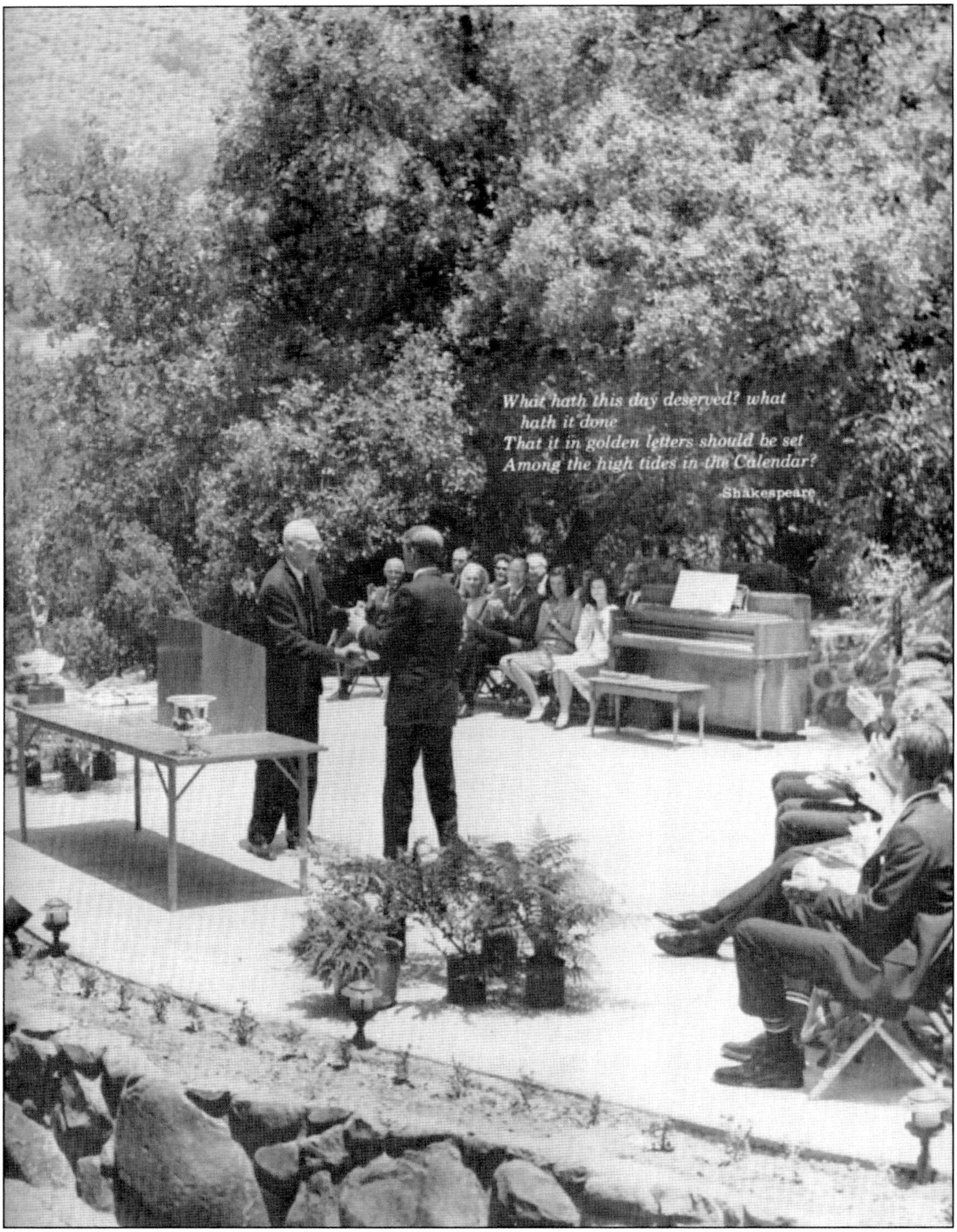

The First Graduation. The dedication of the Upper Campus was held May 8, 1965, with a speech by William L. Wheaton, director of admissions at Pomona College. In his speech, Wheaton extolled the efforts of all who had contributed to the completion of the Upper Campus—from Wallace Burr's vision to the pouring of the last layer of concrete in preparation for the first high school graduation. This landmark ceremony was held just a few weeks later, in June 1965. Class president Dok Smith is shown accepting his diploma from the headmaster, Wallace Burr. Smith later became head of the Upper Campus from 1976 to 1986 and headmaster of the Lower Campus from 1986 to 1990.

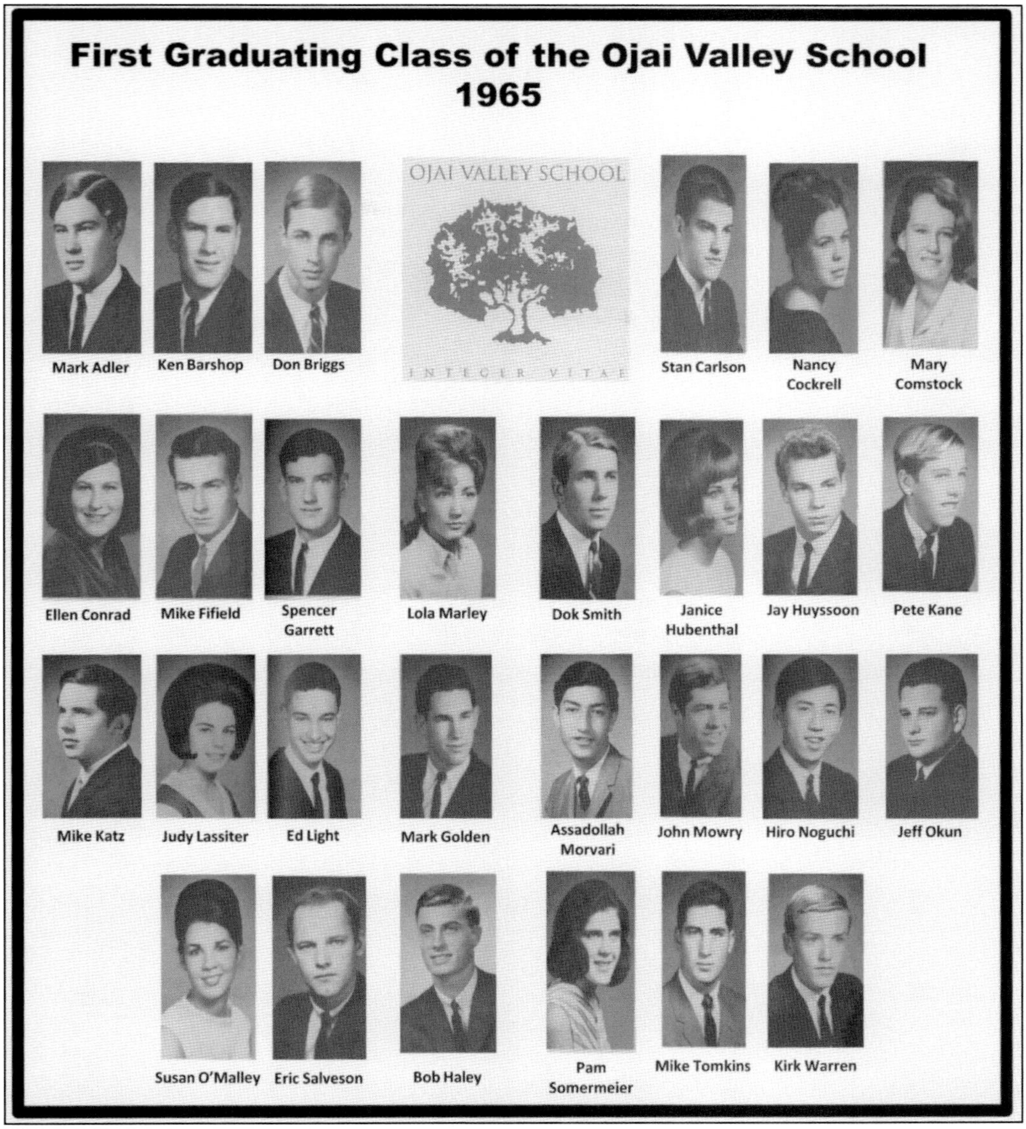

June 1965. The first graduating class of 28 students stepping across the stage of the newly completed amphitheater at the Upper Campus was a milestone for Ojai Valley School. Nine of the original ten boys who moved into Bristol Dorm in 1962–1963 saw their vision to the end. Headmaster Wallace Burr's dream had been fulfilled. Members of the class of 1965 graduated from a fully developed campus with new and unsurpassed facilities and teachers. They shared the unique experiences associated with building and inaugurating a new campus, memories no other class could ever repeat. These pioneers blazed new trails for future classes to follow, and they formed lasting friendships. Now, the desire of ninth-grade students to complete their high school education at OVS had become a reality.

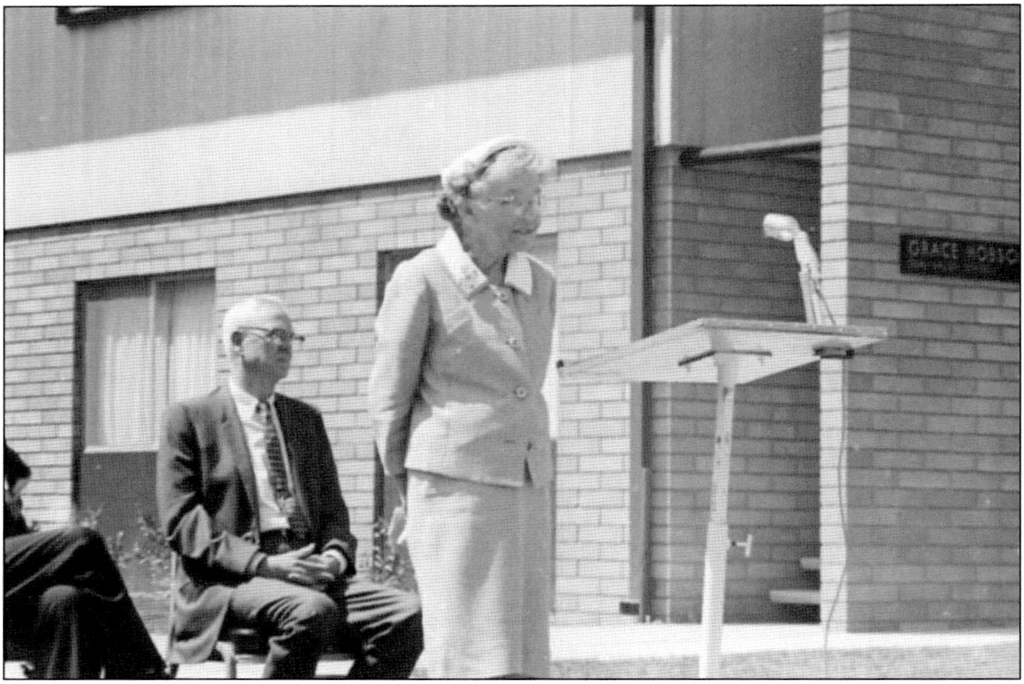

UPPER CAMPUS FAMILY IS COMPLETE. The Grace Hobson Smith House, a two-story dormitory for girls that overlooks the rolling hills and the Ojai Valley, was completed in time for the 1966–1967 school year. This was made possible through contributions from Grace Hobson Smith, a parent and grandparent of OVS students and one of OVS's most generous benefactors. The dedication ceremony was held on the lawn just outside the dorm. Smith was present to receive accolades from students, faculty, and parents as they offered words of appreciation and thanks.

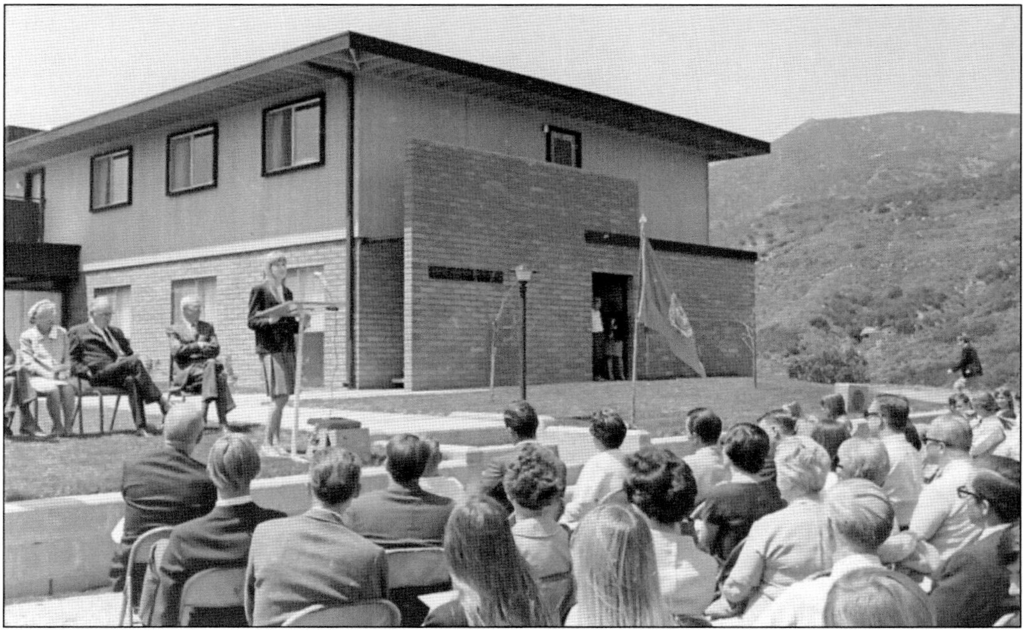

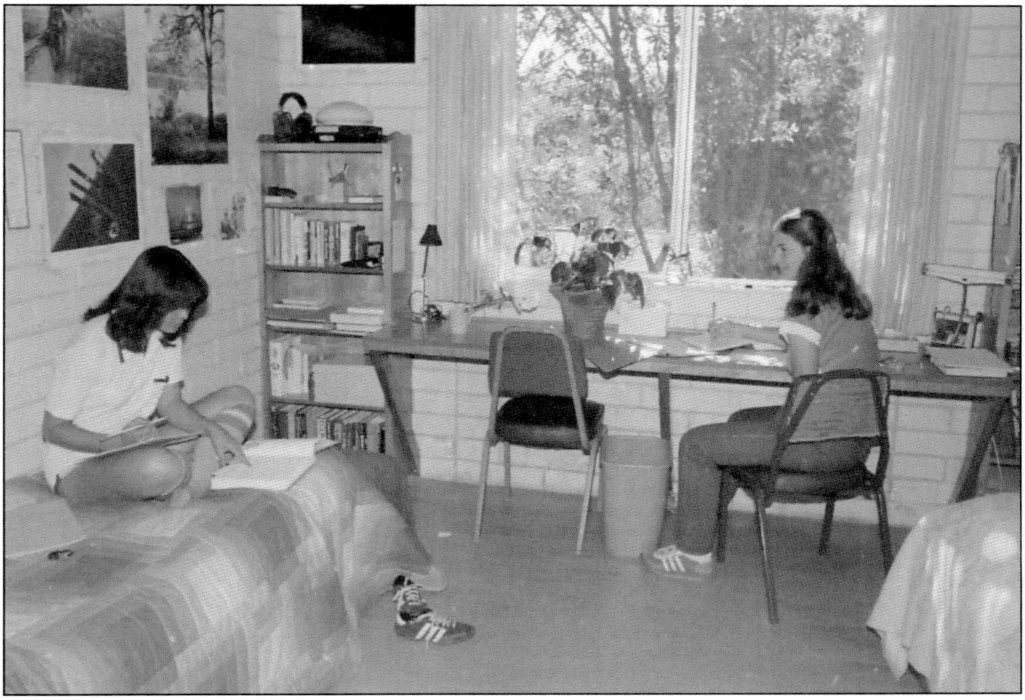

New Living Quarters. The rooms in the Grace Hobson Smith House on the Upper Campus were far more spacious than the 1950s-vintage accommodations at the Lower Campus. Two girls shared a room and were responsible for its cleanliness. Girls were given some latitude in decorating, and many added posters, photographs, and even plants to personalize their living space. Those with horses had additional responsibilities before classes, while others found an extra few minutes to catch up on their reading or review for a test.

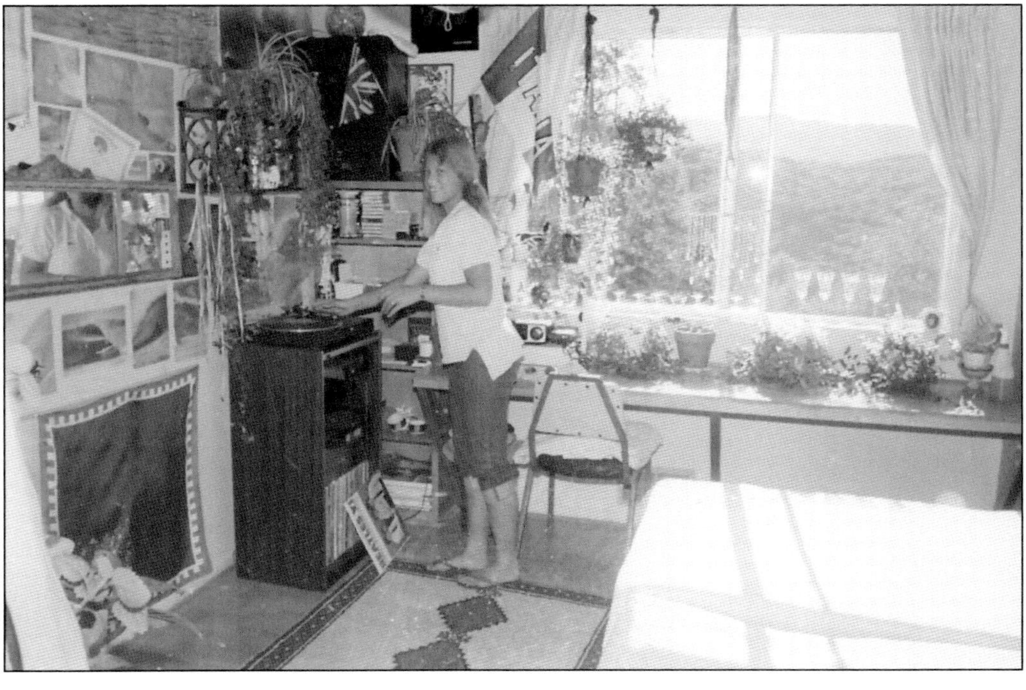

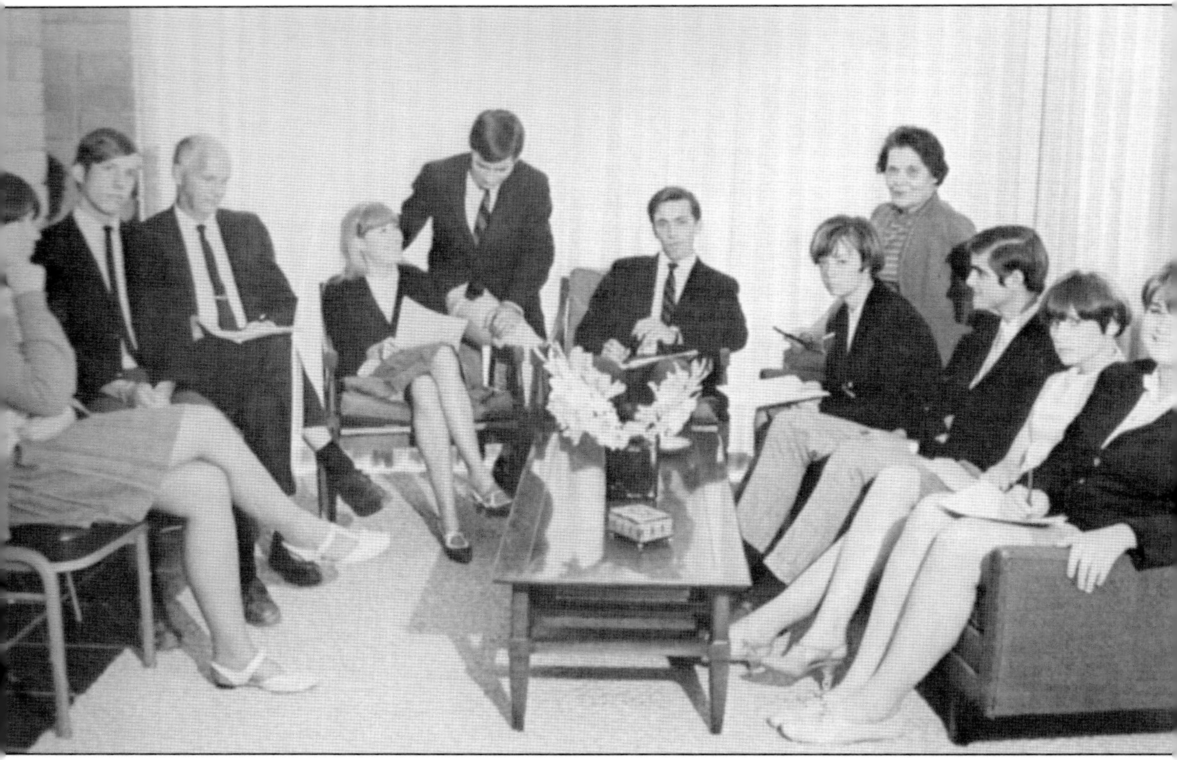

Council of Ten. In the 1960s, unrest over the Vietnam War and the burgeoning drug culture had an effect on the entire nation. Rebelling against authority and tradition became commonplace. No school was spared, private or public. There was great anxiety over bridging the gap between students and adults. Wallace Burr remarked, "I am very concerned about the rebellion of youth. I am dismayed and often displeased. What I would like to see them do is offer some constructive alternatives." In order to bridge this gap between faculty and students, a unique system of faculty-student representation on a governing council called the Council of Ten was started at the Upper Campus. Besides governing, the Council of Ten was in charge of scheduling events such as off-campus trips and concerts. Above is the 1967 council in session. This council served as a precursor to today's student council.

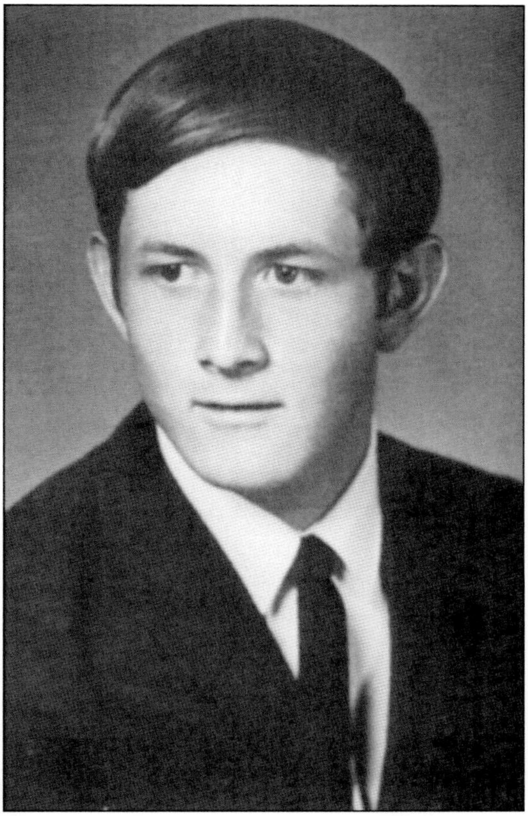

Watching OVS Grow. In 1989, Carl Cooper (L64, U68) was appointed head of school of the Upper Campus. He is pictured at right as a member of the fourth graduating class in 1968, and below in 2004. Like his father, Robert G. Cooper, who had been hired by Wallace Burr in 1951, Cooper developed a great love for the development of the school. Sitting on the stage for 27 commencement ceremonies, Cooper has watched as graduates relentlessly pursue knowledge and understanding, following the two elements promoted by Wallace Burr—"the love of truth and the spirit of charity"—as well as Yeomans's goal of students "striving to be lifelong learners." As the school enters its second century, Cooper still serves and lives at the Upper Campus with his wife, Jody (L71, U74).

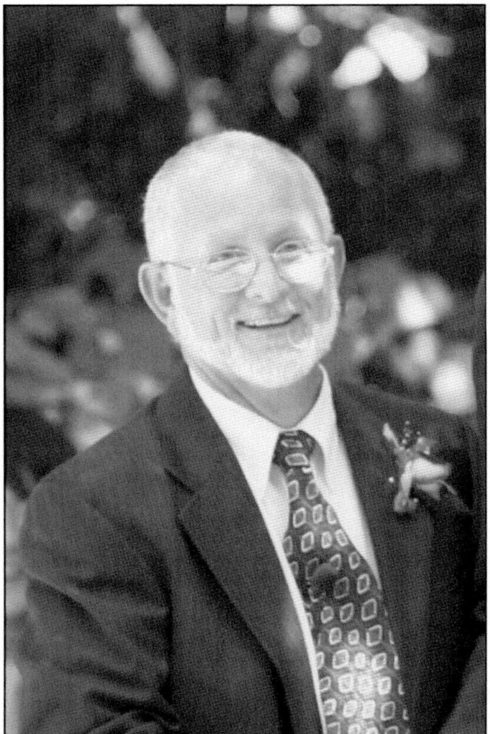

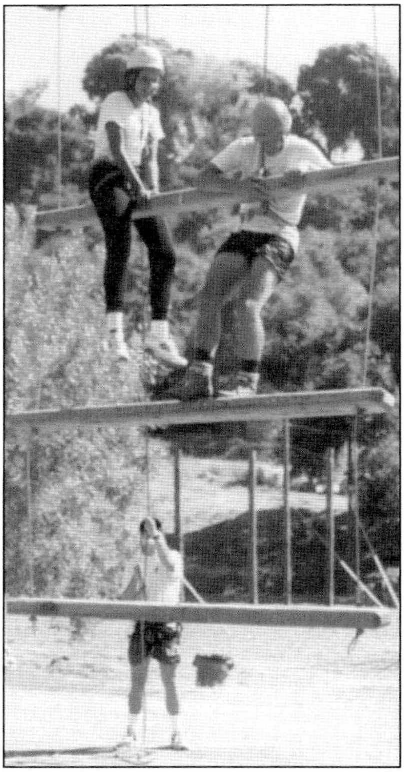

Outdoor Challenges. In 1996, a ropes course consisting of several towers and cable walkways was constructed at the Upper Campus. This approach to learning had been used by Outward Bound and the military with much success. It provided a challenge for the students and allowed them to instill confidence in themselves and build teamwork skills. In addition to the ropes course, athletic fields and a swimming pool were added to help make the Upper Campus more inviting. The distinctive athletic facilities and extraordinary view of the valley helped broaden the appeal to prospective students who might otherwise think the campus too remote.
In 1982, the senior class built an outdoor chapel overlooking the valley as its class gift. Here was a designated place for meditation, religious services, and weddings. These locations, set in the middle of 195 acres, were surrounded by stunning vistas.

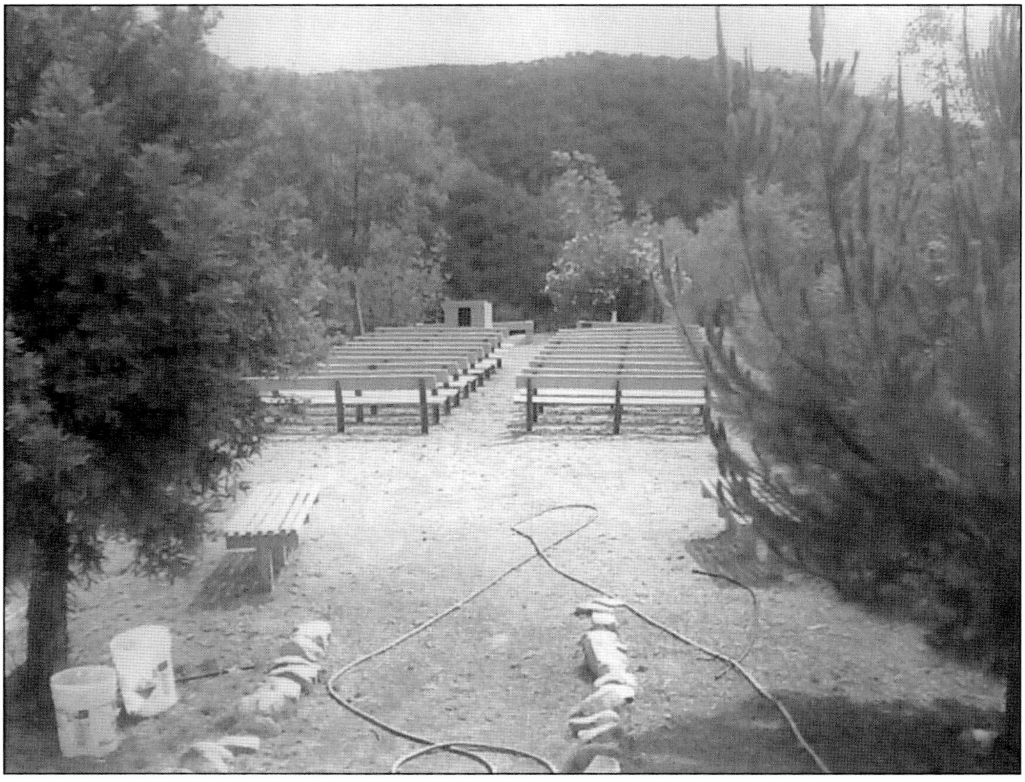

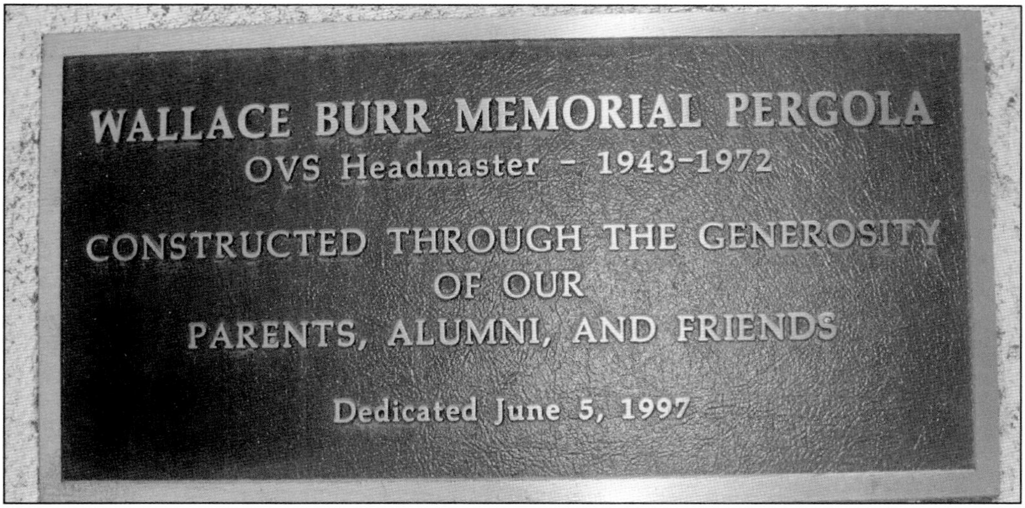

A TRIBUTE. In 1997, the newly constructed Wallace Burr Memorial Pergola, built using generous donations from parents, alumni, and friends of OVS, was dedicated at the Lower Campus. A plaque commemorating Burr's dedication and the generosity of donors was placed just outside on the wall. Everyone knew how much Wallace Burr loved to have students cook and eat outdoors. In addition, reunion celebrations always include a feast on the pergola that is prepared by the kitchen staff and cooked on an outdoor barbecue. This comfortable atmosphere would have pleased Burr, who enjoyed festive affairs and loved to barbecue.

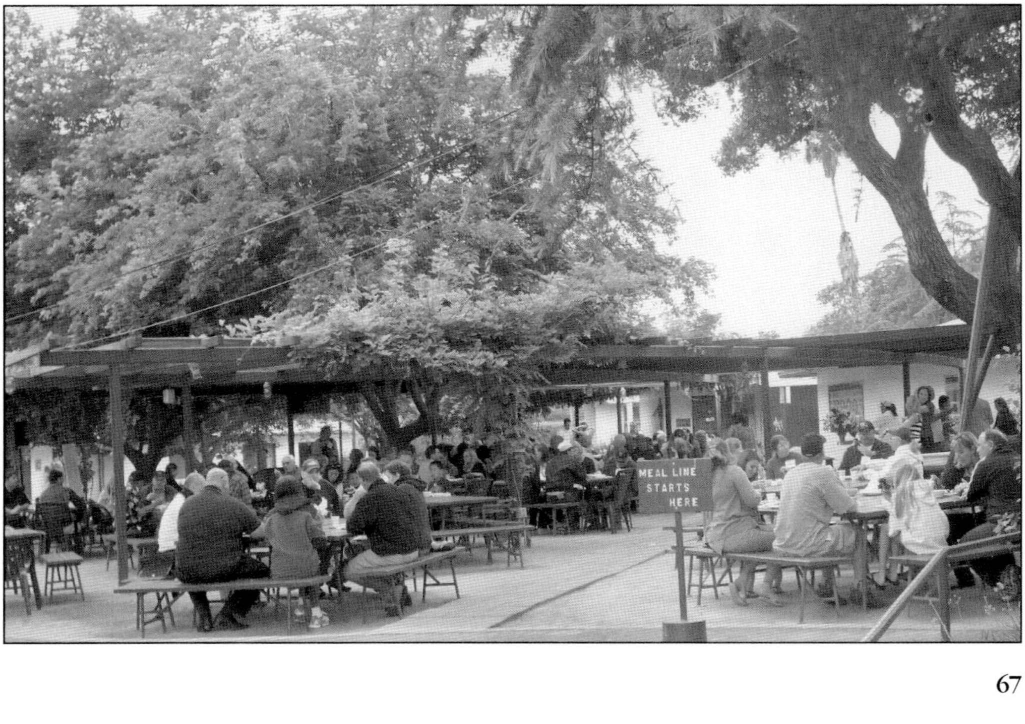

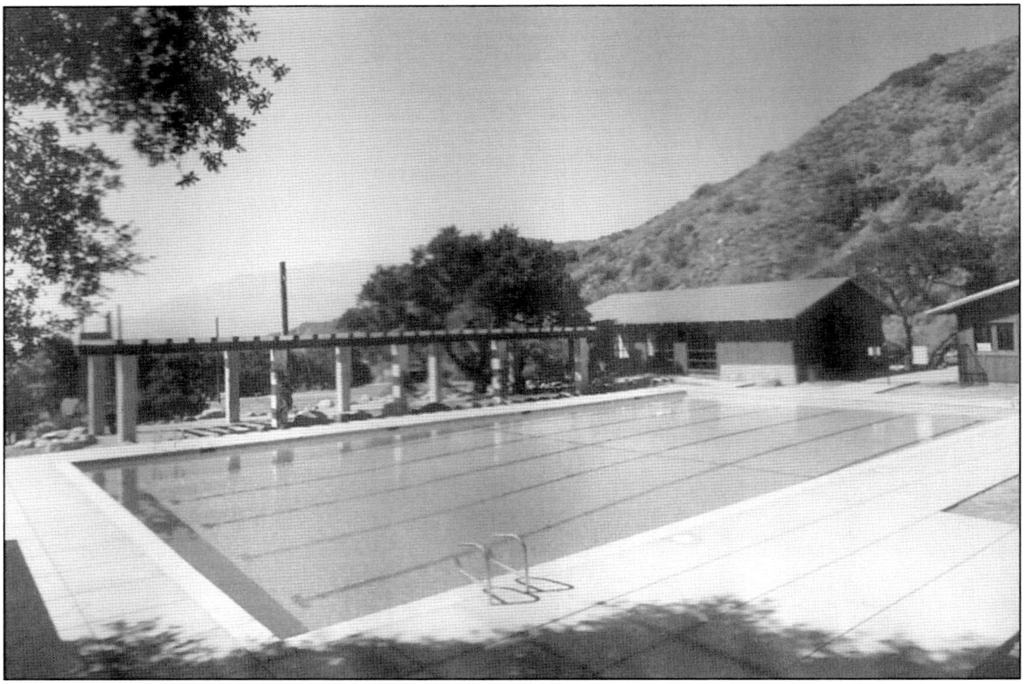

AN UPPER CAMPUS ACTIVITIES CENTER. A swimming pool, field house, and weight room were completed in 1999. The pool was a refreshing reprieve during the hot spring and early fall months. All new additions were made possible through the generous donations of alumni, parents, and friends. In 2005, the school completed construction of the Lucila Arango Science and Technology Center at the Upper Campus (below). Each of these additions, completed under the leadership of Mike Hermes, helped to advance Wallace Burr's vision of a stand-alone high school to complement the kindergarten-to-eighth-grade facility at the Lower Campus.

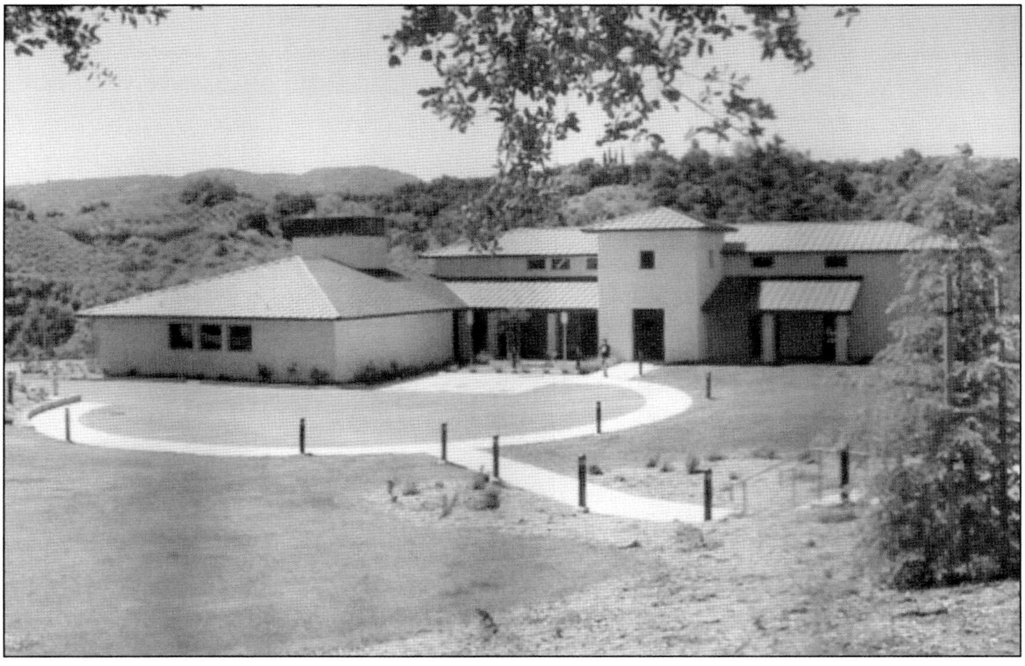

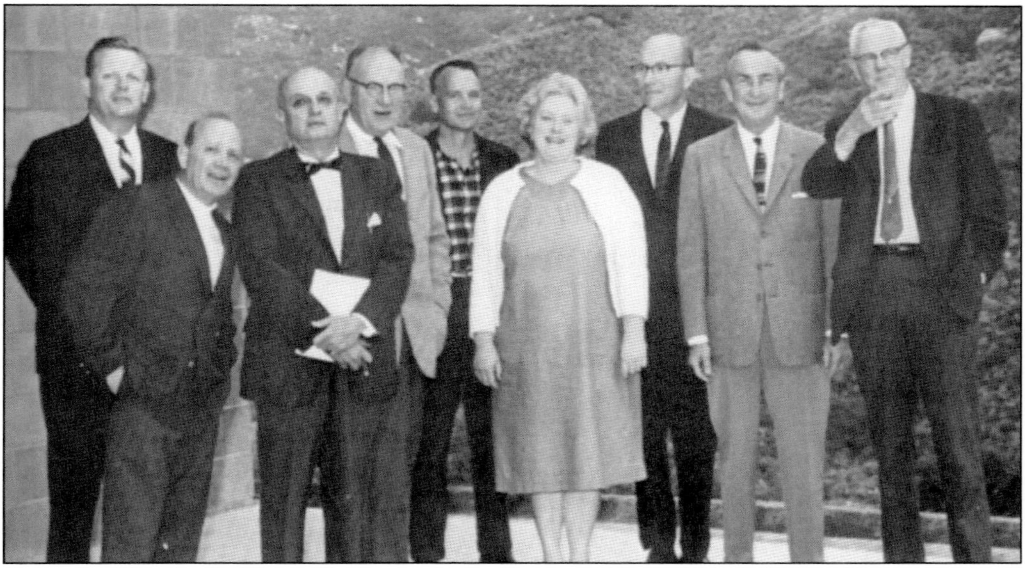

SCHOOL LEADERS. The first OVS Board of Trustees was created in the summer of 1925. Above, from left to right, are the members of the board in 1967: William Myers, George Glass, Benjamin Nordman, Anson Thacher, Rodney Smith, Harriet Herrick, Wil Marcus, Cliff May, and Wallace Burr. Not pictured are Joseph Nesbitt and A. Carl Kotchian. By the mid-1970s, the country and the school had settled down somewhat, and all returned to educating children in a calm environment. School board members wanted children to continue to be challenged physically, mentally, and ethically through expectations, schoolwork, social rules, self-governance, camping, and sports. Below are the 2011 members of the OVS Board of Trustees, 100 years after the beginning of the Bristol School. They are, from left to right, (first row) Pat Farber, Dawn Edwards, Bob Cooper, Ron Rose, and Jack De Nault; (second row) David Trudeau, Andy Helman, Bill Hair, Spencer Garrett, and Michael Hall-Mounsey.

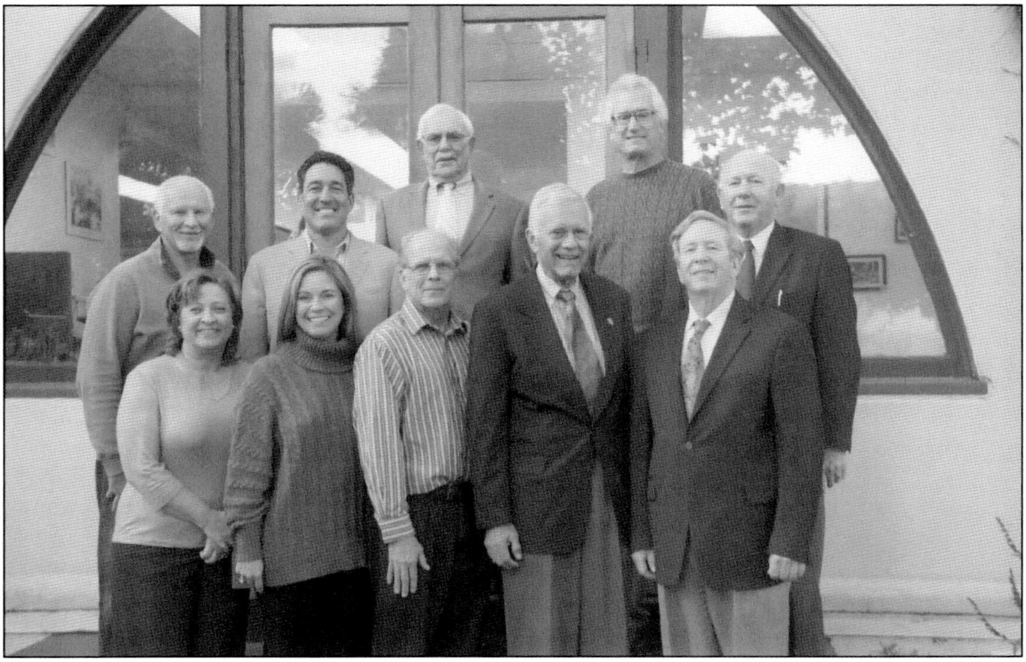

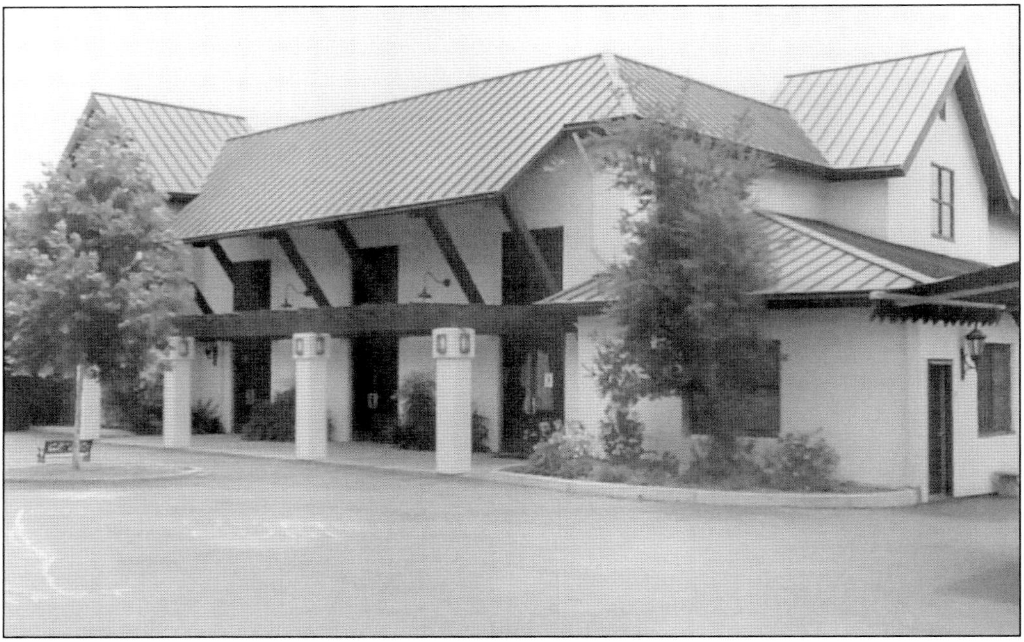

Greenberg Activities Center. The construction of the Greenberg Activities Center in 2006 was one of the most extensive projects at the Lower Campus since the 1923 erection of Frost Hall. This performing arts structure, another product of Mike Hermes's vision, was built over the location of the first Lower Campus pool. The new indoor venue has a fully functional stage with lighting and sound systems for plays and lectures. Removable seating allows an open floor for a variety of uses. This venue is ideal for performances or large gatherings (such as the alumni dinner at the centennial celebration, shown below). It also includes rehearsal and practice facilities.

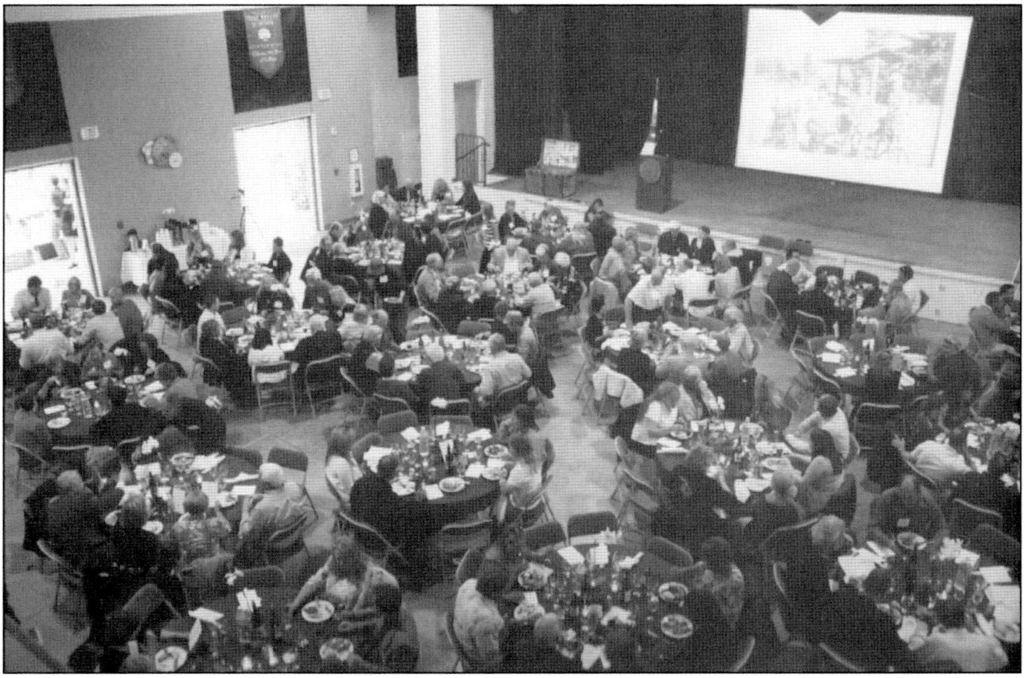

Six

The Hermes Legacy

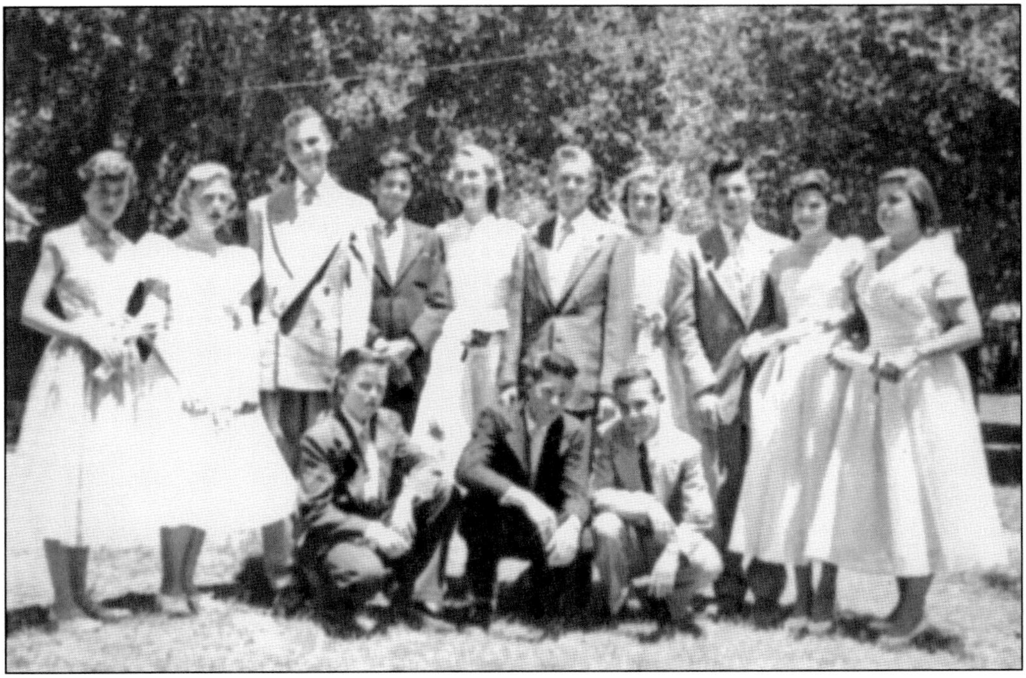

Michael David Hermes. Michael Hermes, whose parents were teachers at the nearby Thacher School, was familiar with the private school environment. He entered OVS in 1946 and attended second grade there, as well as seventh through ninth. Graduating from the Lower Campus in 1953 as president of his ninth-grade class (first row, center), he was also the recipient of the school's leadership award. Hermes graduated from Midland School in 1956 as president of his senior class. He returned to OVS as a staff member in 1962, and his initial roles included dorm parent and coach at the Upper Campus. Hermes always had a love and a vision for the school's future at the Upper Campus. His influence on the school, especially its academic programs and building development, cannot be overstated.

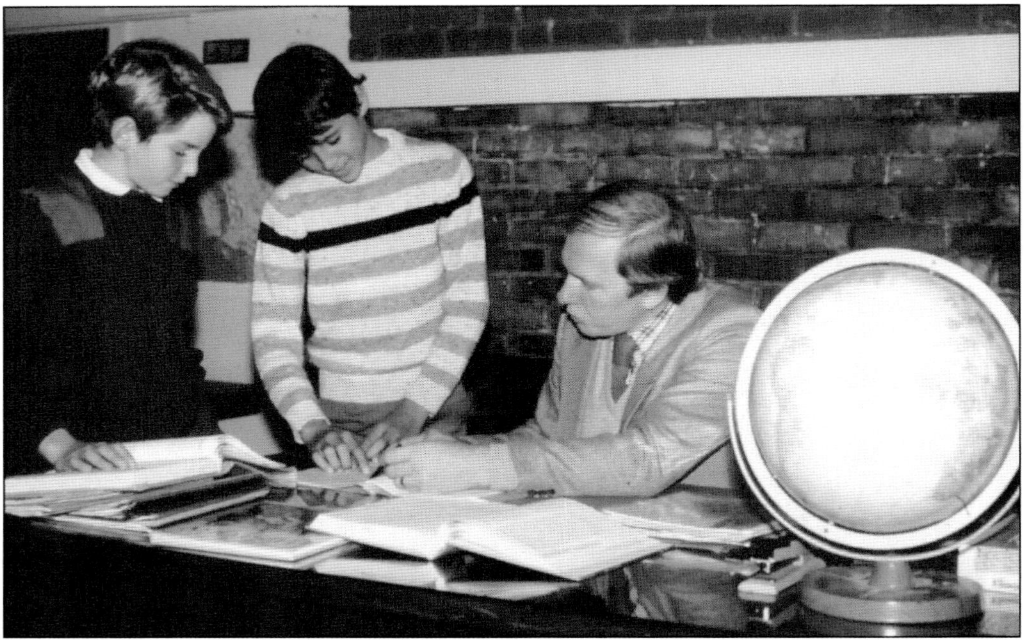

Academics. The OVS academic curriculum began with Yeomans's almost exclusively experiential approach and has developed into a more technology-focused program that befits a 21st-century educational institution. Above is a special social studies session for Lower Campus students with Michael Hall-Mounsey, who began as a teacher and coach in 1981 and is now president and chief executive officer of the school. Expanding enrollment increased the need for Advanced Placement classes at the high school. Nightly two-hour study hall remains a requirement for resident students. Below, math instructor Duncan Wallace explains algebraic principles to his middle school class. High school math instruction begins with algebra and concludes with Advanced Placement math, which includes calculus and statistics.

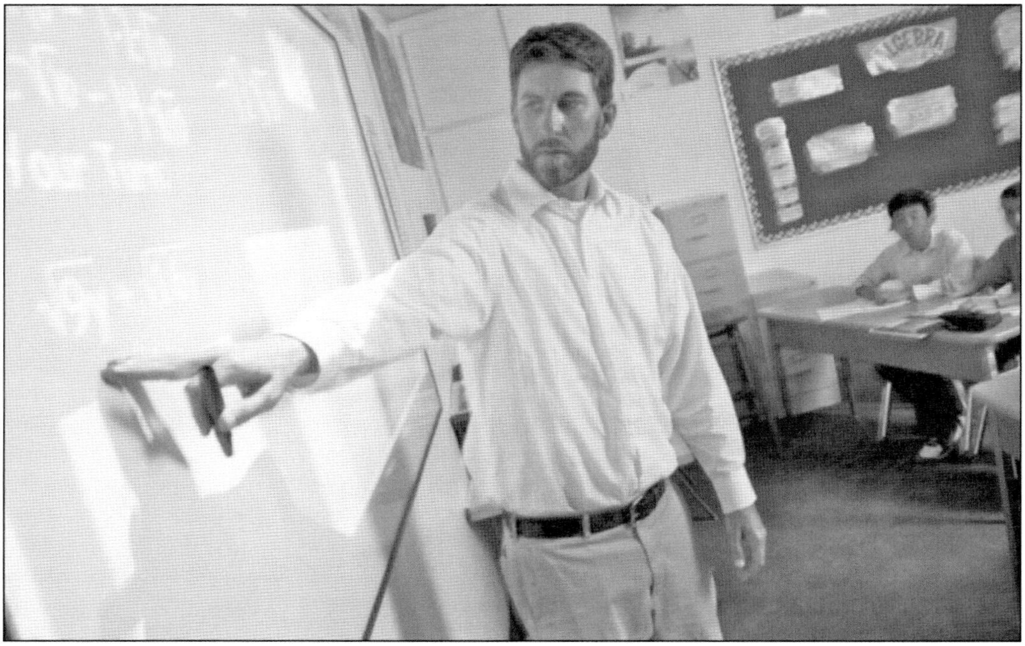

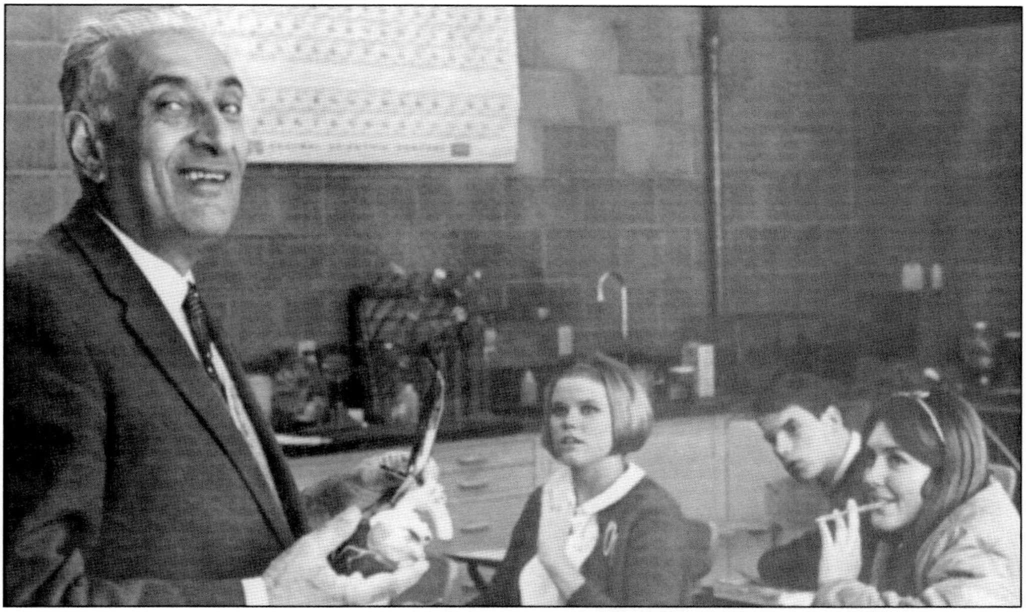

Arts and Science. Small class sizes (10 students or fewer) were and are the norm for OVS. This allows more personal attention for students and private tutoring if required. A strong college-preparatory curriculum includes Advanced Placement and honors coursework. Minimum requirements include English, math, social studies, foreign languages, lab sciences, and fine arts. Biology labs, such as those taught by Dr. Ahmad Parsa, seen above, bring science to life and encourage student participation. Parsa was considered the French, science, and biology guru in the 1960s. At right, former teacher Jessica Thompson has students looking on with great anticipation during a science experiment.

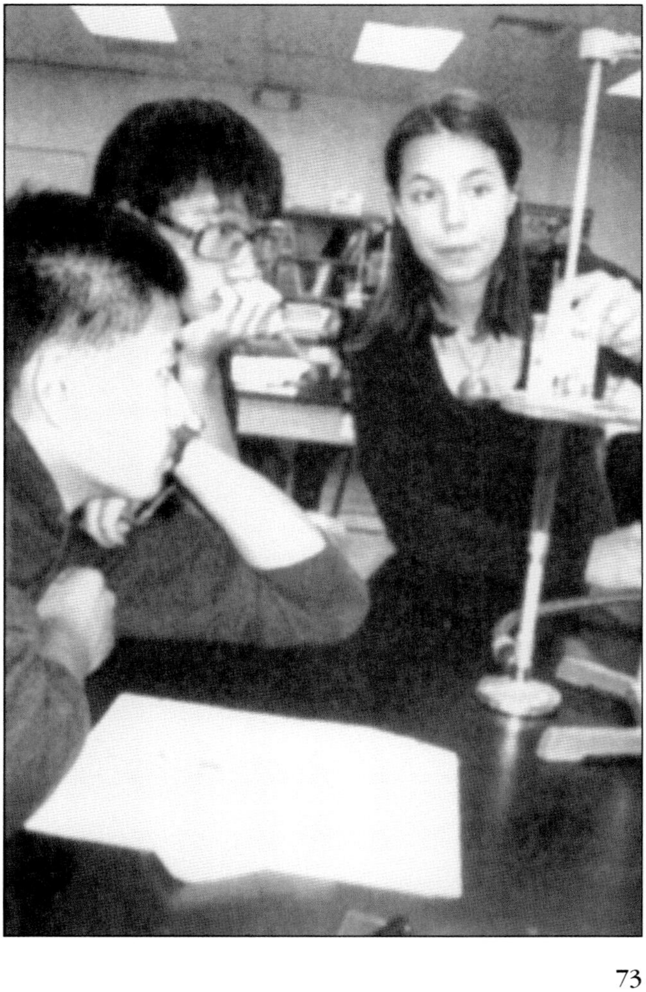

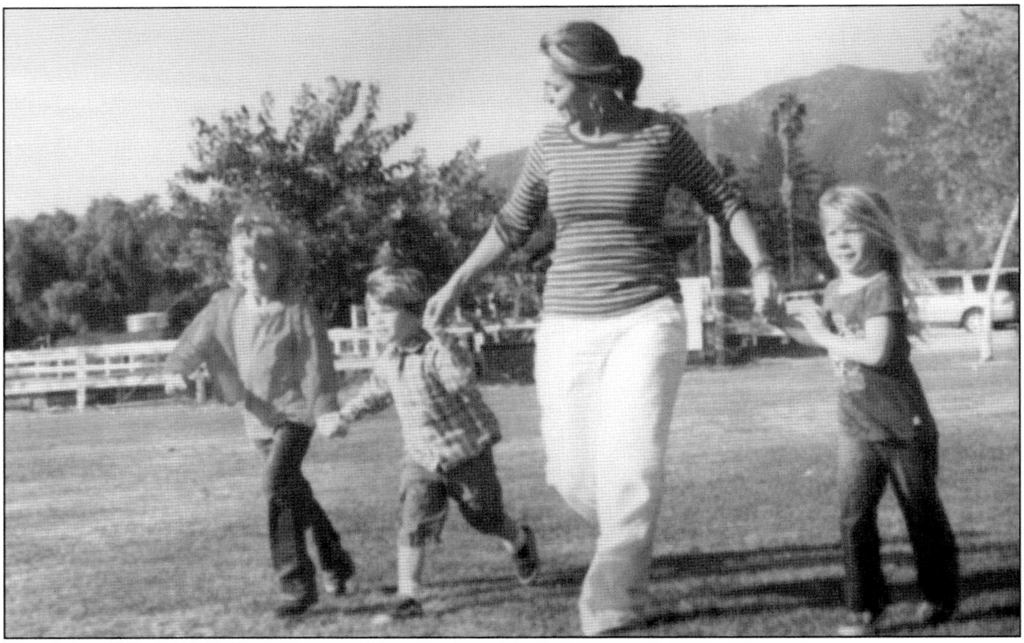

THE YOUNGEST STUDENTS. The kindergarten program began at OVS in 1935, but it was discontinued after three years. In 1990, kindergarten was reintroduced and was available for day students only. Classes were held in the original 1923 academic building. Learning was individualized in the academic areas, and art, music, and barnyard activities were included. With the recognition that younger children are much more adept at assimilating languages, Spanish and Chinese instructions are now included in the elementary curriculum. Hiking and field trips round out the schedule. Children develop self-respect and good sportsmanship while learning to get along in a cooperative setting.

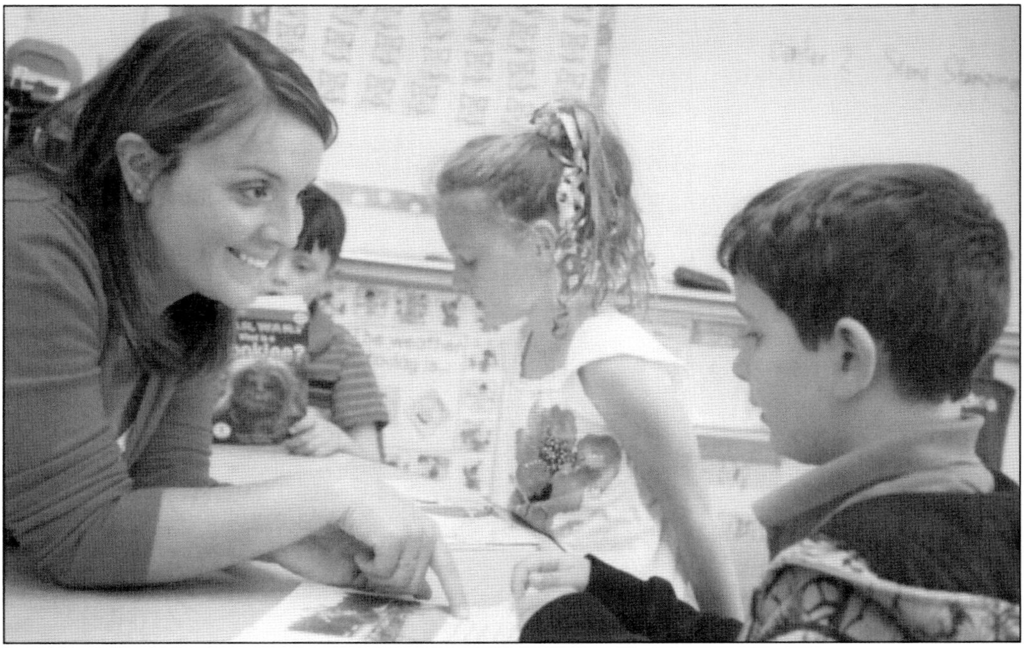

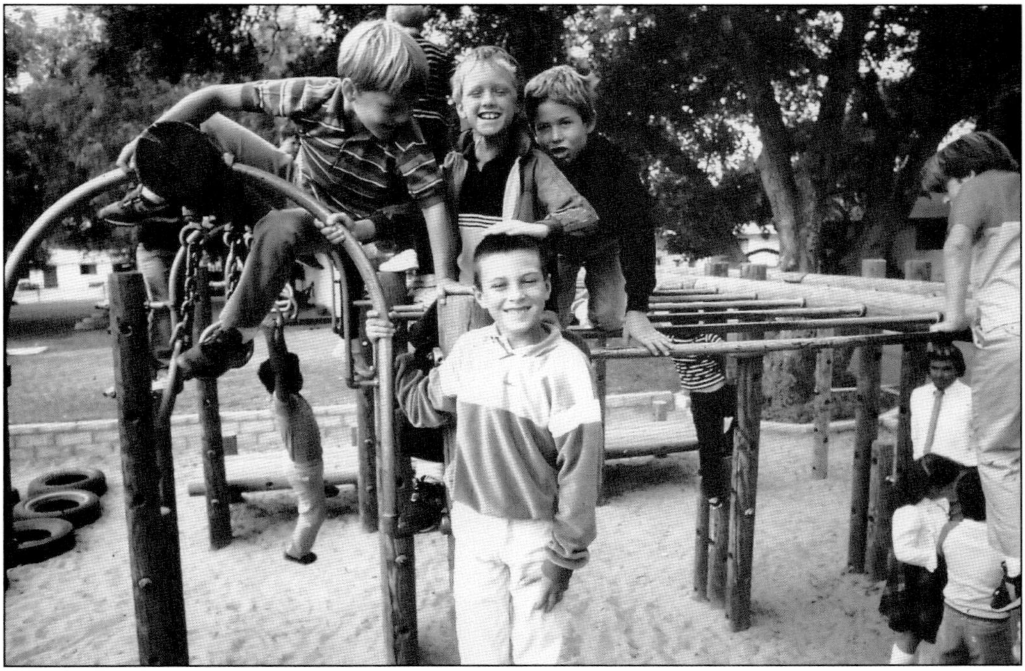

The Art of Play. In this image, elementary children play on Lower Campus playground equipment generously donated by family and friends. Yeomans believed that children are never too young to appreciate the outdoor environment.

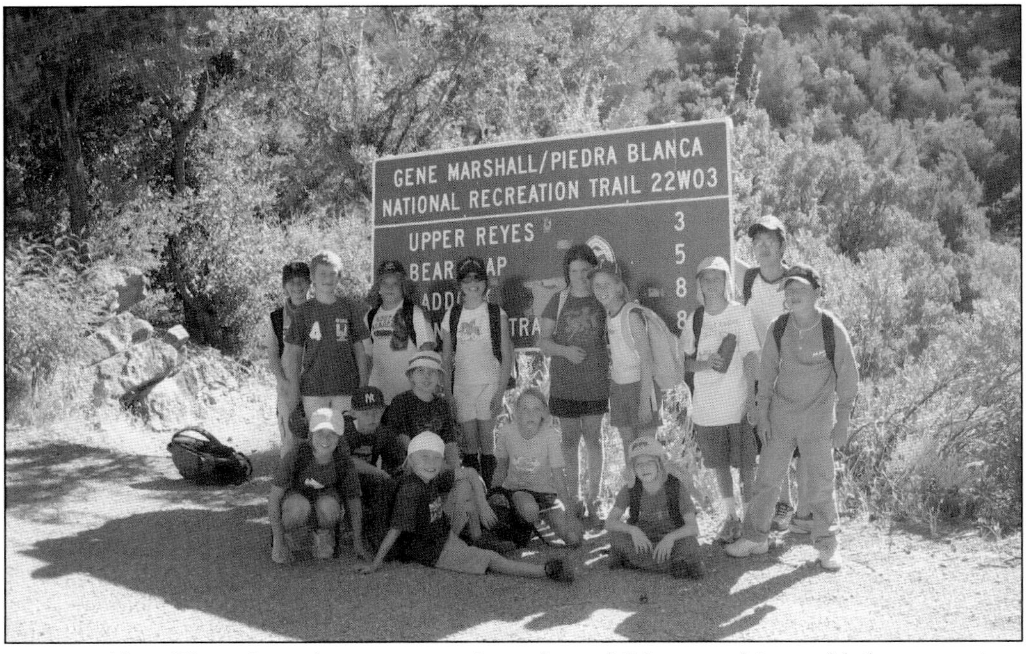

Camping Trip. There is no better way to introduce children to this world than camping, as shown in this image of a group of fifth graders preparing for a trek to Piedra Blanca in 2005. They will set up tents and spend a few nights in the great outdoors. Student trips (also discussed in chapter 8) include horseback camping and drives to remote locations where hikes can begin.

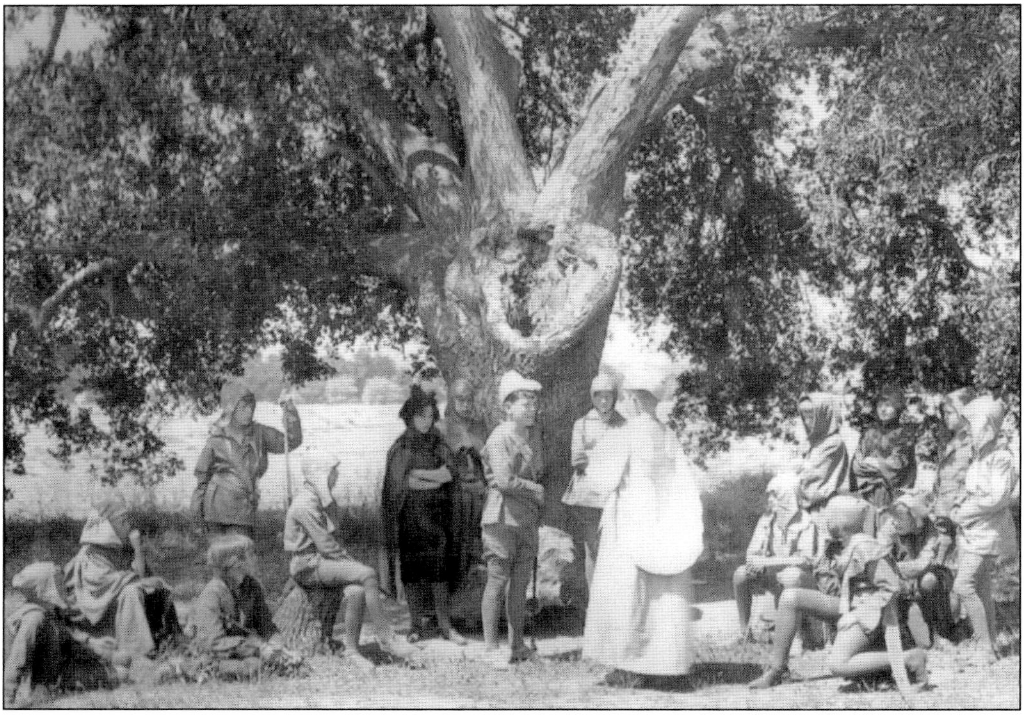

Drama. The image above is from a 1927 performance of *Robin Hood*. Very much in keeping with the importance Yeomans placed on a strong connection with Mother Nature, some plays were performed in a natural setting beneath the school's stately oak trees. Below is a 1938 performance of *A Winter's Tale*. Also in keeping with Yeomans's hands-on approach to education, the children helped make their own costumes for these performances. Plays were yearly events anticipated by students, faculty, parents, and members of the community.

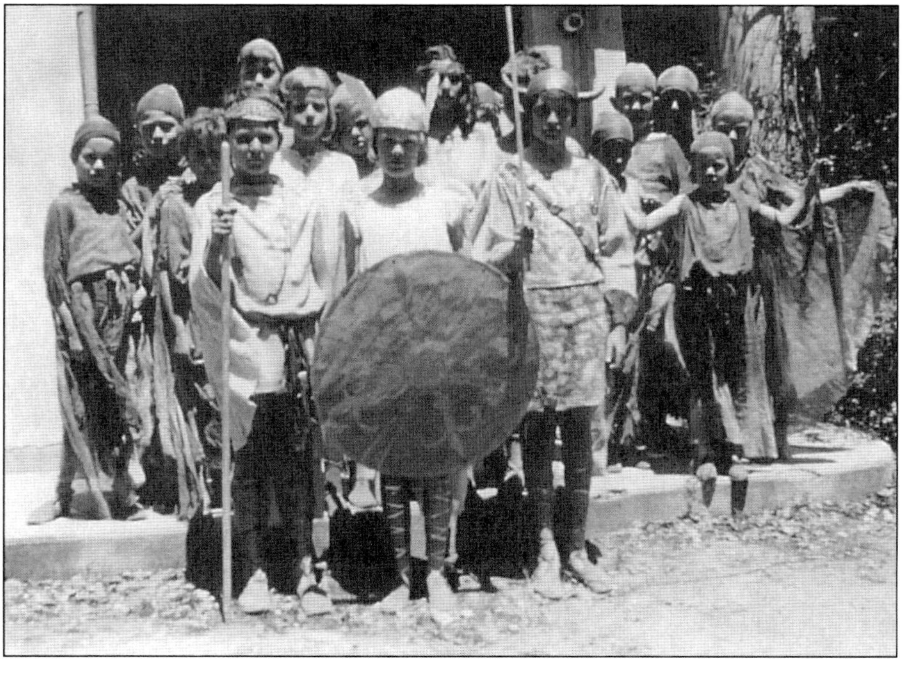

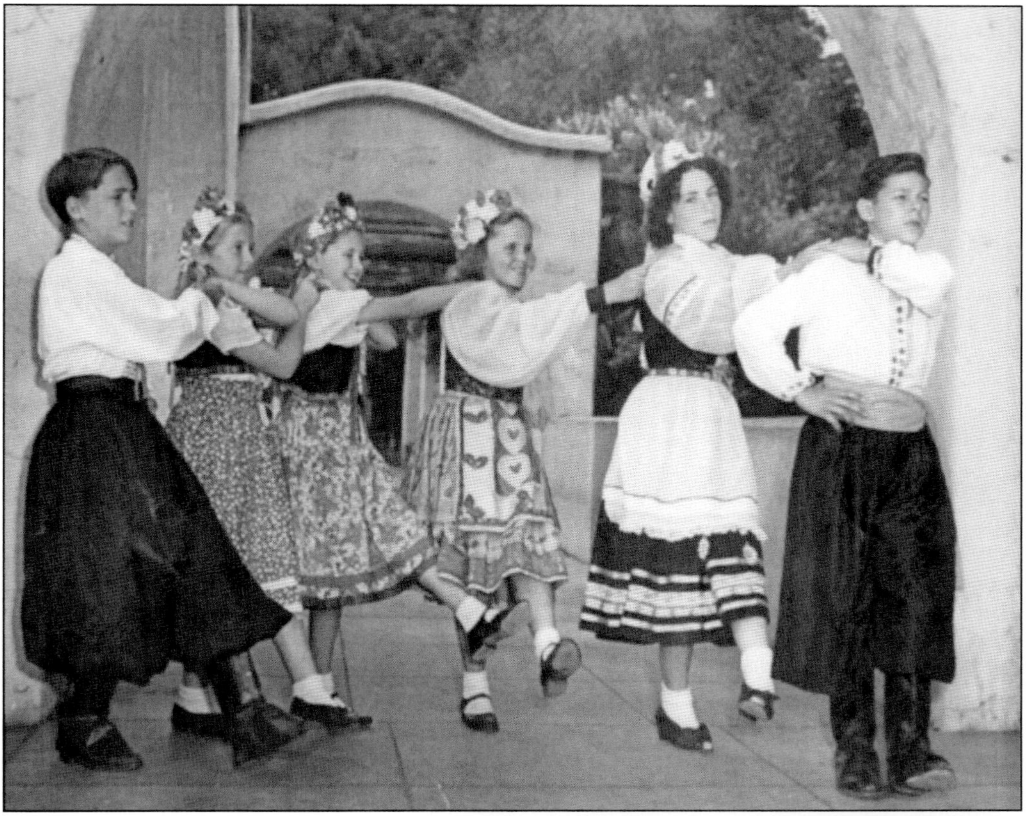

Special Events. In 1946, OVS students perform Ukranian dances to display their talents during the Ojai Music Festival. Scott Eicher (right, L65, U68) ages 20 years in 20 minutes in *The Lottery*, performed in 1968 under the direction of J.B. Close. This play, based on a 1948 short story by Shirley Jackson, tells how the town elder, Old Man Warner, encourages an annual tradition of stoning one of the townspeople each year—a paper marked with a black dot and picked from a box determines the town member to be stoned that year; this is strangely reminiscent of the current Hunger Games trilogy.

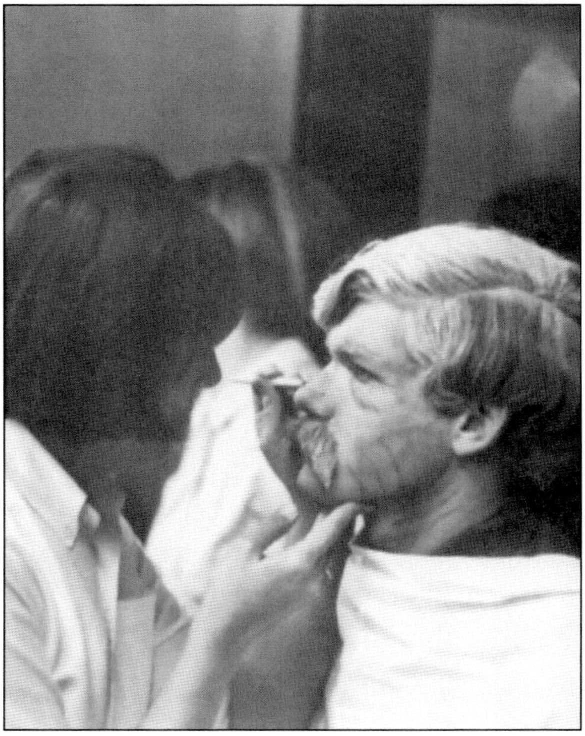

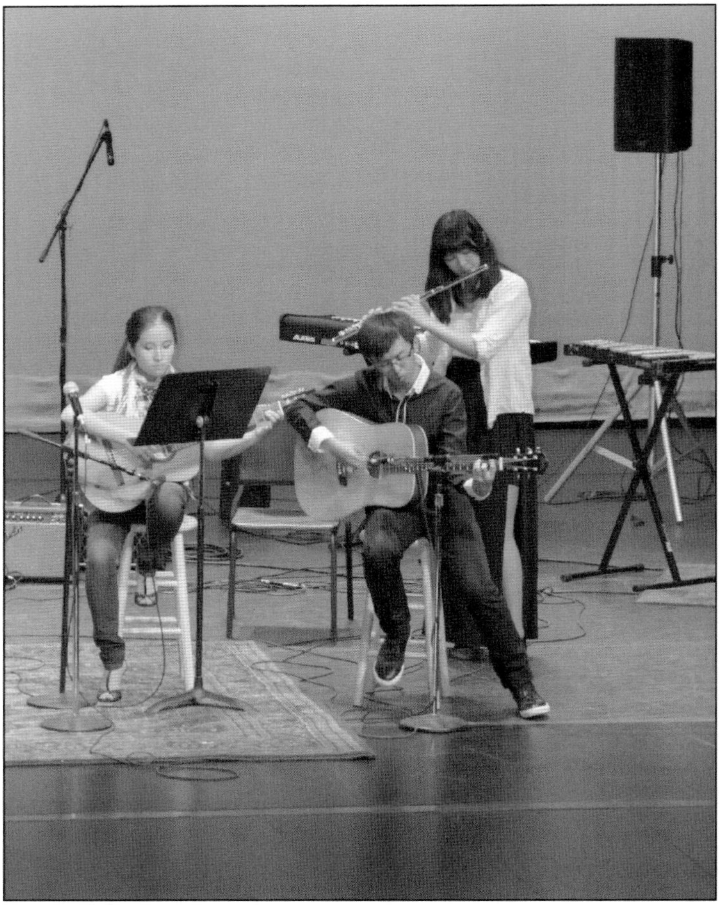

Practice Session. The arts were another cornerstone of Edward Yeomans's philosophy, to which the school remains committed more than 100 years later. The curriculum still includes fine arts, drama, arts and crafts, and music, using the latest capabilities and technology. In the image at left, three students practice for an upcoming recital, or perhaps just for their own enjoyment. Lucy Kim, pictured below, performs a flute solo in 2011. Instrumental instruction, musicals, solos, and choral groups are available to all students.

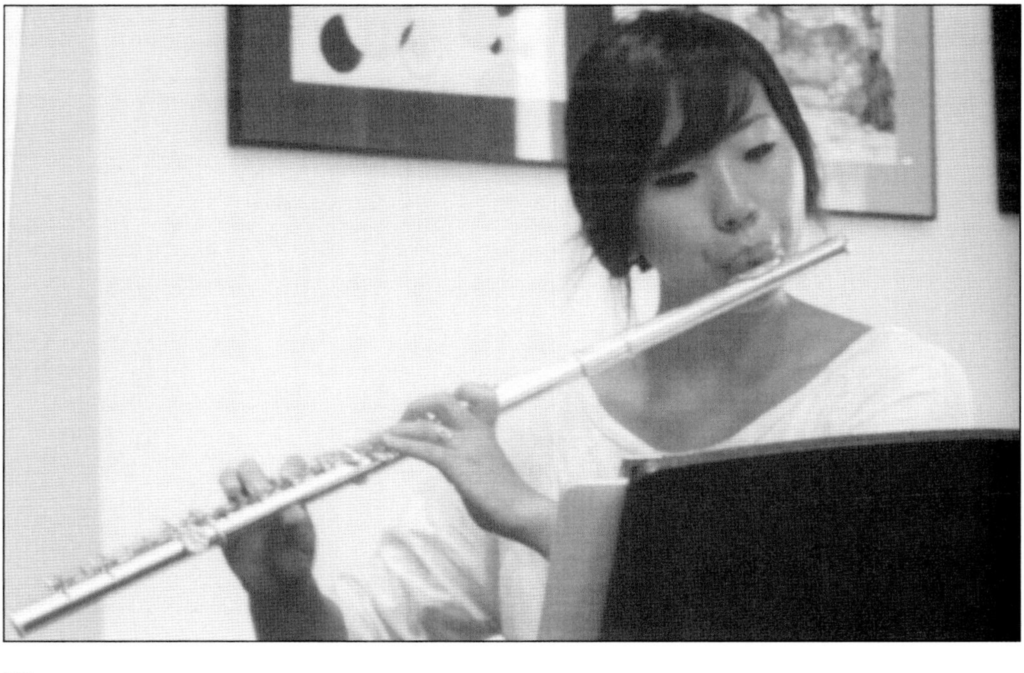

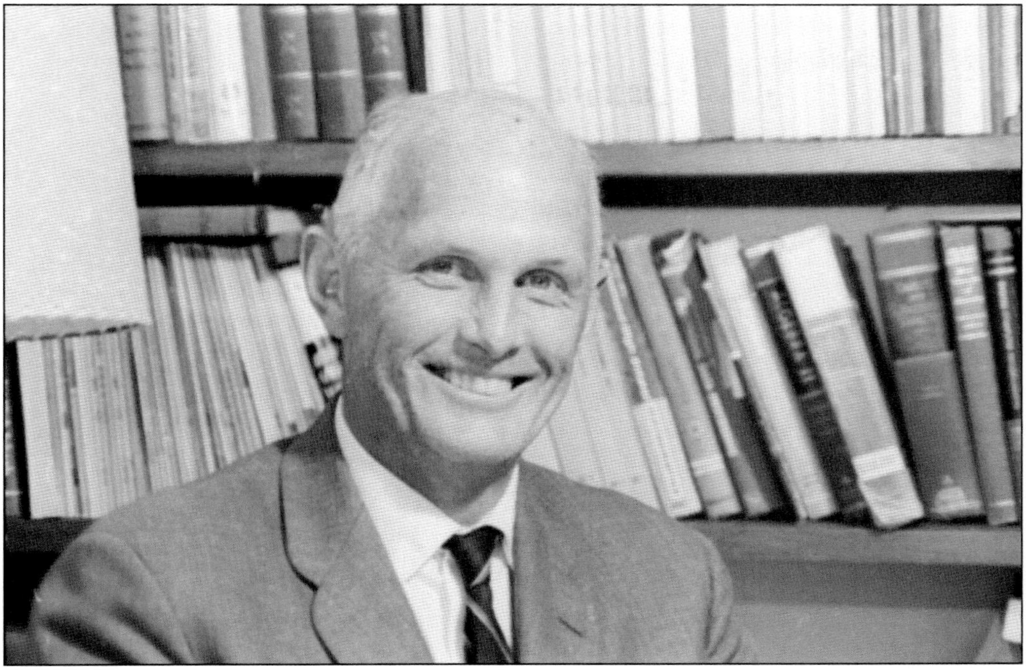

Director of Upper Campus. Robert Cooper, hired by Wallace Burr in 1951, loved physical education and believed in discipline, teamwork, fair play, and good sportsmanship. He insisted that students be responsible for their actions, and he was highly respected. His arrival marked the beginning of interscholastic athletics at OVS. Boys would rush to the courts at lunchtime to shoot baskets with "Coop," and they looked forward to his Sunday touch football games.

Family Man. Cooper said, "One of my reasons for coming to OVS was the chance for my family to participate in the camping program." During his 23 years of service, Cooper taught many subjects and made memorable trips down the Sespe. He and his family moved into a newly constructed home on the Upper Campus in 1964, when he became the director of the Upper Campus. Cooper retired in 1974.

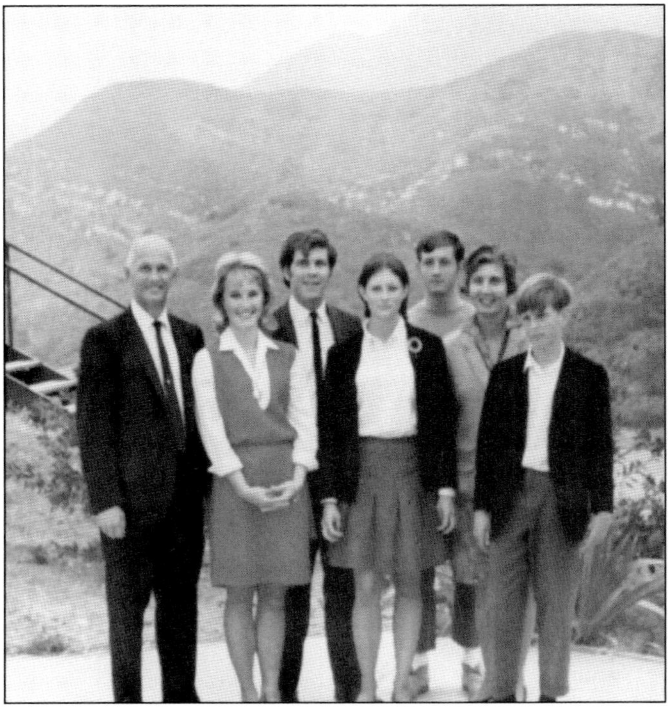

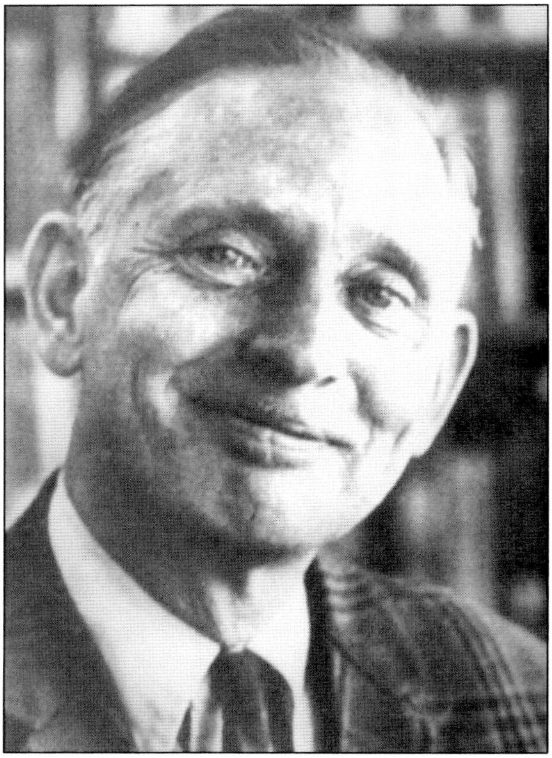

Junius Benham "J.B." Close. J.B. Close came to OVS in 1956. As shown on the next several pages, he typifies the versatility of the OVS faculty. After graduating from Yale, he taught at The Thacher School from 1947 to 1949. He was known for his command of the English language and his love of the theater. Close, a wonderful reader of stories, blessed many assemblies with his readings of *Peter Rabbit*, *Winnie-the-Pooh*, and tales by Edgar Allan Poe. Students were spellbound every time he stepped up to the podium. Close referred to himself as "Toad" and affectionately called some students by special terms of endearment, such as "Moo," "Igit," "Mim," and "Milmoss."

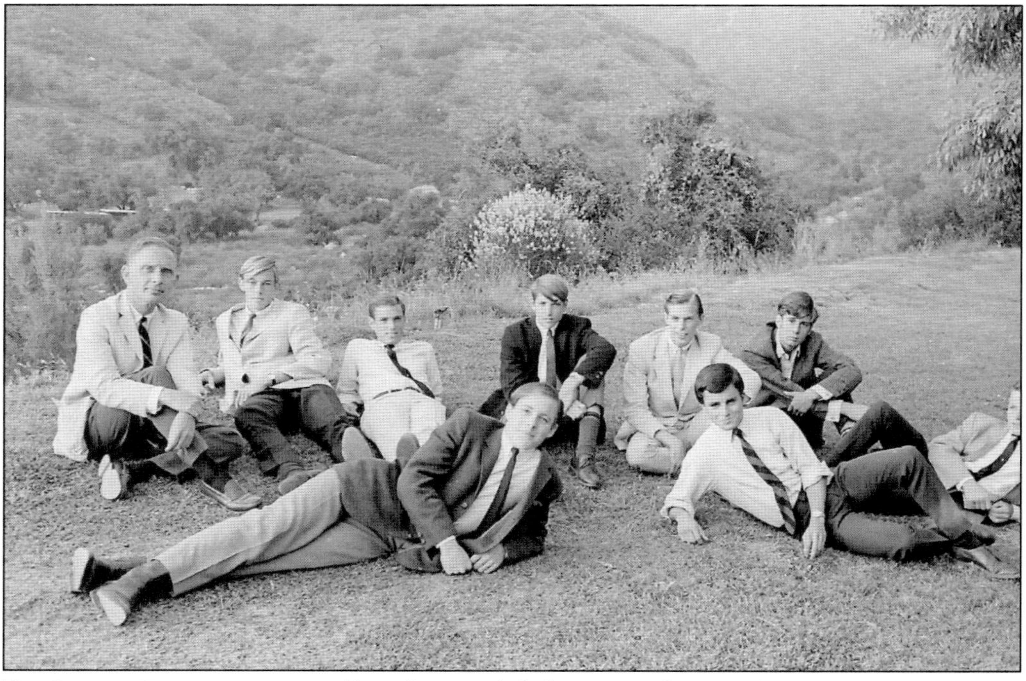

The Bristol Highlanders. J.B. Close frequently led a group of upper class camping enthusiasts known as the Bristol Highlanders on camping trips. Shown here, from left to right, are (first row) Ed Littlefield and Steve McPherson; (second row) Close, Craig Christensen, Jeff Ehrlich, Jon Van De Venter, Keith Carradine, Bill Huysoon, and Bill Irvine.

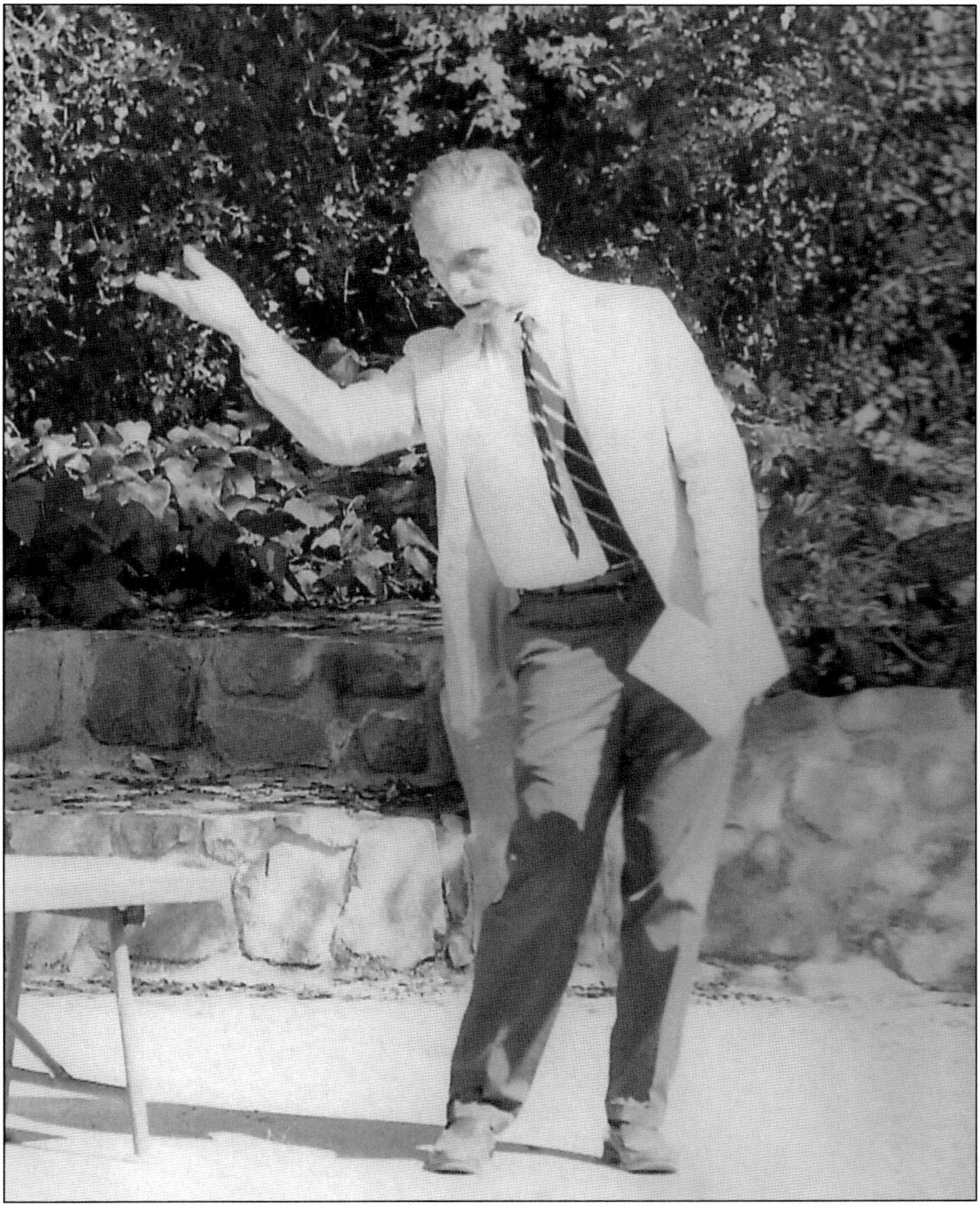

The Drama Master. "No matter what he read, he gave vigor and color to his stories with his British accent and his obvious enjoyment," said Terri Travis Skidmore (U66). "His love of English literature was inspiring to us all." J.B. Close directed magnificent school dramatic productions, including *The Lark*, *Aria da Capo*, *The Madwoman of Chaillot*, *The Lottery*, *My Three Angels*, and *The Taming of the Shrew*. All of his dramatic offerings were performed outdoors (Yeomans would have been proud), either in the Upper Campus amphitheater or on the stage of the music building on the Lower Campus. Close's humor was dry; but his laughter, contagious. If something struck him as funny, he would throw his head back and fill the room with laughter. It was an honor to have him for an instructor and a friend.

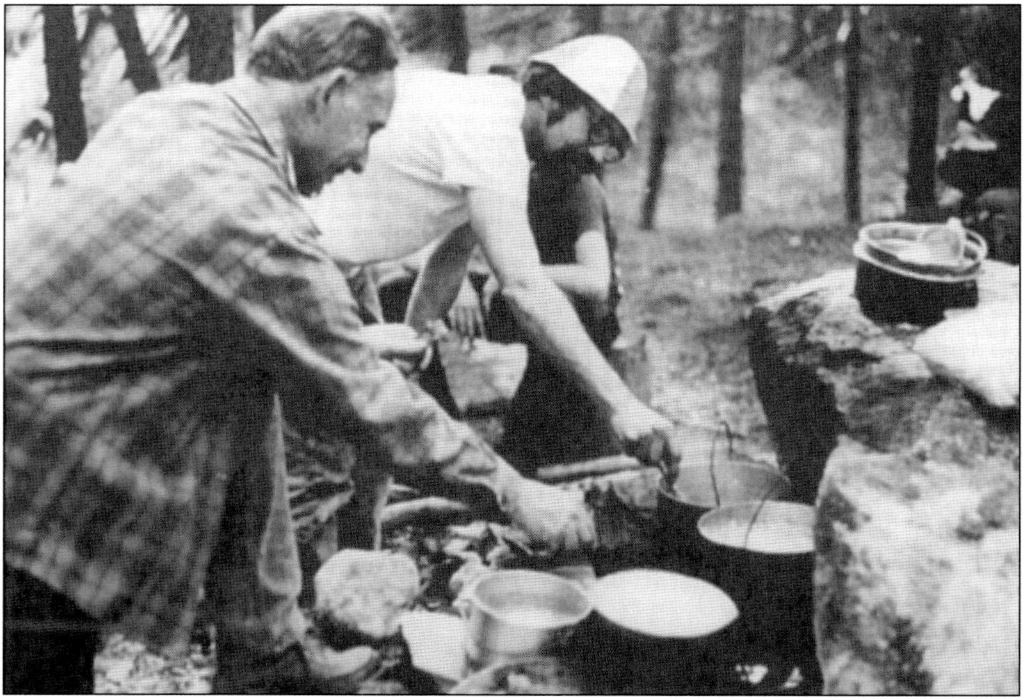

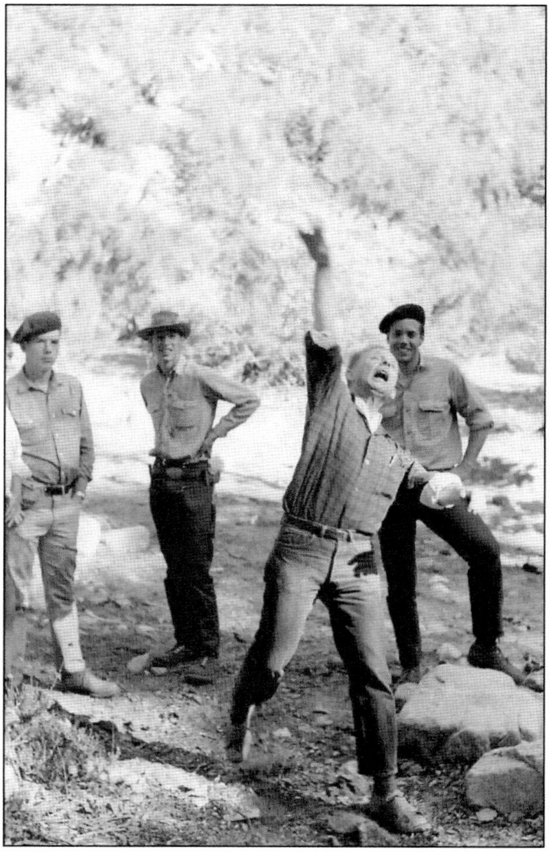

Master Chef. Close exhibited outstanding camp culinary skills. He once prepared *cordon bleu* curried chicken and saffron rice for 20 very hungry campers. He made Russian glop from beef and sour cream and a stew with green peppers and red tomatoes he called "Portuguese Poop." He is also remembered for preparing baked Alaska with a blowtorch and fashioning an oven out of tin foil to create pineapple upside-down cake. His was truly gourmet cooking.

Onion Toss. Camping with Close was an experience full of life lessons and unforgettable memories. Here, he throws the ceremonial onion at a departure ritual at Spruce Falls. This served to appease the supposed camping gods to ensure a repeat visit and as a thank-you to Mother Nature. Close was a soft-spoken, slightly rumpled man who inspired everyone. His students will always remember his infectious laughter, his most endearing quality.

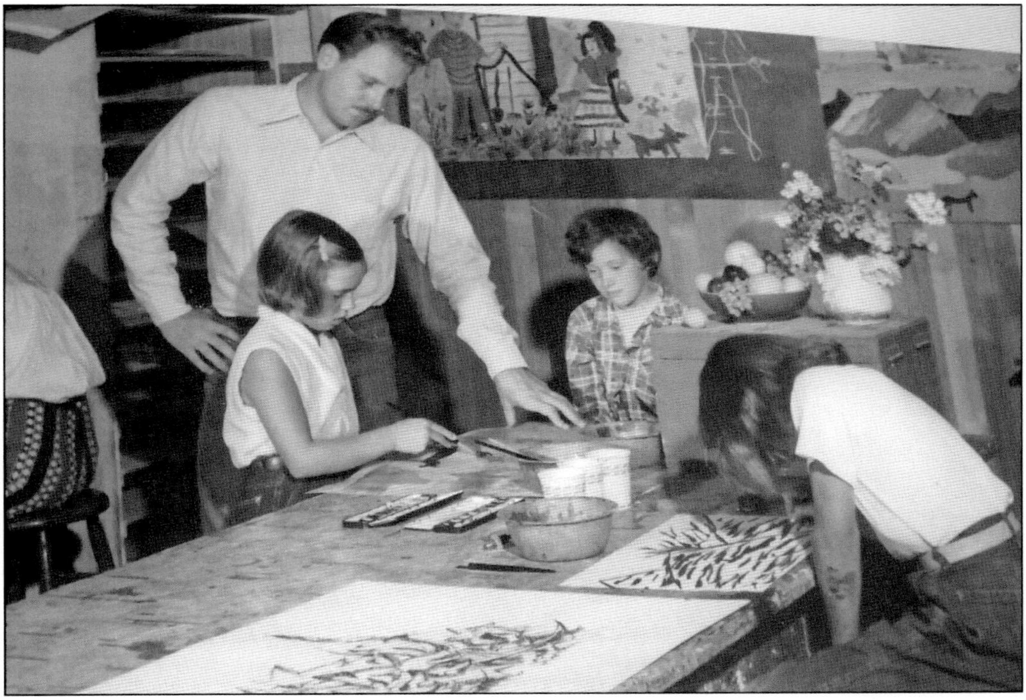

Otis Wickenhaeuser. Otis Wickenhaeuser was a multitalented man whose demeanor commanded respect. He taught Latin, Spanish, English, history, civics, and art (above). The fact that he received his elementary education in Italy and Austria probably explained his abiding love of languages. While working as a teacher off and on from 1954 to 1973 at the Upper and Lower Campuses, he became a camping enthusiast. He found a passion for hiking and camping trips, where he felt more liberated (although some of his young charges may have felt rather burdened with their heavy packs and sleeping bags). Camping was a particular joy, especially when he and J.B. Close were creating camp cuisine.

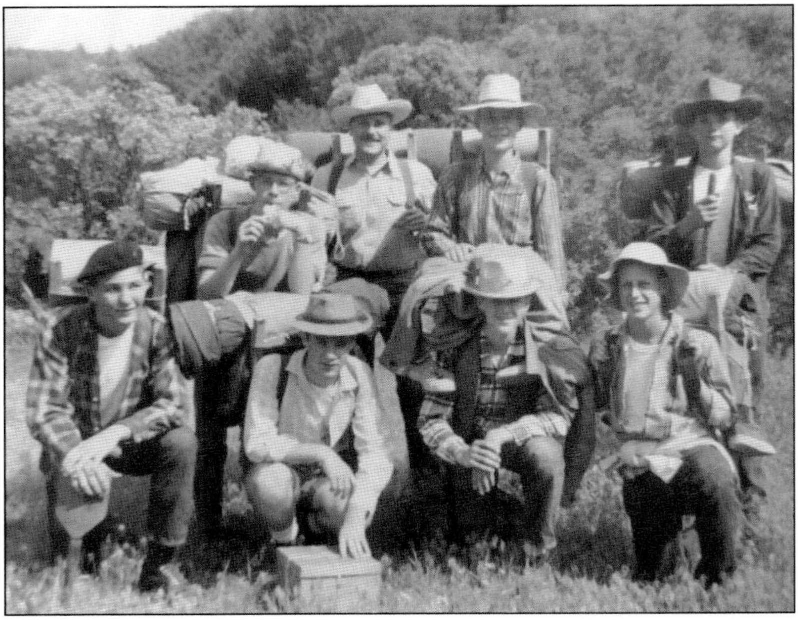

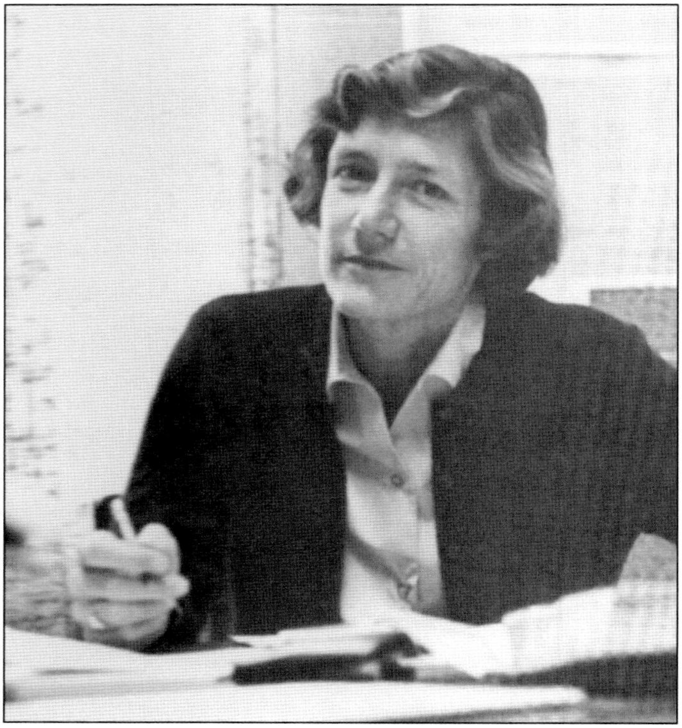

Joyce Biscoe. Known for her courage, dedication, and integrity, Joyce Biscoe came to OVS in 1964 with a master's degree in guidance and college counseling. After substituting in an English class, Biscoe fell in love with the subject matter. She soon became the head of the English department. Prior to her retirement in 1985, she was instrumental in starting the Advanced Placement program at OVS.

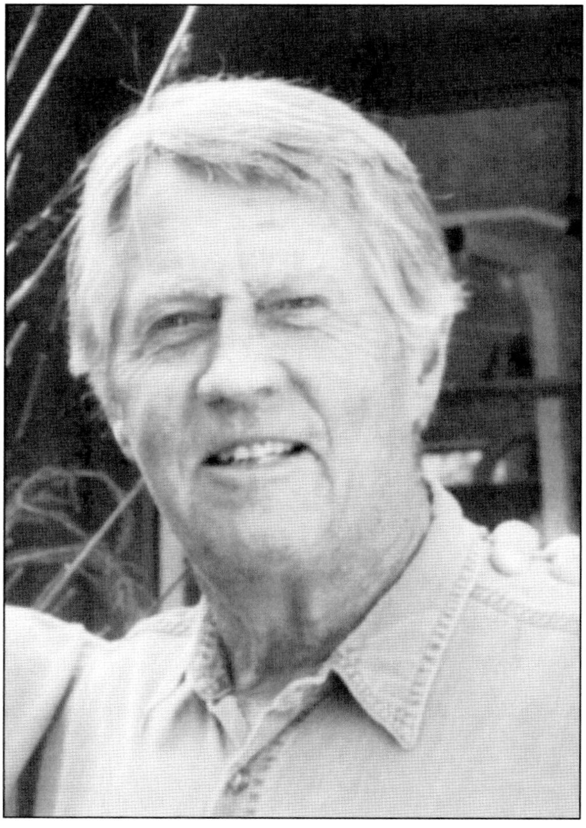

Gary Dinkins. This longest-serving faculty member taught at OVS for 45 years and touched the lives of hundreds of students. His cross-country and track teams won several Condor League titles. Gary taught Latin, French, Spanish, US history, world history, and geography, and his artwork can still be seen on display at the Upper Campus. One of his favorite quotes was "Not all who wander are lost."

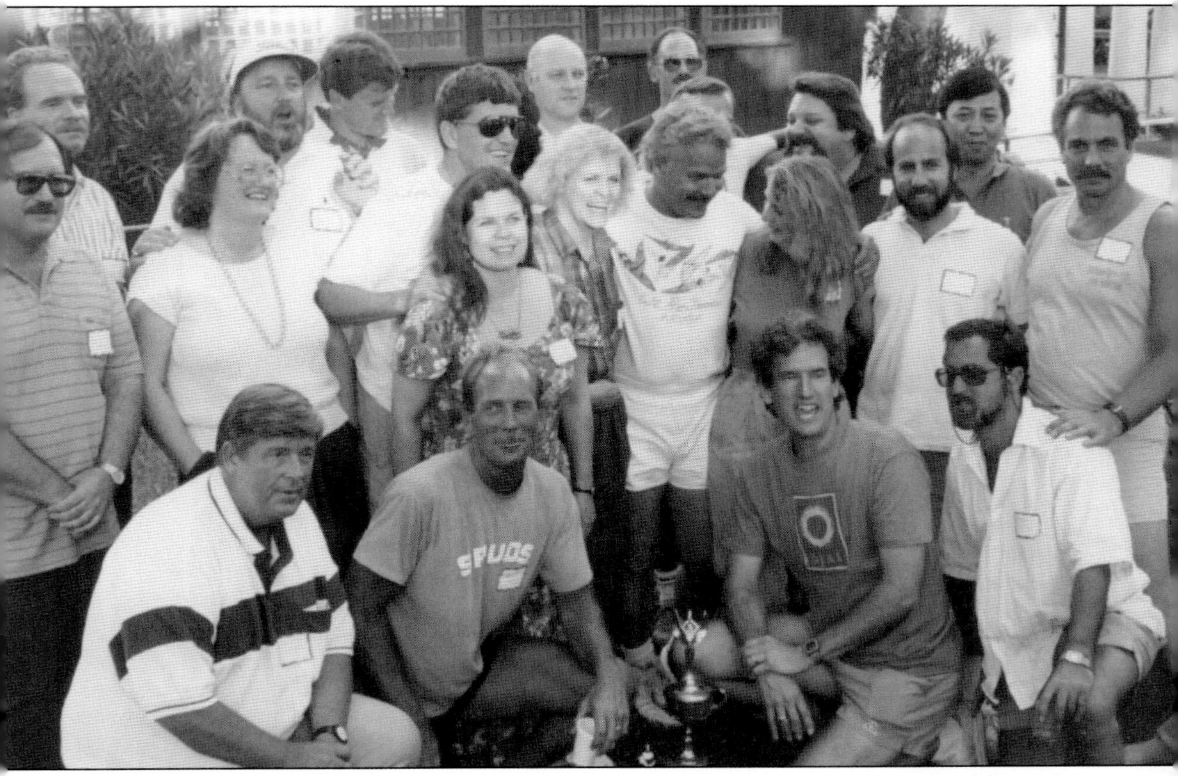

First Graduates Return. The beginning years at the Upper Campus were magical for Mike Hermes and the boys. Daily wild rides up and down the undeveloped roads from the Upper Campus to Lower Campus in "Petunia" were an adventure. According to Albert Beach, the first year on the Upper Campus will always stand as a banner year: "It started with one man's daring decision and another man who knew what a group of kids could do if they pulled together." In 1975, Hermes became president and chief executive officer of the school and put the institution on sound financial footing. He also served on the OVS Board of Trustees. He traveled the world as a recruiter for OVS. Hermes served from 1962 to 1967 and again from 1972 until his passing in 2011. Under his stewardship, tens of millions of dollars were raised to upgrade existing facilities and construct new facilities such as the Donlon Pool Complex and Greenberg Activity Center at Lower Campus and the Arango Science and Technology Center at Upper Campus. Here, Hermes (first row, far left) is surrounded by members of the first graduating class from 1965.

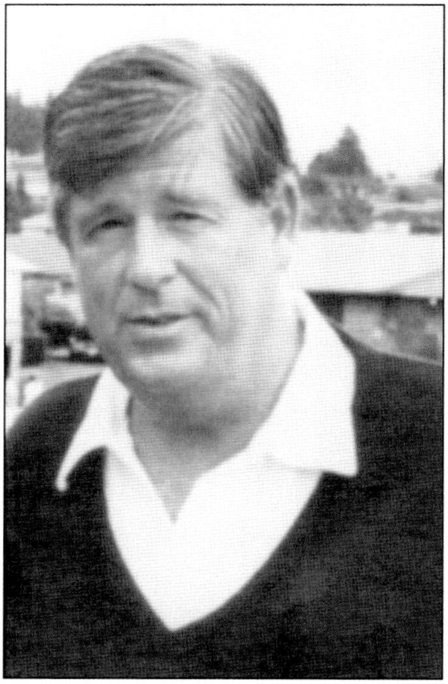

The Hermes Legacy. Edward Yeomans had a vision of an educational institution that would allow young children to learn by experiencing the real world. Wallace Burr extended that vision to include older students. Mike Hermes brought Burr's vision to life by putting the school and both campuses on a solid financial foundation and by successfully recruiting students from not only Ojai and the greater Los Angeles area, but from all around the world. Under Hermes's dedicated leadership, both campuses grew to full enrollment, and many new educational programs and extracurricular activities expanded and prospered. Without his energy and devotion to the school, OVS would not be the highly regarded independent college-preparatory school it is today. All of the students who attended the school during his remarkable 42-year tenure, and all of those who have attended since then, owe a debt of gratitude to Hermes. The plaque on the Hermes Quad at the Lower Campus honors his memory and many contributions to the school.

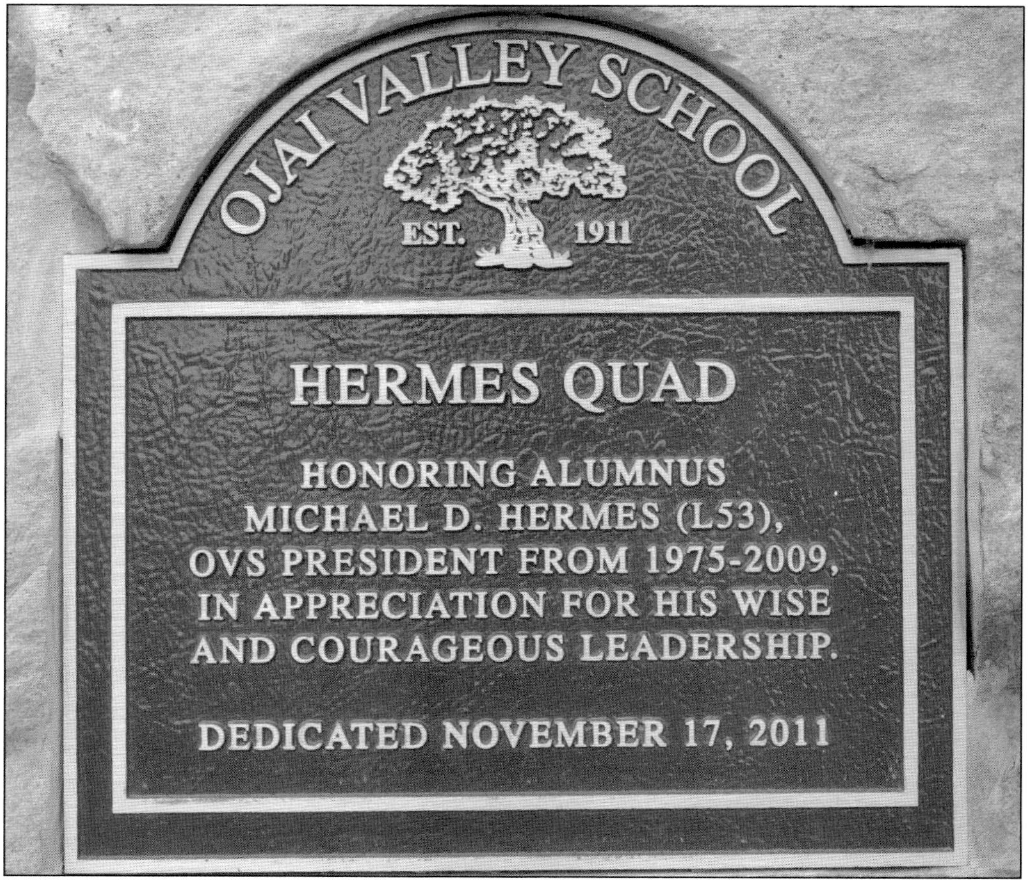

Seven

Horse Program

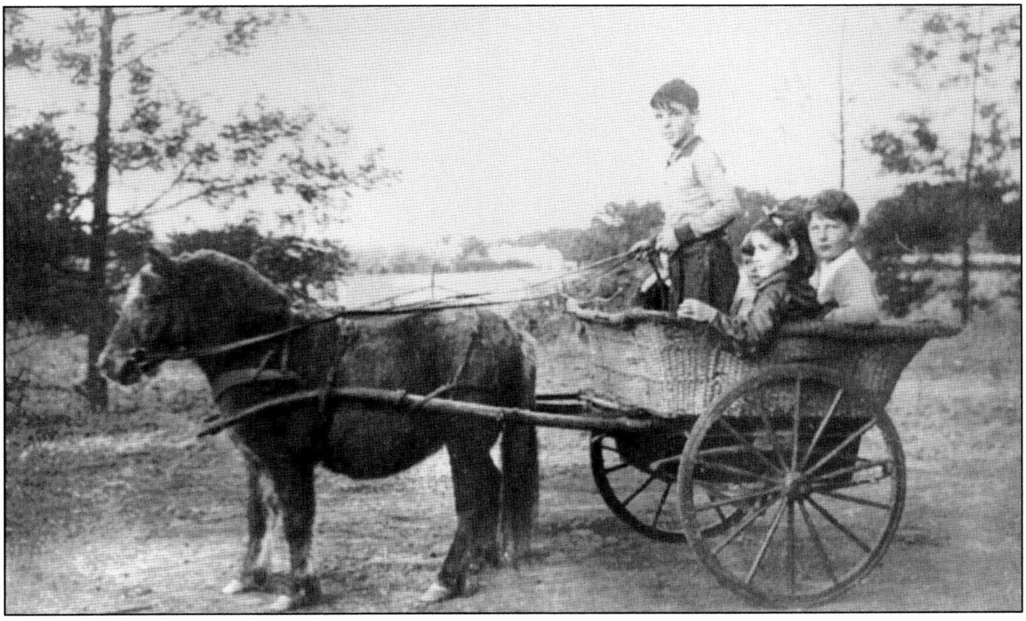

Pony Rides in the Early 1920s. Even before horses played a central role in the school's activity program, there was always a desire brewing to incorporate them. Yeomans and his colleagues realized that Sherman Thacher, founder of The Thacher School, was right when he said, "There is something about the outside of a horse that is good for the inside of a boy." If a child could not communicate with teachers or peers, there was always a sense of magic between children and horses. The equestrian program continues to be one of the strongest and most popular extracurricular programs offered.

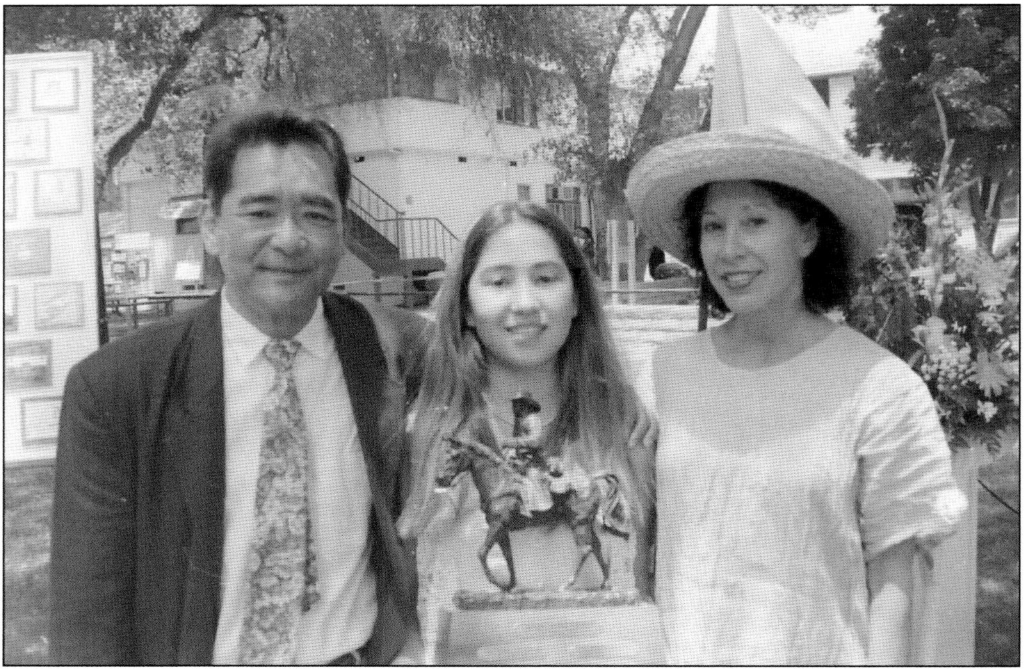

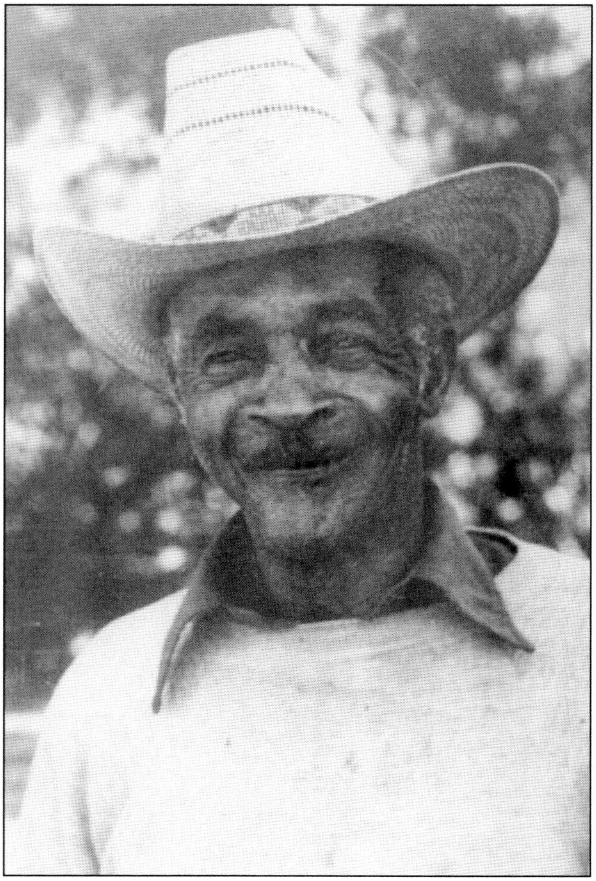

HORSE PROGRAM. Wallace Burr, recognizing the importance of a horse program, purchased horses and constructed a barn in 1946. In 1950, he hired Paul Pittman (left) to develop a comprehensive riding program. Most students had minimal experience with horses prior to coming to OVS. However, under the strict but encouraging supervision of Pittman, novice riders quickly learned the basics of horsemanship. Within a short time, Pittman instilled in the children a love for horses and a respect for nature. Camping trips—which included riding, hiking, and swimming in the Sespe River—became a new vehicle for attracting students from urban areas. The Paul Pittman Horsemanship Award is still presented annually to the worthy student who demonstrates the commitment to and values of the OVS equestrian program. In 1994, Laura Sato (L94, pictured above with her parents) was the recipient of this award at the Lower Campus graduation.

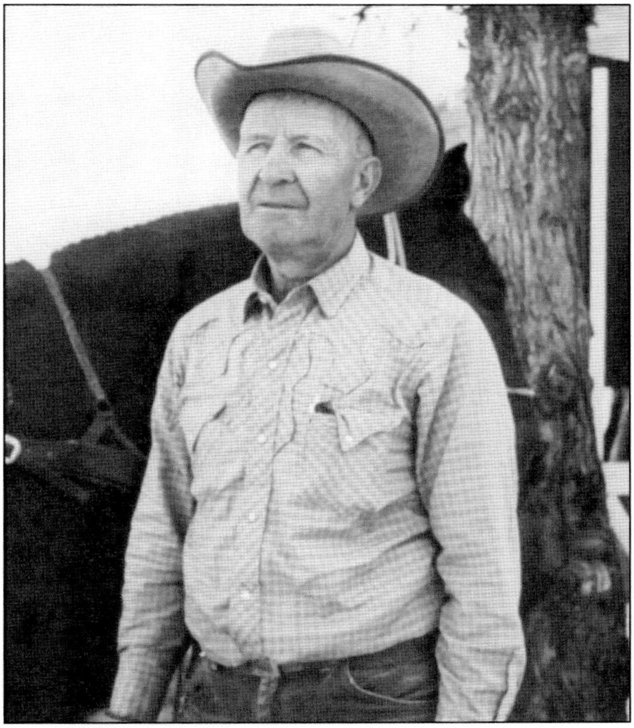

Valuable Teachers. Along with daily room inspection, stalls and corrals were inspected as well. This reinforced order and self-discipline for student riders. Up until the 1970s, play days and events on horseback were conducted on weekends at Soule Park and the OVS gymkhana field. Once they were certified as "safe riders," children were allowed to ride all over Ojai without supervision (though permission was always required). Joe Singleton (pictured), riding master from 1958 to 1966, was a crusty old cowboy who taught children safety and responsibility and to take pride in their horsemanship. A horseback trip with Singleton was an experience and became a treasured memory.

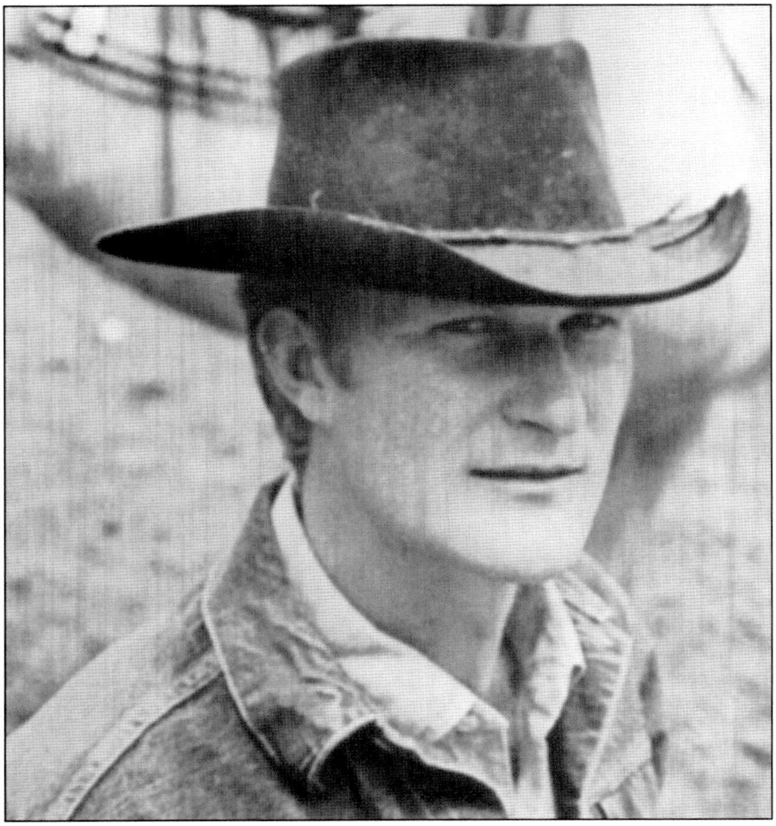

New Riding Master. Following in his father's footsteps, Ron Singleton (pictured) took over as the OVS riding master in 1967 and served until 1975. He proudly continued his father's principles in the OVS riding program. Stanford Ballou was riding master from 1975 to 1983.

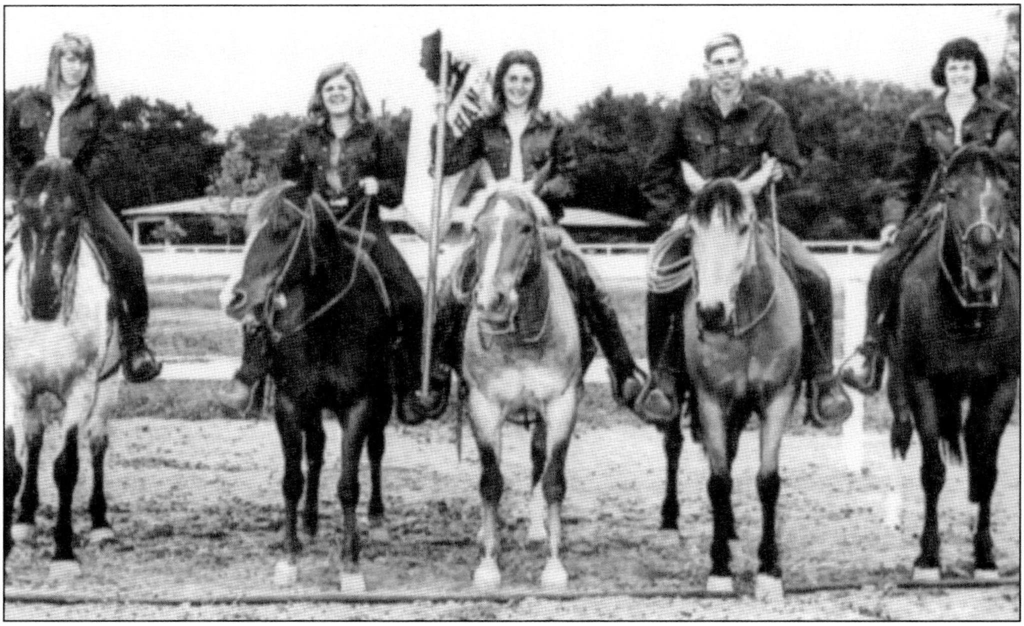

GYMKHANA. Above is the 1965 gymkhana team— from left to right, Judy Frazier, Susan Barnard, captain Doris Pfeiffer, Fred Fickert, and Pam Somermeier. Gymkhana events such as barrel racing, figure eight, and pole bending were offered weekly to students. Equestrians were encouraged to participate in local horse shows and gymkhanas at Ojai's Soule Park or at The Thacher School. Budding young riders were totally responsible for the feeding, exercising, and grooming of their steeds. Children could bring their own horses from home or ride a school horse, and they learned quickly that there was joy in the hard work that horses and camping trips presented. The total care for an animal at this young age builds strong character.

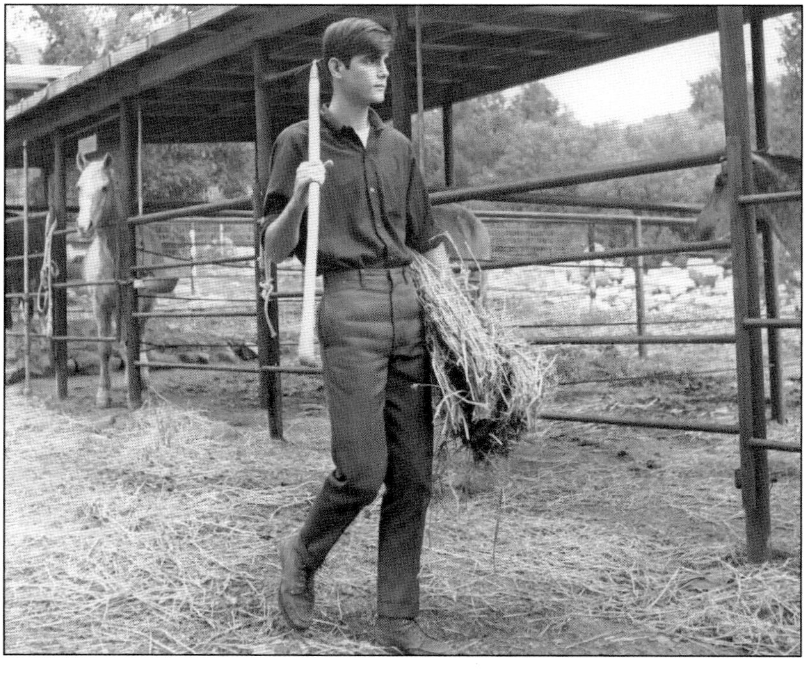

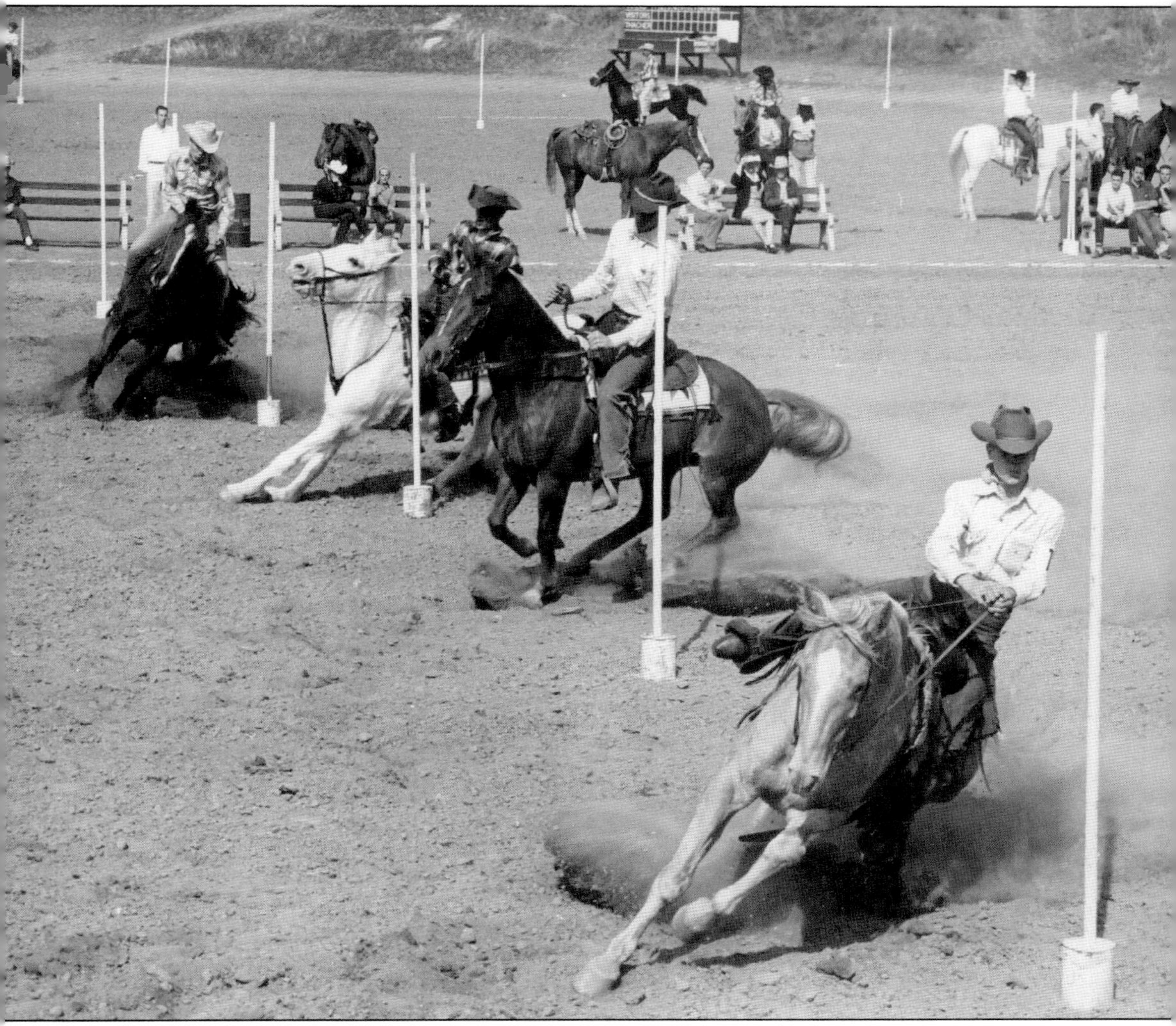

Western Riding. Gymkhana consists of speed pattern racing and timed games. Events include barrel racing, pole bending, figure eight racing, and the quadrangle stake race. Gymkhana competitions were regularly held on weekends with the nearby Thacher School. Horsemen and -women from OVS were consistently competitive in many of the classic gymkhana events in the 1960s. (Thacher archives.)

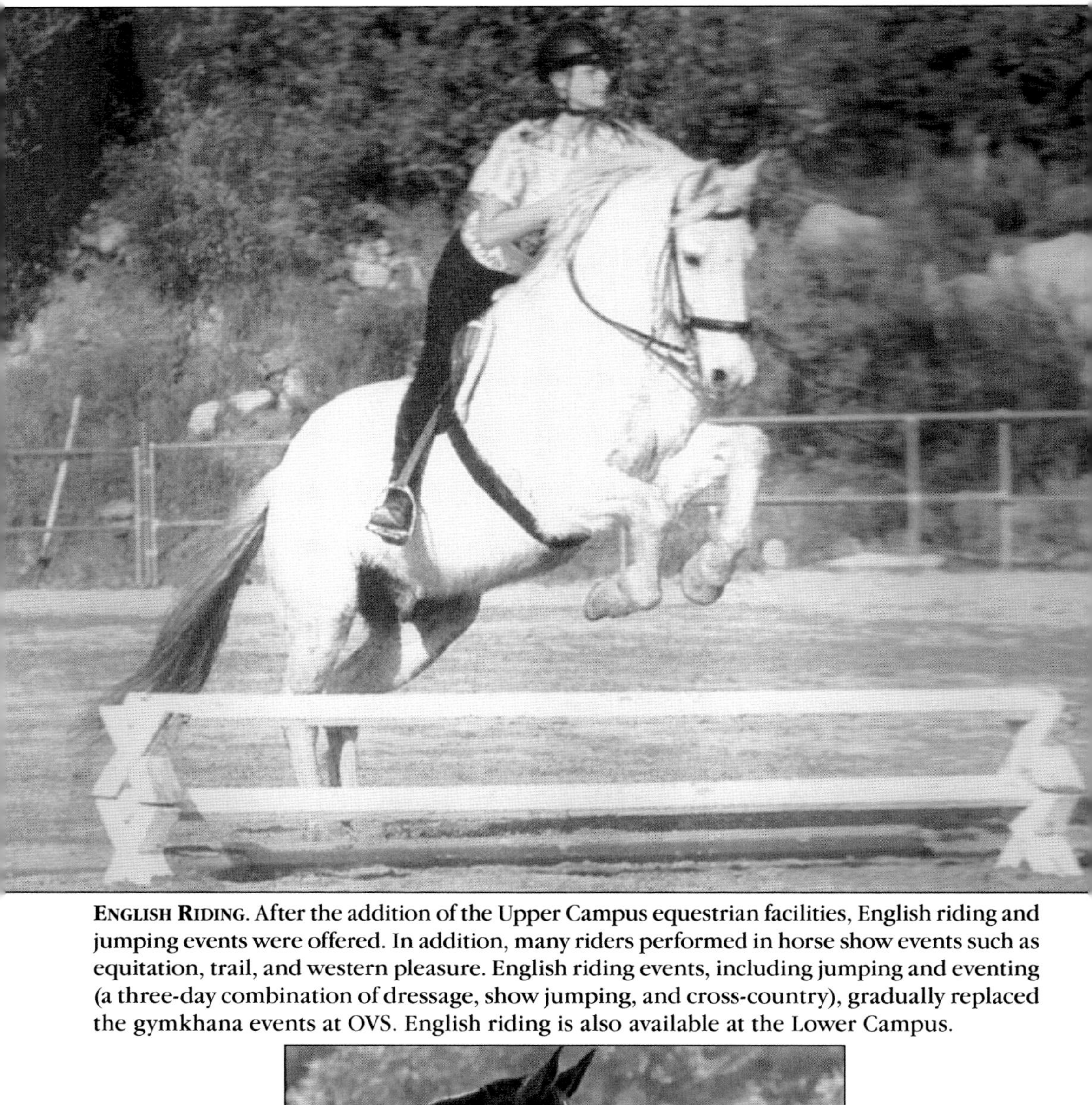

English Riding. After the addition of the Upper Campus equestrian facilities, English riding and jumping events were offered. In addition, many riders performed in horse show events such as equitation, trail, and western pleasure. English riding events, including jumping and eventing (a three-day combination of dressage, show jumping, and cross-country), gradually replaced the gymkhana events at OVS. English riding is also available at the Lower Campus.

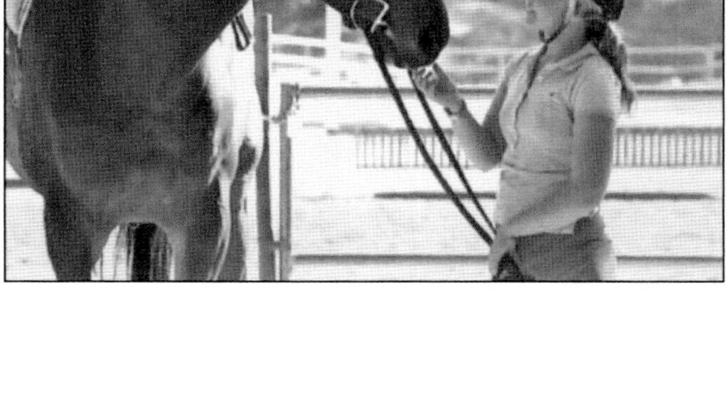

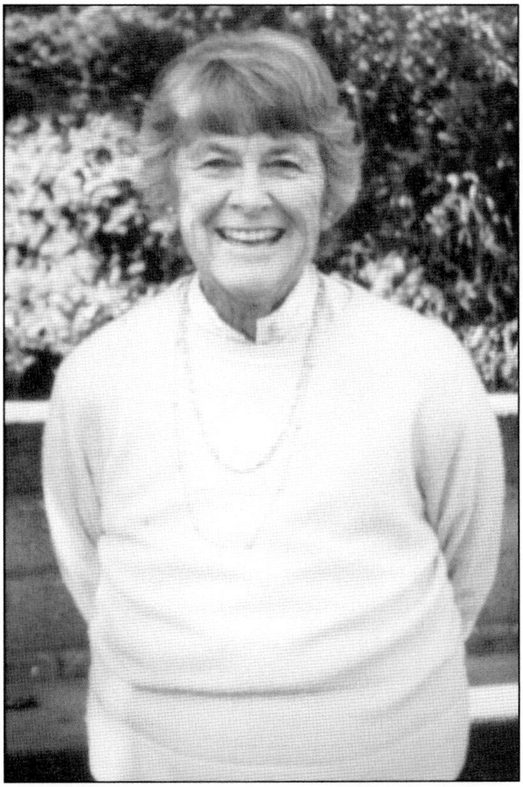

Riding Masters. Alumnus Greg Coulson took over as riding master from 1978 to 1986. Terry Wilson (right) served as equestrian director from 1986 to 2011. Under her guidance, student Tiana Coudray fulfilled her lifelong dream of performing in the 2012 London Olympics with her horse, Ringwood Magister. In 2009, the newly renovated barn on the Lower Campus was named the Terry Wilson Equestrian Center. The sleek new facility was twice the size of the old 1946 barn. The tack room was enlarged, and a veterinary treatment room was added, providing excellent living conditions for horses. A new facility on the Upper Campus also served as an attraction for equestrians.

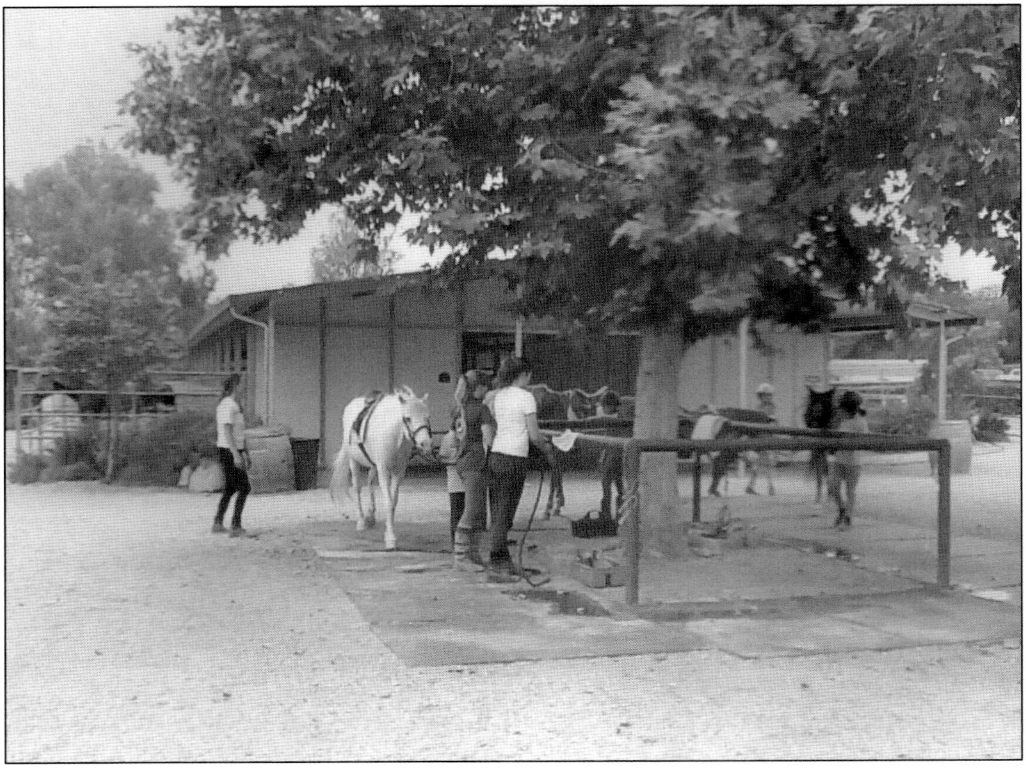

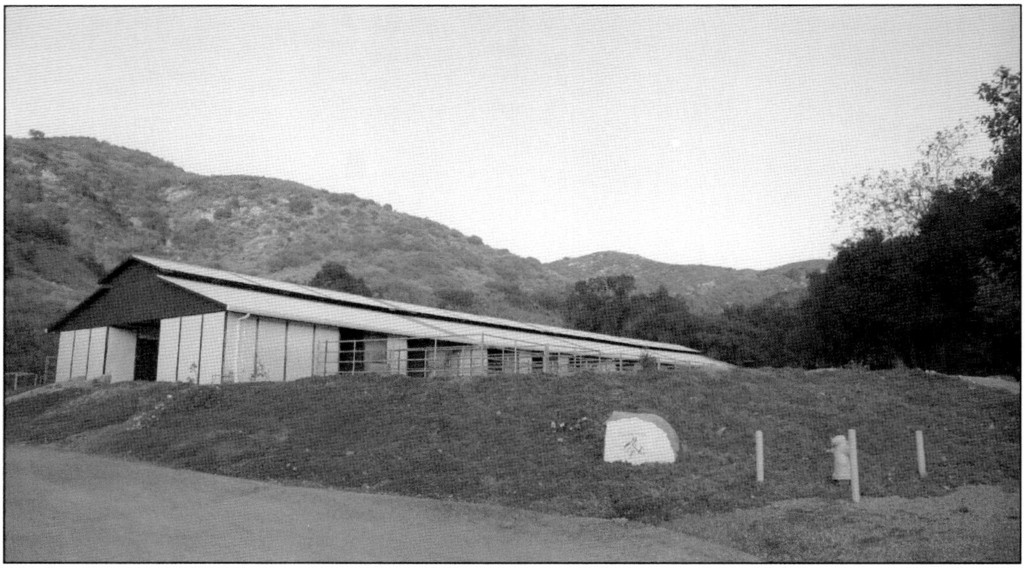

Open-Air Classroom. In addition to the new barn built in 1992 at the Upper Campus, the horse program benefited when Stephanie Gustafson joined the faculty in 2005. Instead of working indoors with textbooks and blackboards, she set aside her doctorate in history and opted for her favorite classroom, the dusty open-air learning laboratory known as the riding ring. She preferred to teach from the back of a horse, on a mountain trail, or in a riding arena. In 2011, Gustafson took over as the equestrian director for both Upper and Lower Campuses.

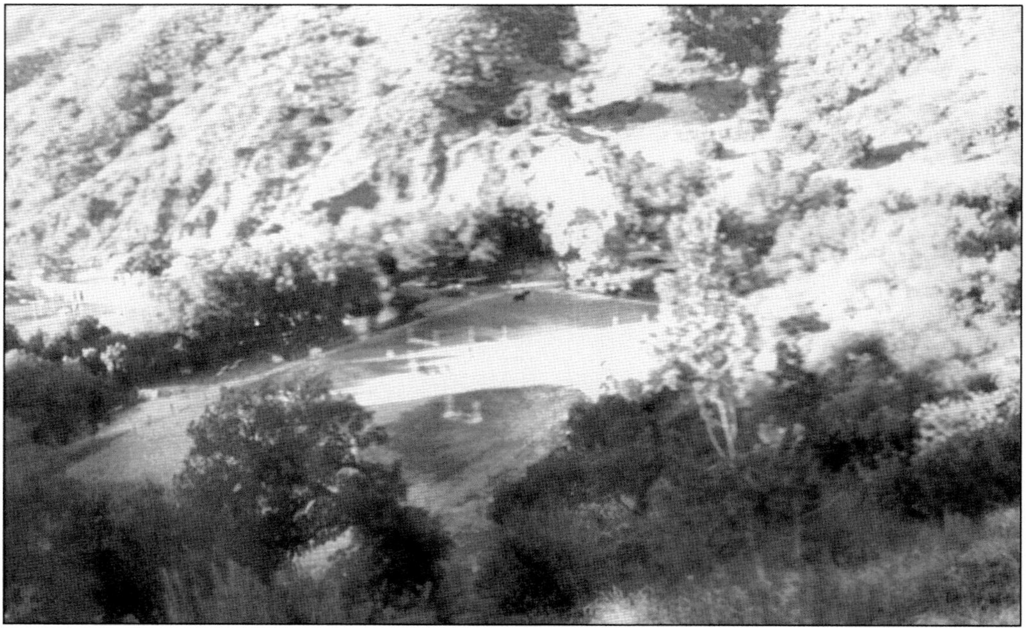

Upper Campus Stables. The Upper Campus equestrian facilities allowed upperclassmen to hone their horsemanship skills. In addition, they could explore trails in the nearby Los Padres National Forest and even blaze some of their own. The setting was magnificent. Students were allowed the freedom to wander with their horses through the rolling hills, with the Ojai Valley just to the west. Memories are made on the trails, in the camps, and in the arena.

Eight

OUTDOOR ACTIVITIES

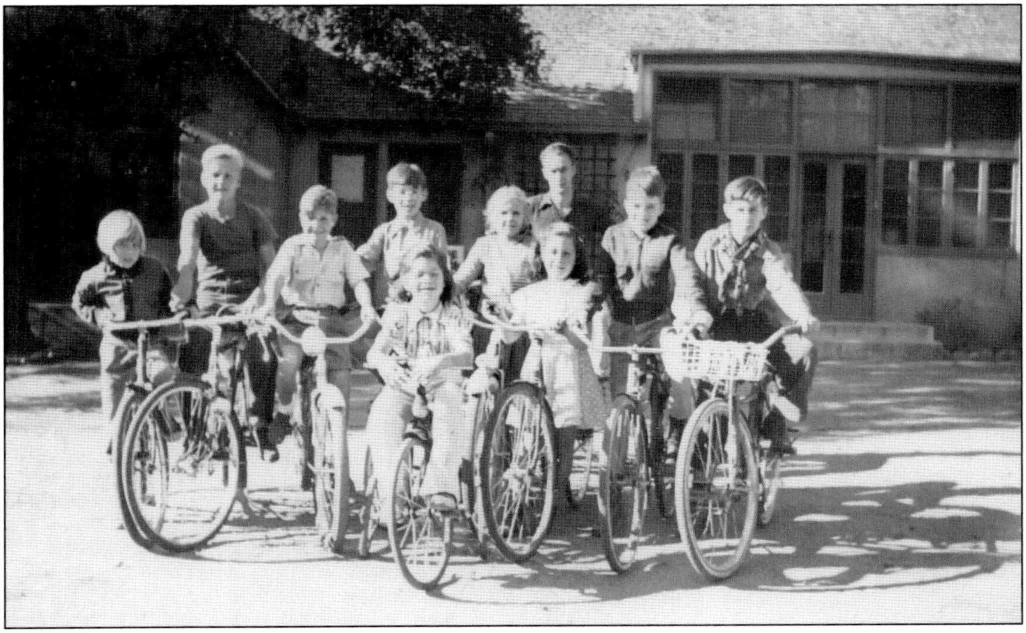

BIKING IN THE 1940s. Children were encouraged to generate their own sources of entertainment. Creating games, pretending to be on a bear hunt in the woods, or simply riding around campus on a bicycle reflected Yeomans's educational philosophy and could be a great source of enjoyment. Life was simple, and a child's imagination could take him or her anywhere. Bike trips to the mountains were common, and there were plenty of caves and canyons for children to explore. Camping became such an integral part of the overall educational program that it was made mandatory. Teachers felt that camping trips provided opportunities for children to learn to cooperate and develop leadership skills, especially when faced with the adverse conditions of Mother Nature. Trips were taken early in the year, and leaders emerged very quickly.

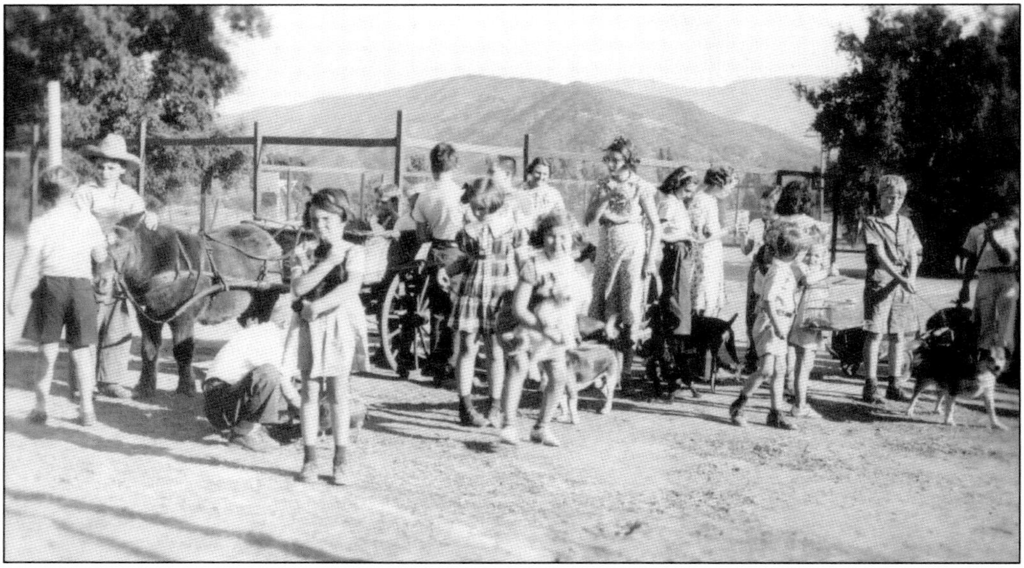

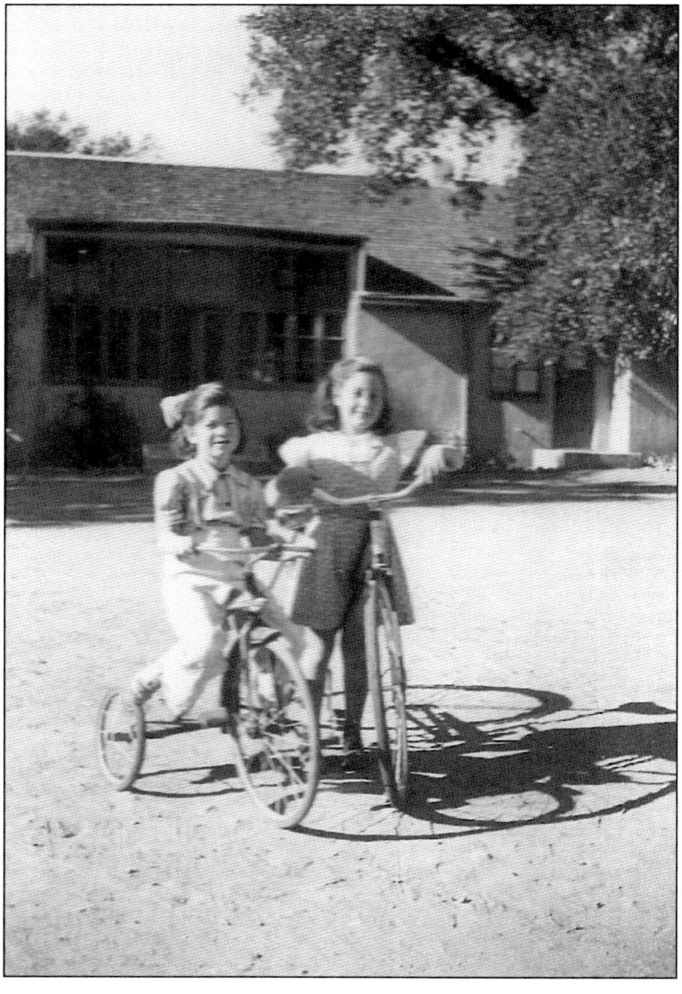

Simple Fun. Outdoor fun in the 1940s included simple pleasures like cooling off in lawn sprinklers in the quad, planning a circus with school pets (above), or riding tricycles and bicycles around campus (left). Everyone participated in the outdoor activities. In addition to riding personal vehicles around campus, children were encouraged to hike in and around the foothills to study the wide variety of flora and fauna. Picnic outings were common. In the days before cell phones, computers, and the Internet, these simple activities were truly memorable.

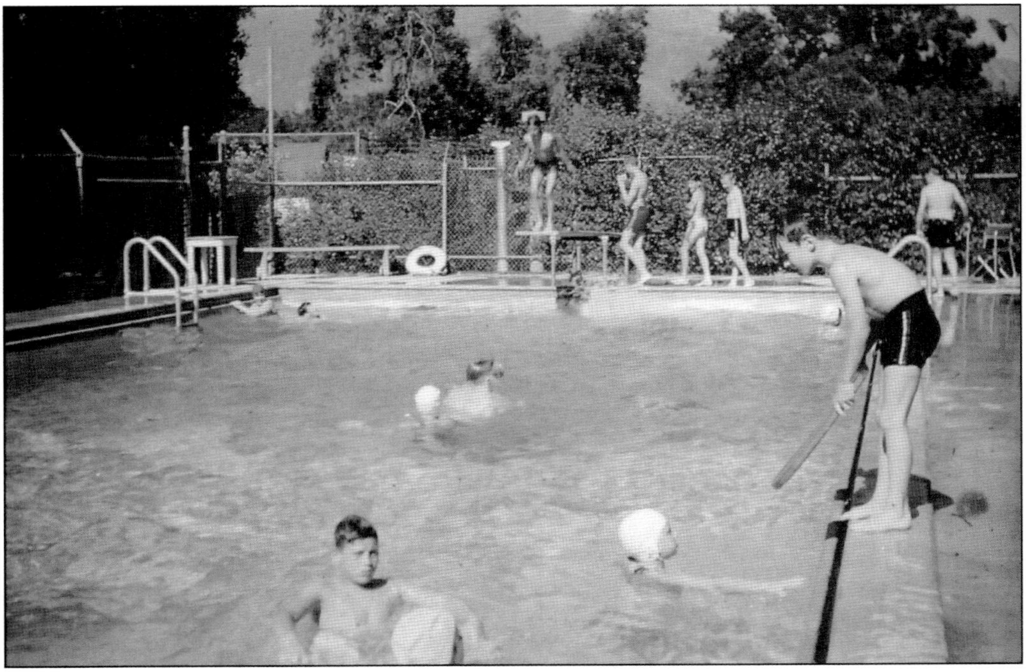

Then and Now. During the Burr years, dramatic changes took place at the school. In 1947, using a donation of $5,000, Burr arranged for the construction of the first swimming pool (above). An additional 3.9 acres were purchased for a graded playing field and gymkhana arena between El Paseo and Ojai Avenue. For years, gymkhana was popular at the Lower Campus, but in the 1980s, the gymkhana field was converted into a grass field. Today, Lower Campus Pony Club teams travel and compete.

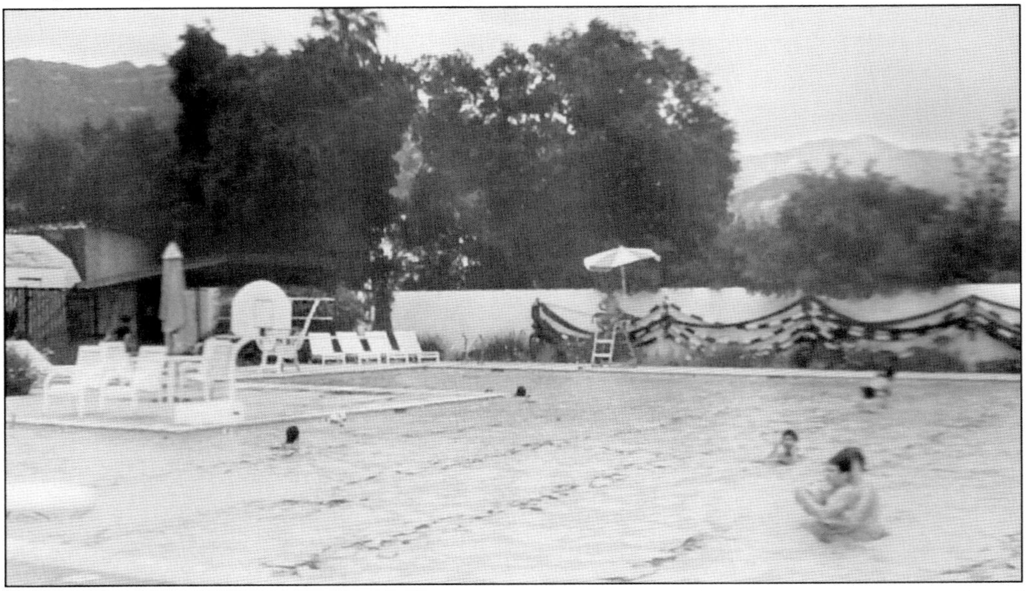

New Lower Campus Pool. The David Donlon Pool Complex at the Lower Campus, completed in 2000, came with showers and dressing rooms. Kindergarteners could now play in the pool and learn to swim. Evening reunion cocktail parties, where alumni can meet and greet over wine coolers and delicious hors d'oeuvres, are held poolside.

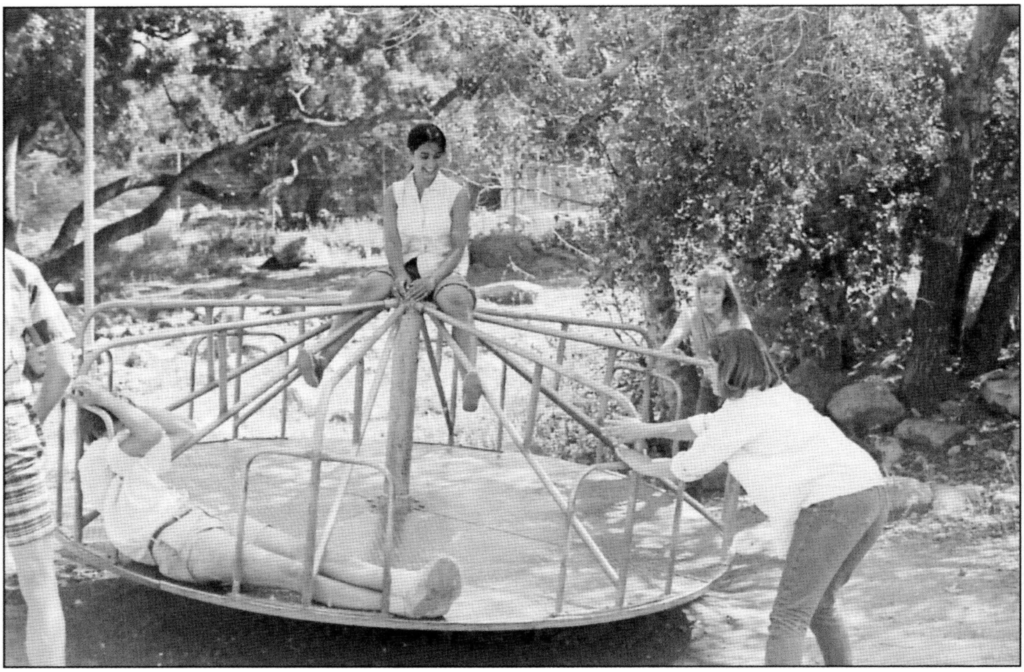

Children at Play. Students worked hard in the classroom yet always found time to just be kids. In the early 1960s, there were horseback rides through the hills and walking trips to town or church on the weekends. Many students used their free time to read, play musical instruments, or draw and paint the scenery of the beautiful Ojai Valley. Life is still simple yet structured, providing little time for idle hands to create mischief. Below, children compete in spring games involving blindfolds and mattresses. Children at the school learn to create their own fun, and community service is encouraged.

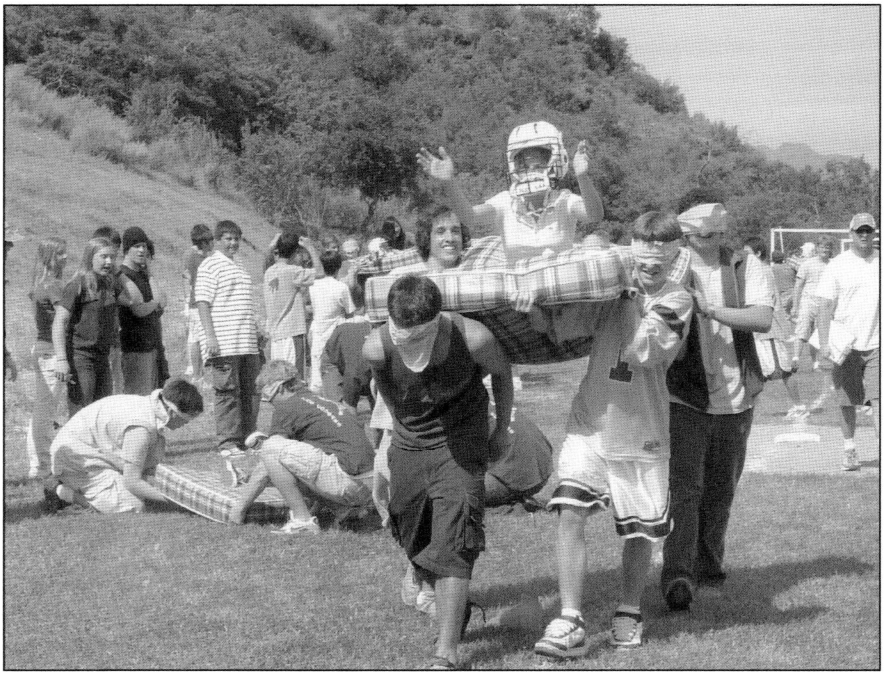

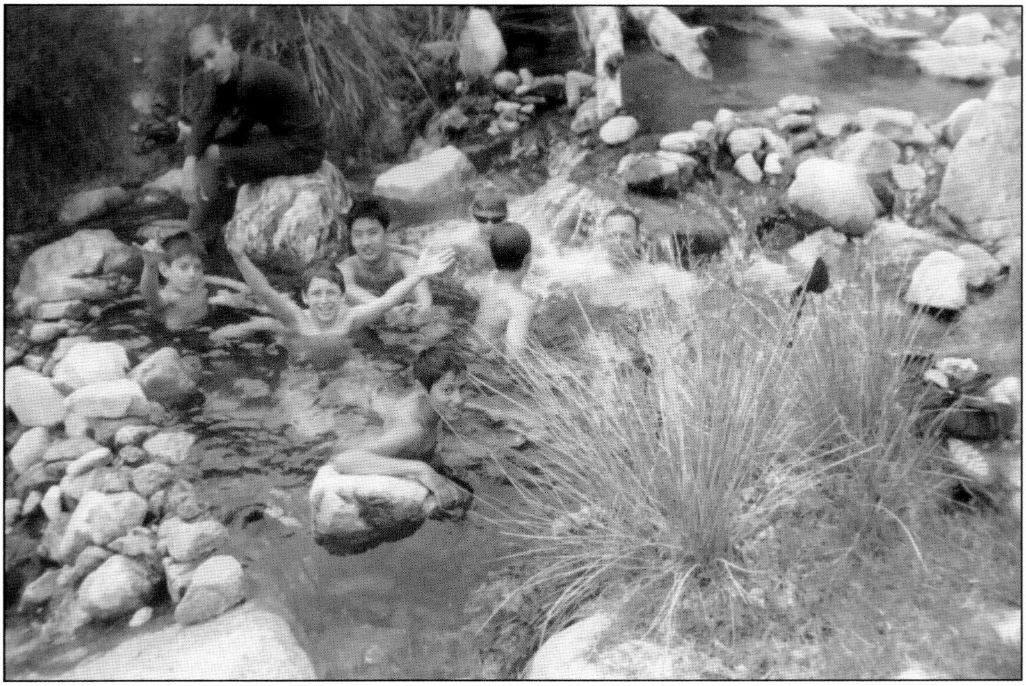

A School Tradition. Many lessons are taught in the great outdoors. Camping became an integral part of school life, and teachers were expected to participate. Weekend camping trips were taken into the Sespe Valley, and annual eight-day camping trips to various sites in the Los Padres National Forest were required for the entire student body in the 1950s and 1960s. Swimming in the Sespe is still a favorite OVS tradition.

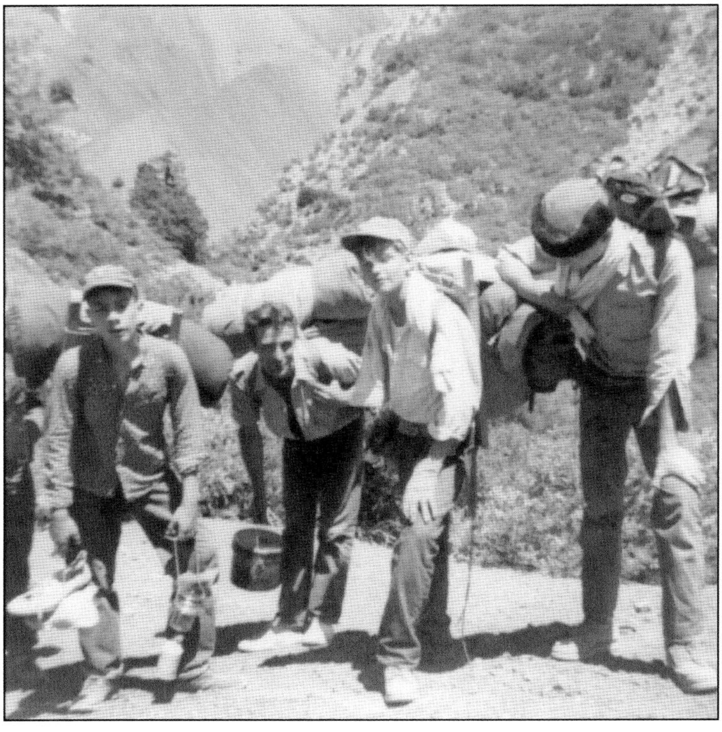

Camping in the 1950s. Campers carried their own supplies for the week on their backs or on horseback and shared the responsibilities of setting up and breaking camp. After long hikes in the mountains, there was nothing more pleasing than the smell of a pine-scented campfire and a hot meal. With only light from the stars or a flickering fire, campers got a sense of being alone in the wilderness. This continues to be one of the defining experiences at OVS.

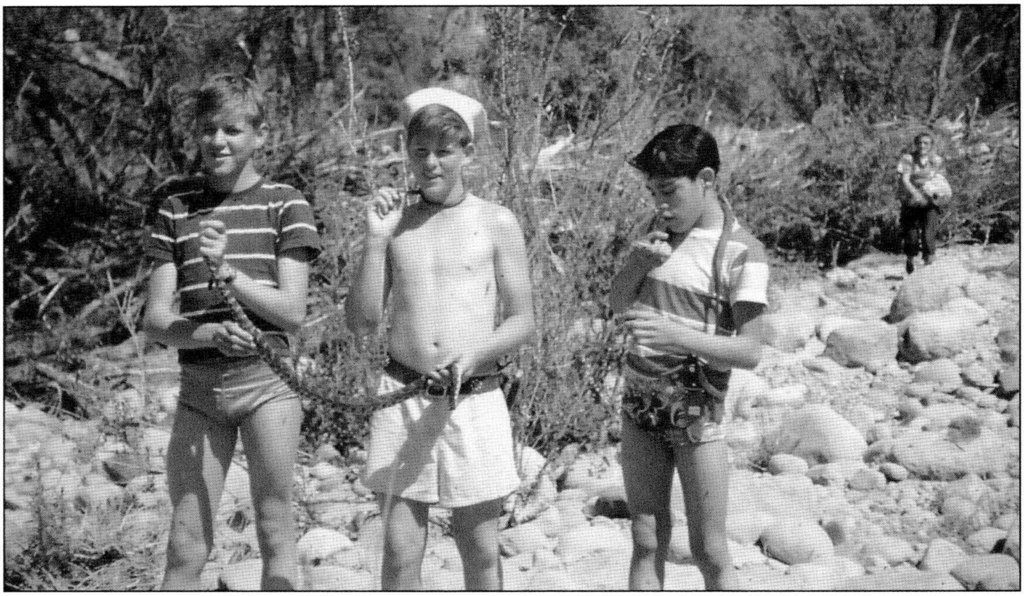

Annual Eight-Day Trips. Yeomans embraced the virtue of understanding nature. In keeping with this philosophy, Burr implemented the annual eight-day camping trip. Sudden downpours sometimes forced one to swim a river he or she had walked across the day before. This 1952 camping trip involved snakes, rocks, and poison ivy. Sitting around a smoky campfire at night listening to ghost stories was the norm.

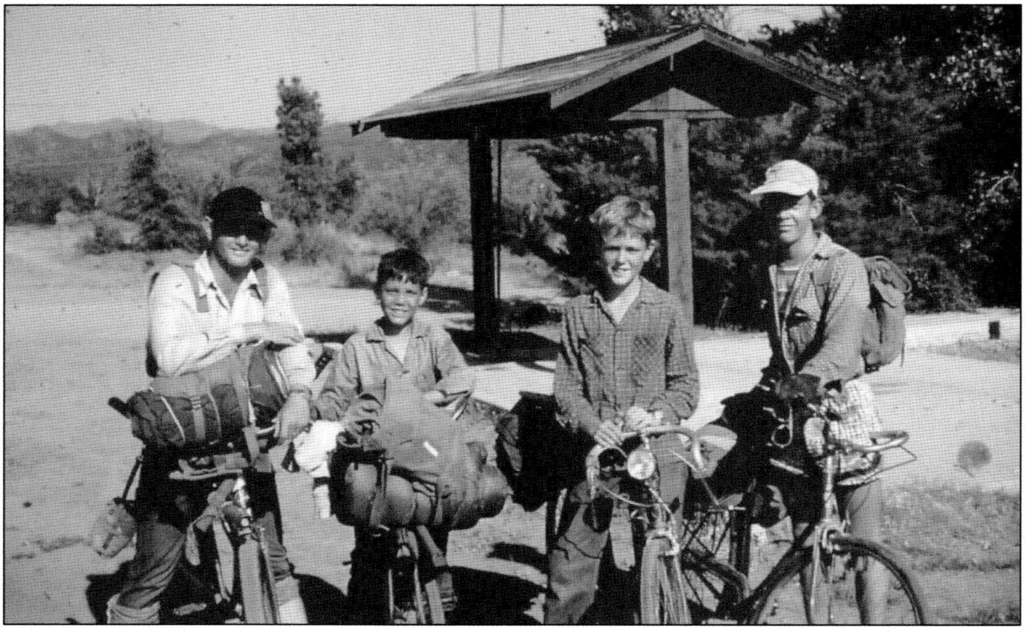

Bicycle Camping. Robert G. "Coop" Cooper's bicycle escapades down the Sespe River were real adventures. On one trip, the campers found themselves in an area that had been flooded, leaving behind a tremendous sand buildup. The boys pushed their bikes until exhaustion overtook them. Fortunately, they managed to reach Hartman's campground for the night. Upon reaching Cottrell campground the next day, they were welcomed with a bath at the hot springs and a day of fishing.

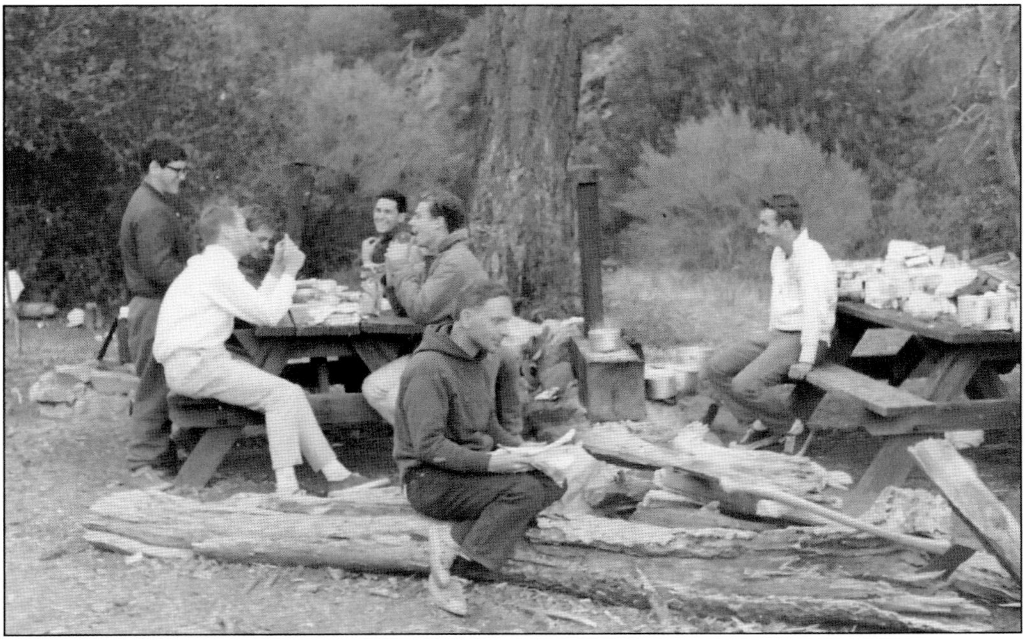

Camping in the 1960s. A hearty breakfast prepared by J.B. Close was a good way to start a day out on the trail. The smell of crisp bacon and steaming coffee on a cool, misty morning could bring any camper out of his warm sleeping bag. Notable camping sites included Lion Camp, Pine Mountain Lodge, Timber Canyon, Hartman's, Twin Forks, and Rose Valley Falls. Horse master Ron Singleton (below left) and Fred Fickert (below right) take charge this morning by preparing grub for 20 famished boys. A favorite camping tale of Wallace Burr's was his fanciful story of the coming-of-age rituals of the Boney Beans, an imaginary Chumash clan.

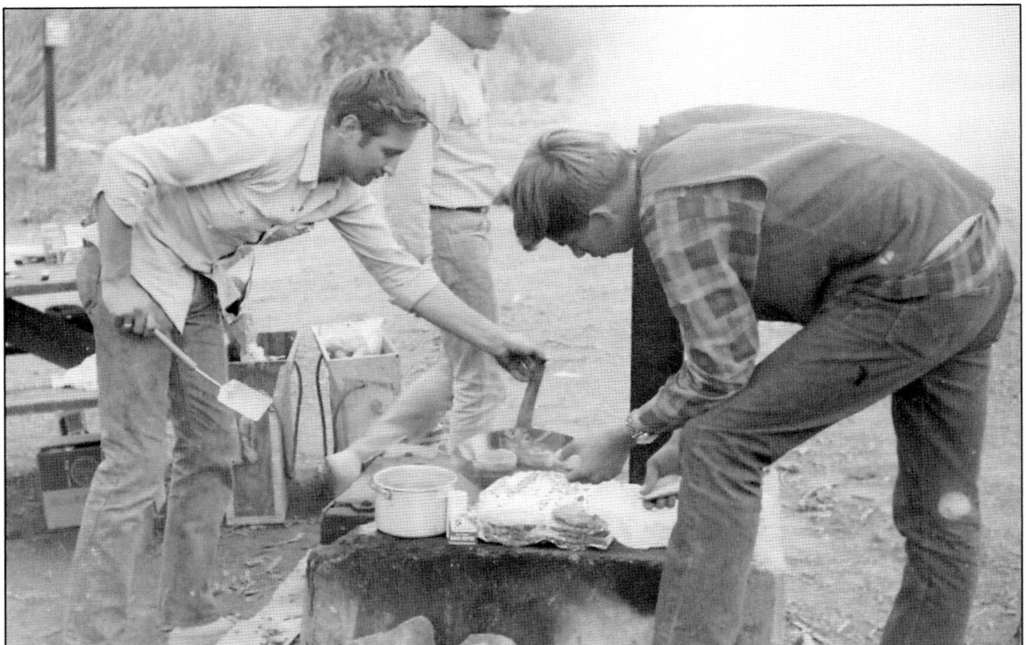

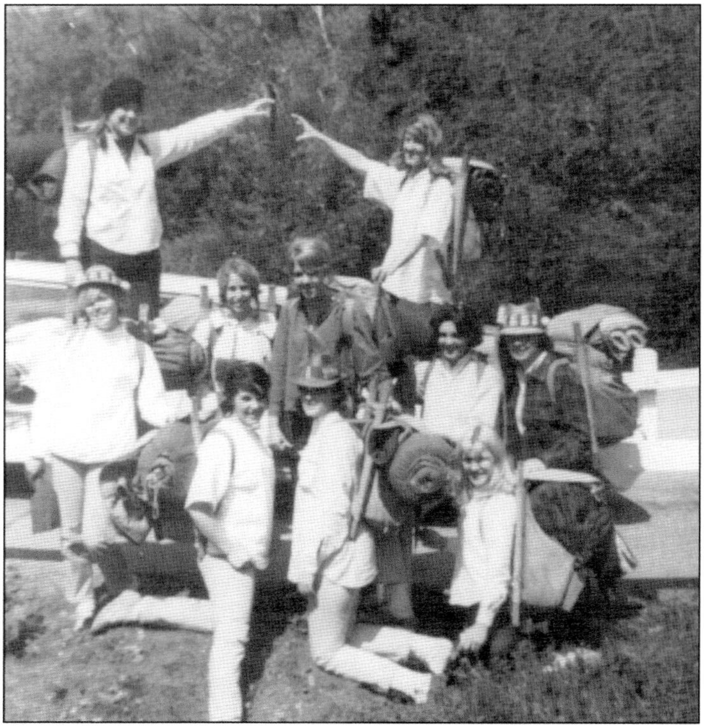

Camping Challenges. Girls' camping trips were as adventuresome as the boys'. Girls carried heavy packs, climbed mountains, set up camp, swam in upstream pools, gathered wood, and prepared food. Songs, ghost stories, and s'mores finished out the night before bed. Experiences and memories like these were unforgettable. Camping trips could take students to unusual places and present them with unexpected dilemmas such as getting caught in a downpour, getting lost, or chasing after runaway horses.

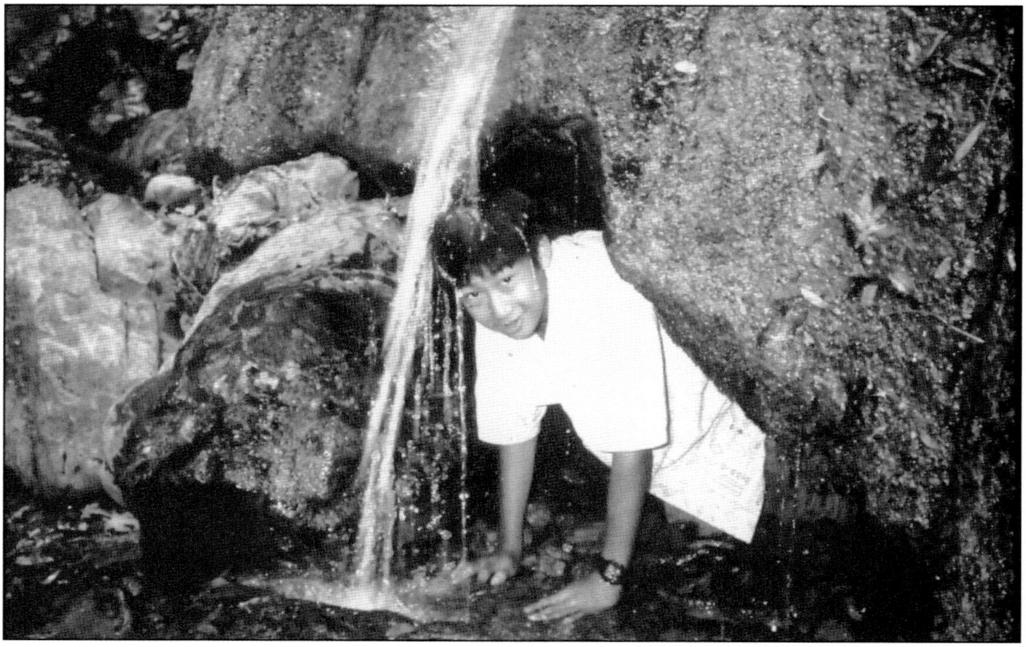

Becoming a Boney Bean. Unexpected twists and turns challenged campers and allowed them to meet nature face-to-face. "Becoming a Boney Bean took courage and resourcefulness. It began by crawling through a dark cave for 10 or 15 feet to a sunlit opening and a scramble through the falling water of Rose Valley Falls." According to Wallace Burr's traditional campfire story, this is what the imaginary Boney Beans might have experienced during their rite of passage.

CAMPING IN THE 21ST CENTURY. Hiking, backpacking, and rock climbing are all good options for the thrill-seeking OVS student. Exciting treks are taken to the Anza Borrego Desert or the Carrizo Plain, an important Native American site and home to a diverse community of wildlife and plant species. The importance of teamwork is emphasized on these trips, during which the hikers/campers traverse the infamous San Andreas Fault with its carved valleys and steep ravines. The campsite at Cone Peak, with its dramatic setting along the treacherous Big Sur coastline, features redwood forests and seven creek crossings. As pictured at right, rock climbing in the Sespe in 2005 is a challenging adventure for Ronny Ferrari.

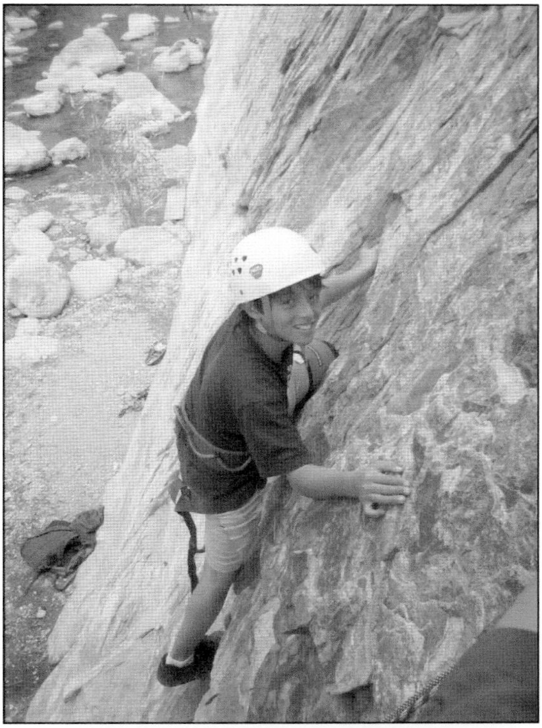

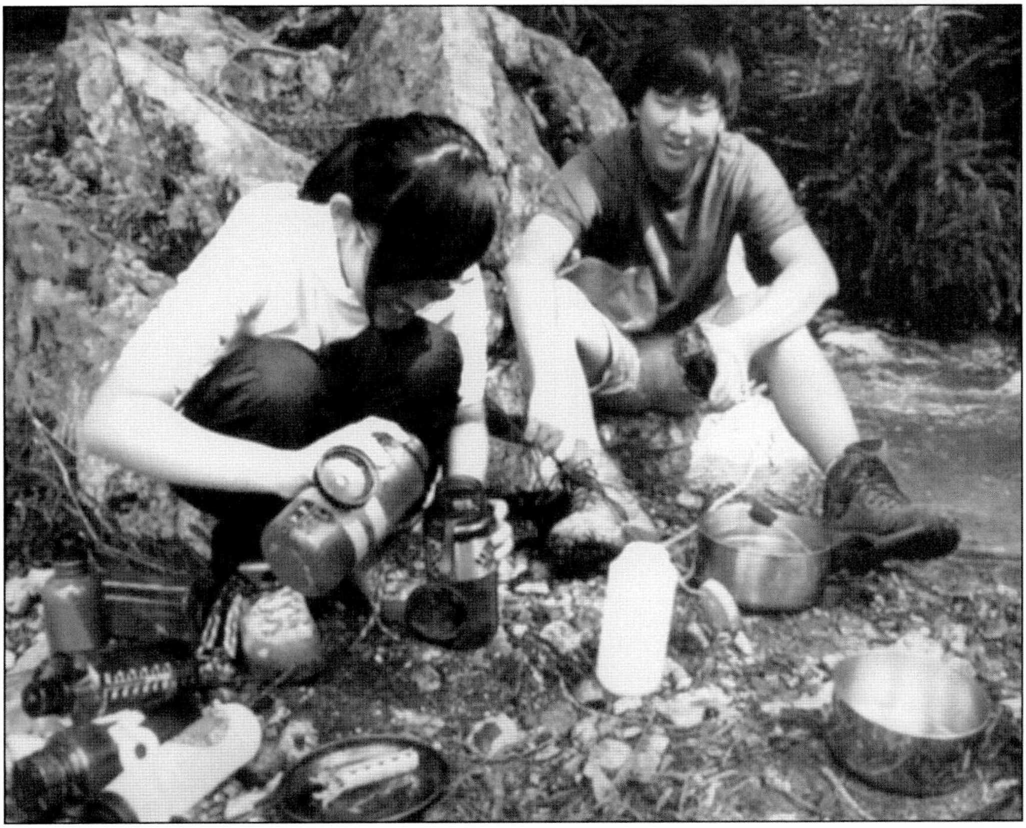

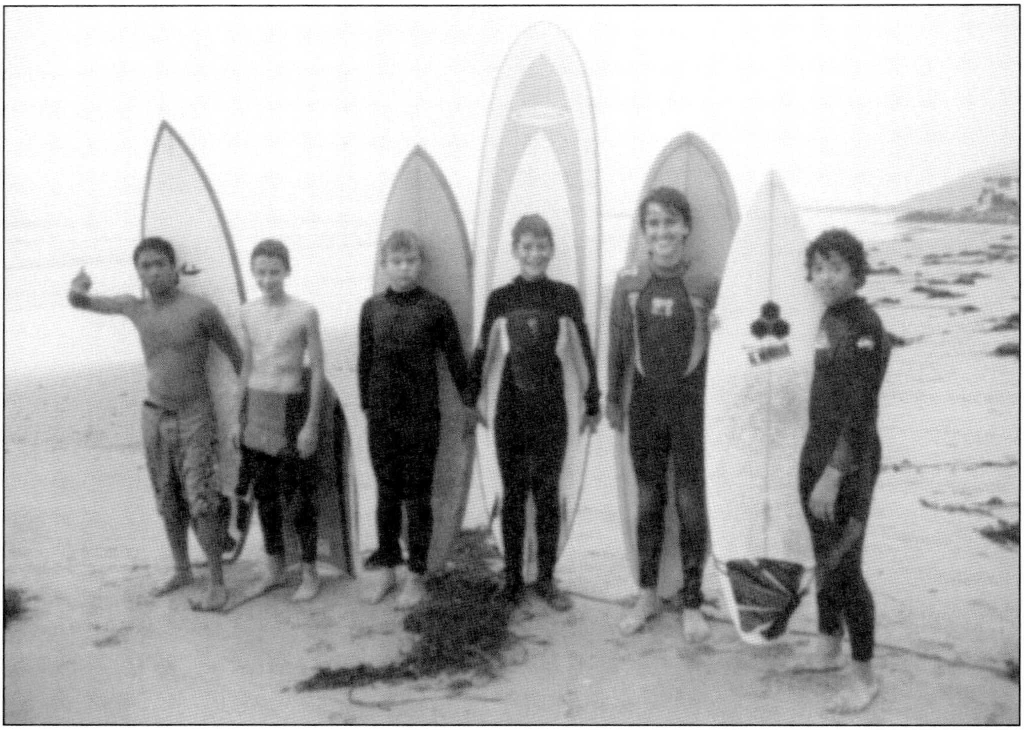

Special Opportunities. In the 1960s, surfing and the Southern California beach phenomenon became a popular part of teen culture. This was inspired by musical groups such as Jan and Dean and the Beach Boys. Under the supervision of older boys or teachers such as Gary Dinkins and Dok Smith, surfing became a popular extracurricular activity, especially during the summer program. Many occasions for excursions to the California parks, coastlines, and wilderness also presented themselves to students. As shown below, one could even commune with nature during outdoor trips.

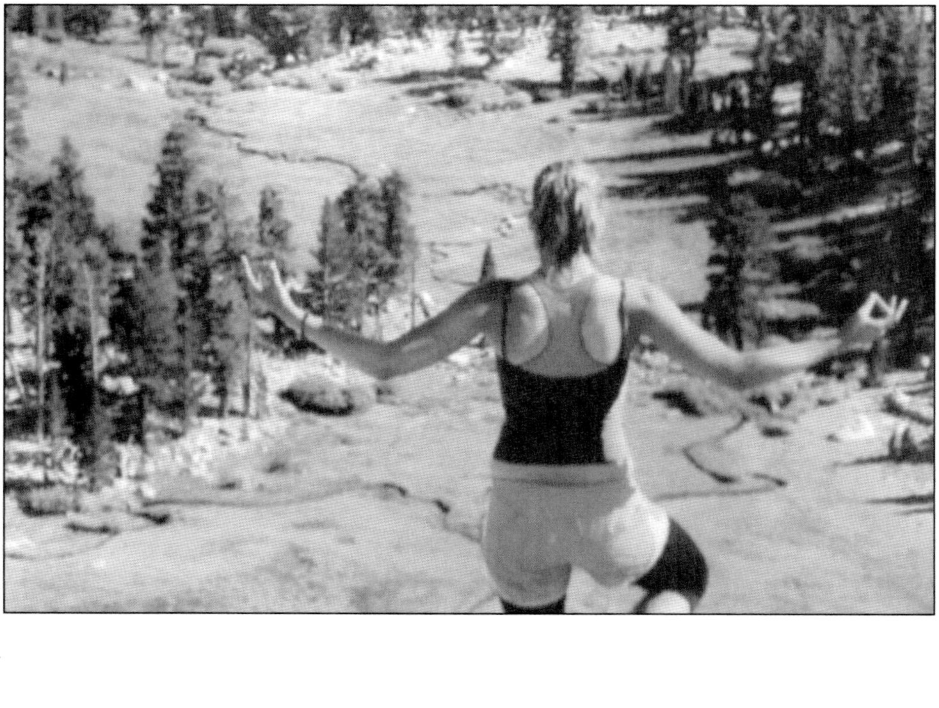

Nine

Athletics

The Outdoor Classroom. The opportunity for children to participate in athletics provides a learning experience outside the academic setting. On the field or court, students learn to be gracious losers and humble winners. Challenges are presented that children must address while maintaining fairness and self-control. Overcoming these conflicts helps to develop boys and girls into healthy men and women. A school mascot, the Spud, made its appearance at OVS in the 1970s and continues to represent the school in a variety of areas, but mostly in athletics. The name Spuds was created by Carl Cooper when he was head of the athletic program. "Spuds are hardy and, without a doubt, a name that is unclaimed by any other school," Cooper said. The girls' volleyball team began to refer to itself as "Spudettes." The Thacher mascot was Toad, Midland's was the Gnats, and Dunn's was Earwigs. The OVS Lower Campus athletes call themselves "French Fries and Tater Tots."

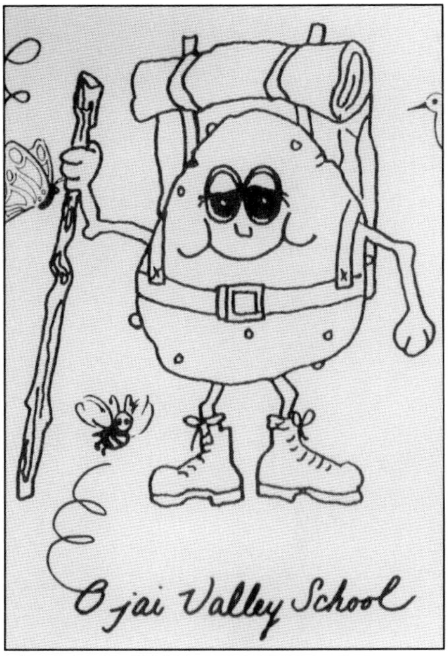

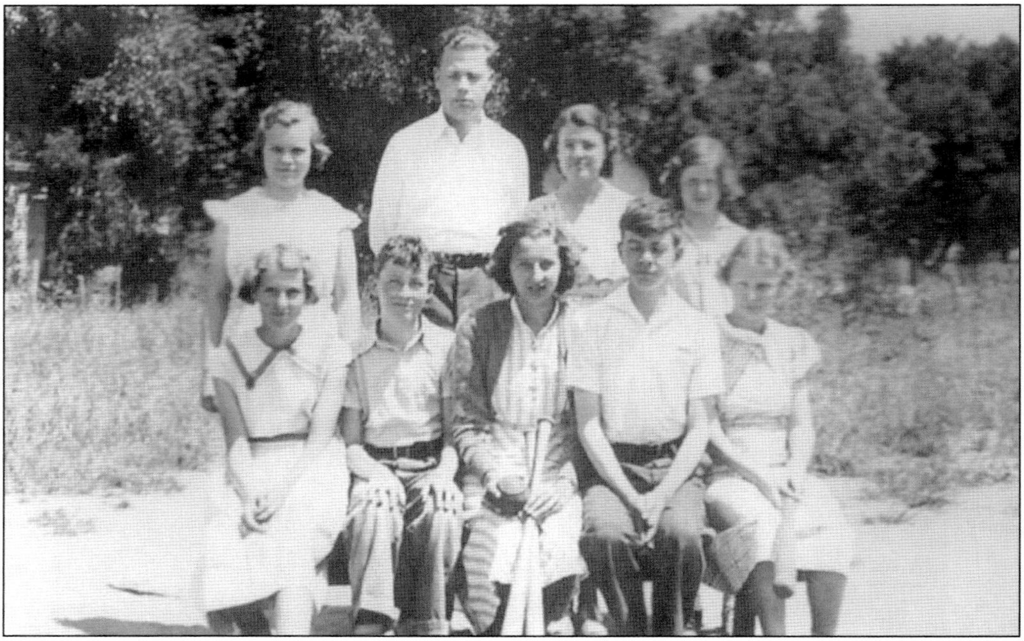

Baseball. The above image, showing of members of the 1936 baseball team, illustrates the interest in sports early on. In fact, intramural baseball was one of the first athletic activities at OVS. Both intramural and interscholastic competitions were encouraged for boys and girls. Today, there are only boys' baseball teams. In the early 1960s, baseball was played on a grass field at the Upper Campus. Today, it remains a popular spectator sport. OVS won the Condor League baseball championship in 1965 and 2004.

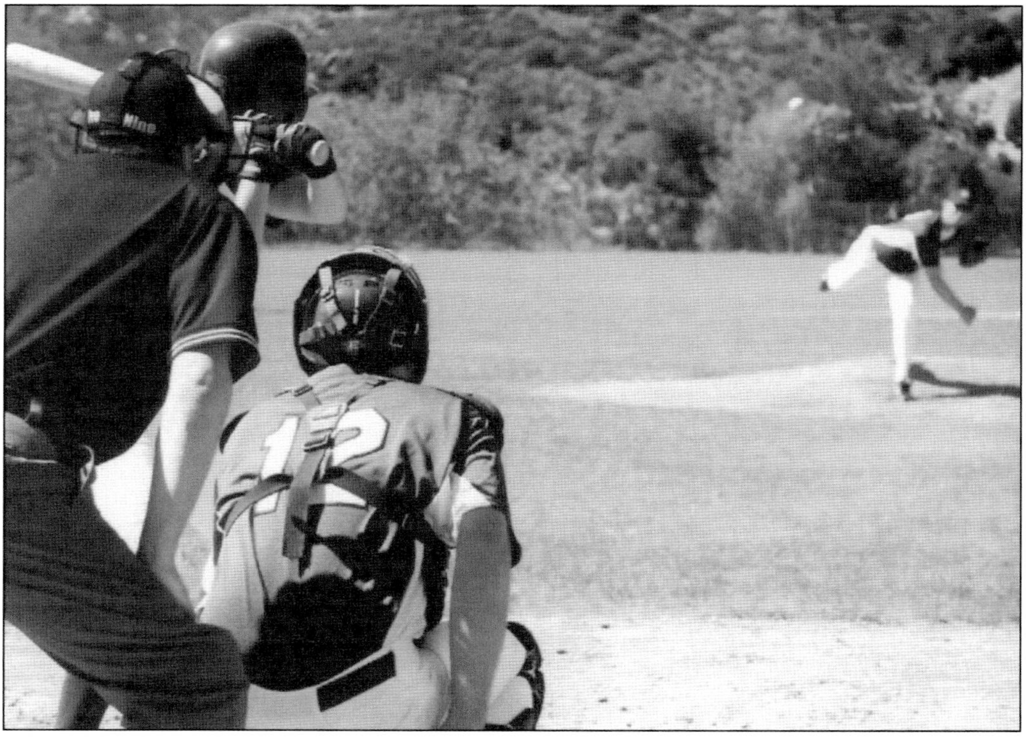

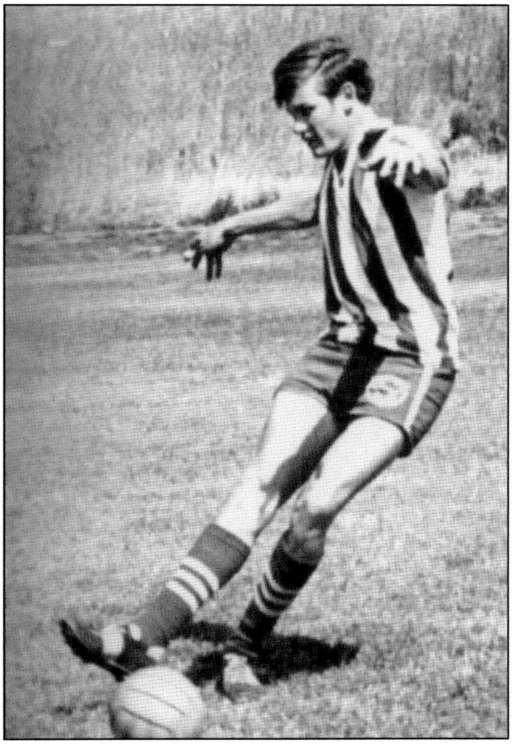

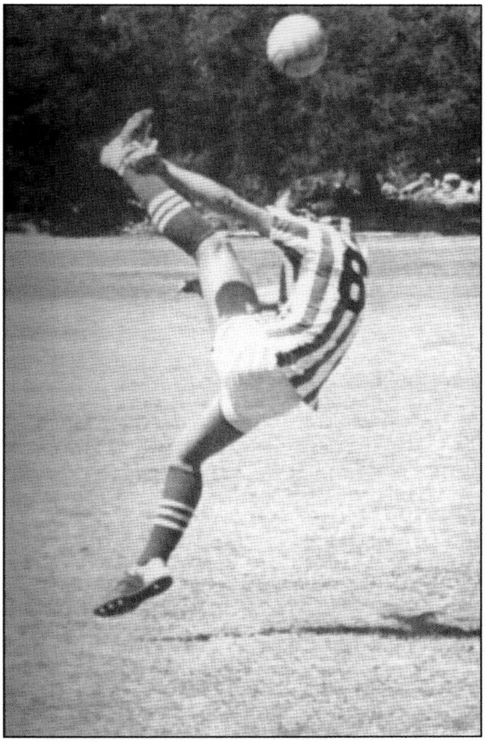

Boys' Soccer. This popular international sport made its appearance in the early 1950s with the hiring of Robert Cooper. Cooper believed in discipline, fair play, and teamwork, and he recognized the educational benefits of exertion, grace in defeat, and humility in victory. Soccer was one of the first organized sports at OVS. Teams played local schools such as Laguna Blanca, Cate, Midland, Webb, Thacher, and Dunn. In 1962, the ninth-grade boys' soccer team went undefeated. Demonstrating soccer skills are Scott Eicher (above left, U68), Pete Kammeier (above right, U68), and Andrew Lee (right, U13). In the early years, the teams were inexperienced, but eventually a legitimate athletic program was established at the school. Its popularity continues undiminished.

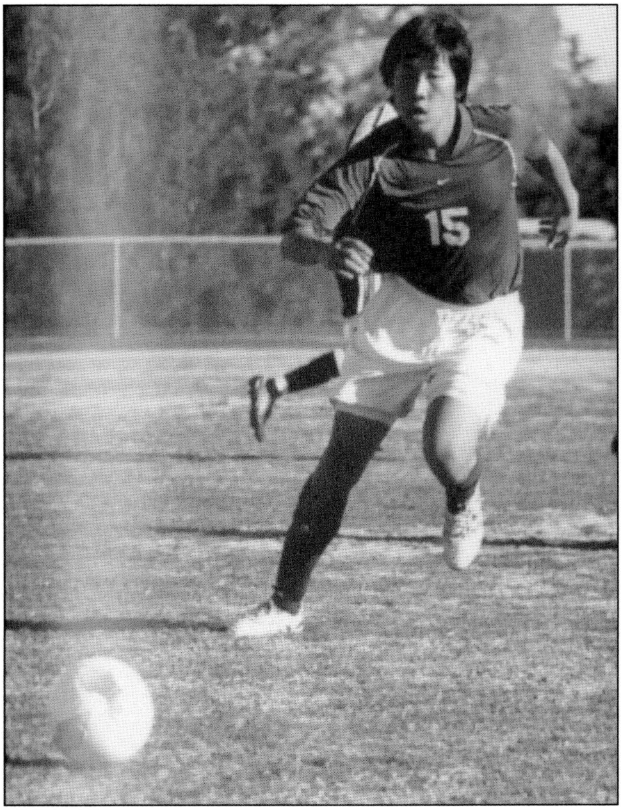

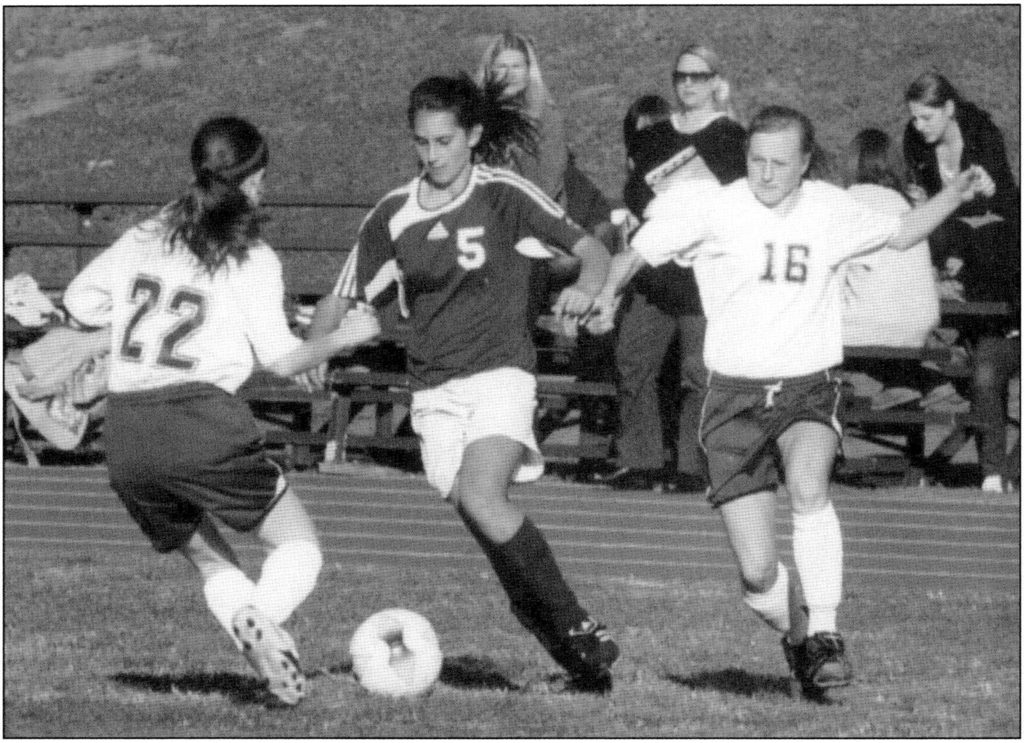

Girls' Soccer. Girls' soccer became popular in the 1960s, especially after the Upper Campus was completed and fully enrolled. In addition, many of the other schools had girls' teams, so interscholastic competition was possible. Like boys' soccer, girls' soccer shifted from fall to winter when the Condor League adopted football. These images show the 2011 girls' team in action. Teamwork and good sportsmanship were always stressed and were far more important than the final score.

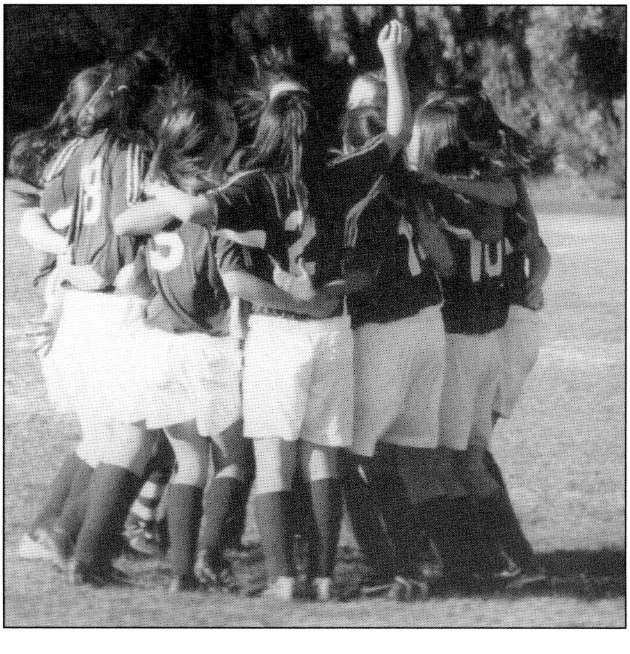

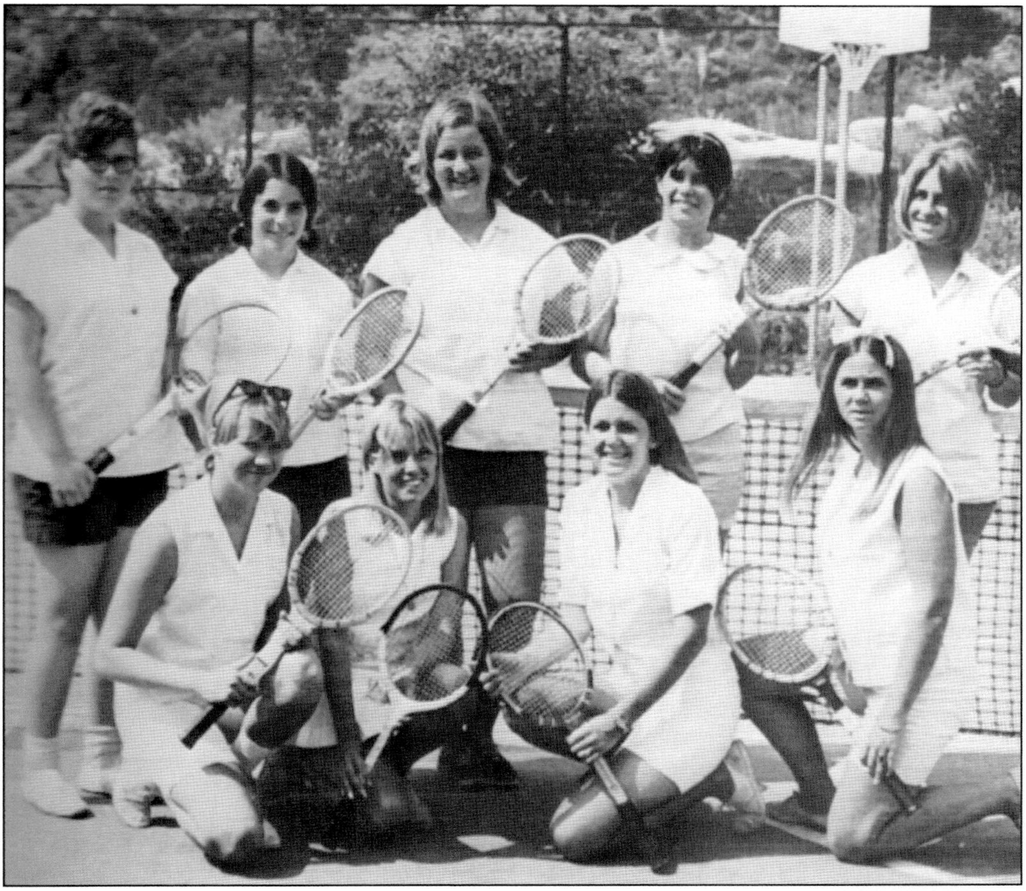

Girls' Tennis. Many students had been exposed to tennis before they arrived at the school. This popular sport was reinforced because the school was in such proximity to the Ojai Valley Tennis Tournament. Above is the 1967 girls' tennis team: from left to right, (first row) Karen Williams, Muffie Block, Jody Boswell, and Joni Doell; (second row) Kathy Stewart, Michelle Ross, Eleanor Rhodes, Betsy Curran, and Melissa Phillips. Coach Fedro Yanez (right) served as tennis instructor from 1965 to 1968 and started the first official teams for boys and girls.

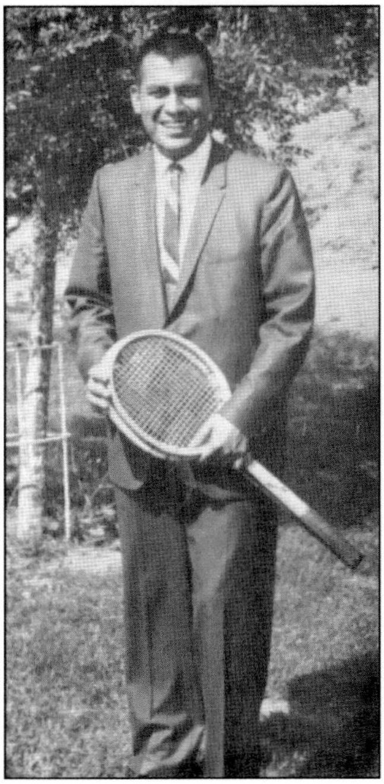

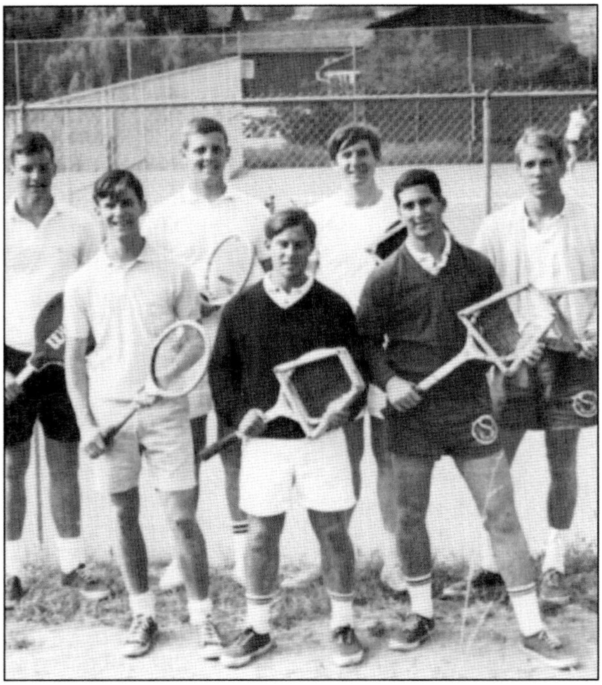

More Tennis. The first Upper Campus boys' tennis team (left) was coached by Mike Hermes in 1964–1965. The team competed with private schools, including Thacher, Cate, Midland, Webb, and Laguna Blanca. Pictured are, from left to right, (first row) Steve McIntyre, Mark Adler, and Mike Tomkins; (second row) Stan Carlson, Roger Haley, Robert Kotchian, and Dok Smith. In 1985, tennis courts were completed on the Upper Campus. Tennis was a Condor League event for girls and boys. John Wood (L29) recalls with pride that he played in the Ojai Valley Tennis Tournament in 1929. The sport remains popular more than 80 years later, and Grace Pan (U00) is shown below taking a swing.

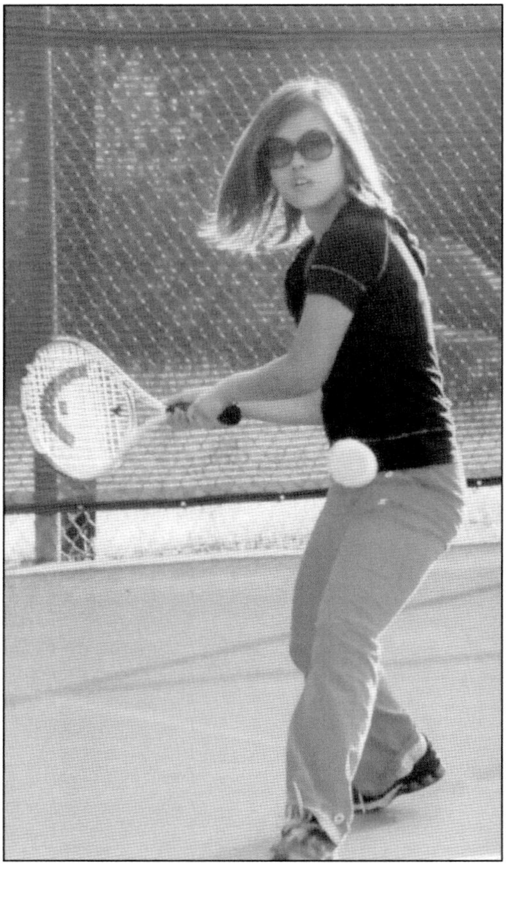

WOMEN'S VOLLEYBALL. This popular American sport is played in the fall. It is quite competitive, and the girls put their hearts and souls into every game. Volleyball finally gave girls the opportunity to participate in another fall athletic event. At right, students play on a new grass court at the Upper Campus. Volleyball is also played indoors in neighboring school gymnasiums, but currently there is no gymnasium on either of the Ojai Valley School campuses. Girls' volleyball, softball, and track did not make an appearance until 1967 or 1968.

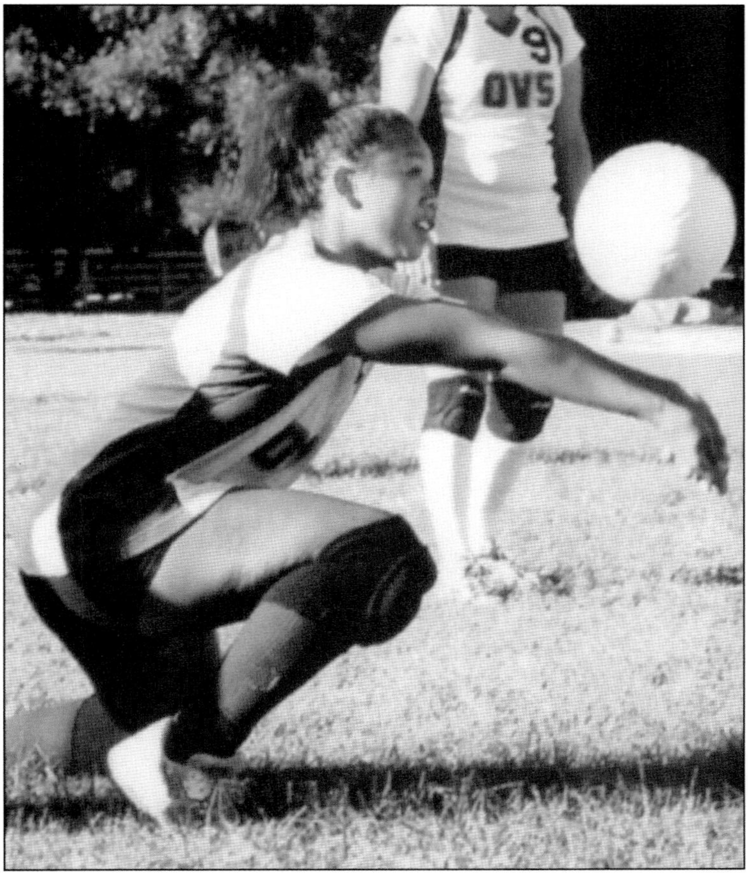

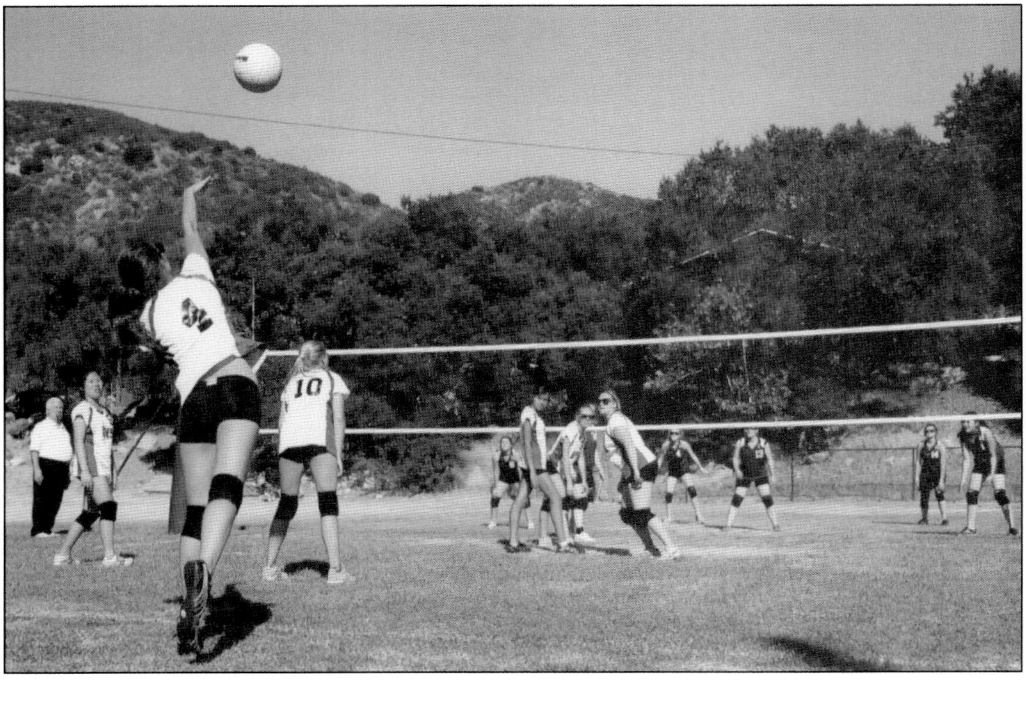

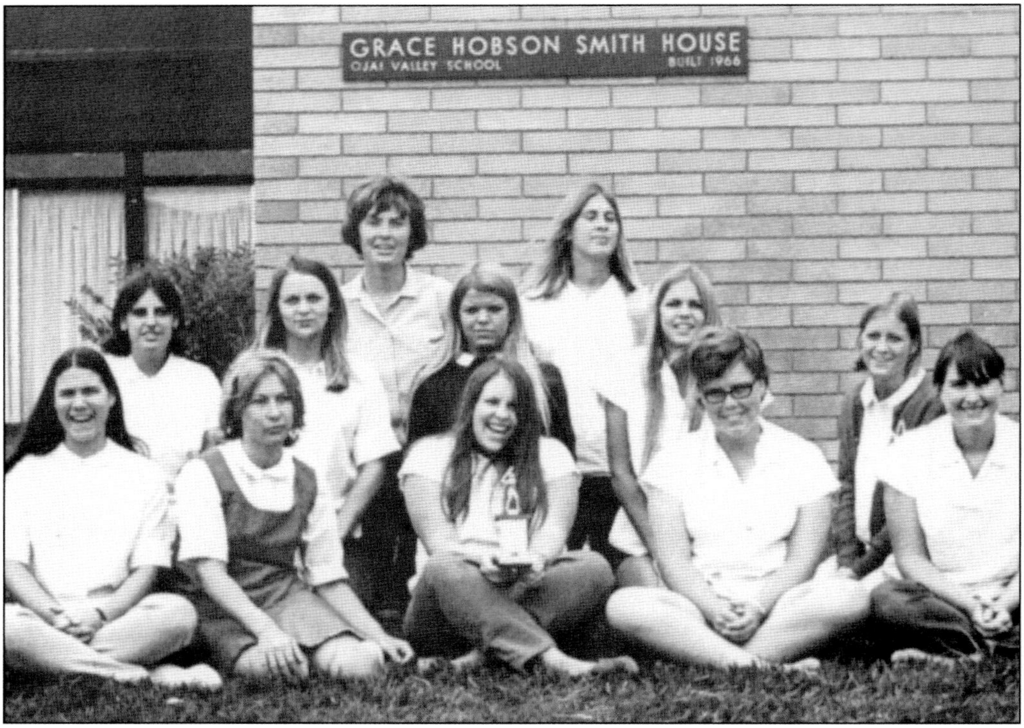

Softball and Cheerleading. Since baseball was not played by girls in the Condor League, girls were given the opportunity to play softball in the late 1960s. Seen above is the first girls' softball team with coach Sharyle Call. Cheerleaders appeared in 1965, and the first girls to cheer for soccer and baseball games were Danny Robertson and Janice Hubenthal. Over the years, cheerleaders became more involved in cheering for other sports. In 1968, these active girls made an appearance at most sports events, cheering their teams to victory. Seen below are, from left to right, Joni Doell, Gina Vitousek, Jennifer Bayless, and Stephanie Mefford. These girls cheered for both boys' and girls' games.

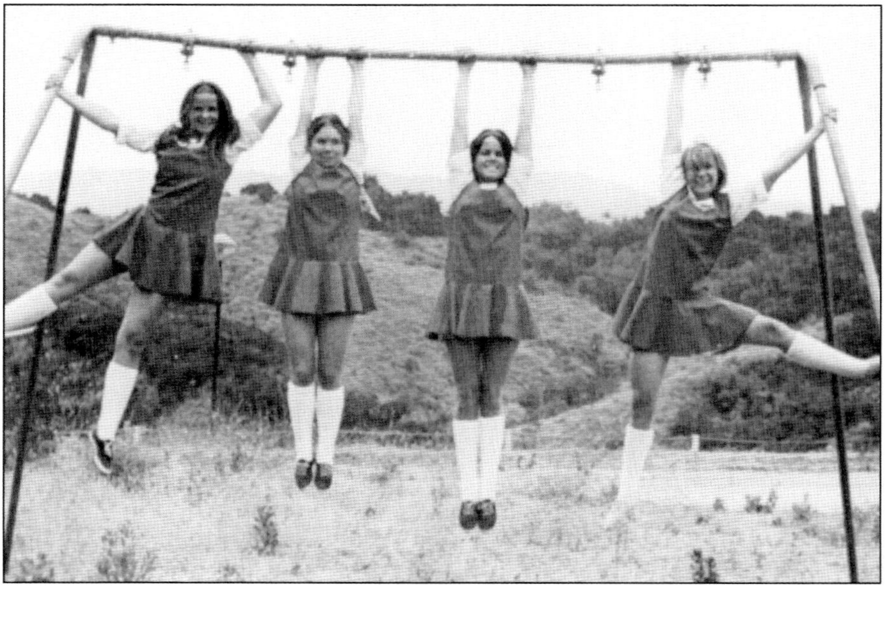

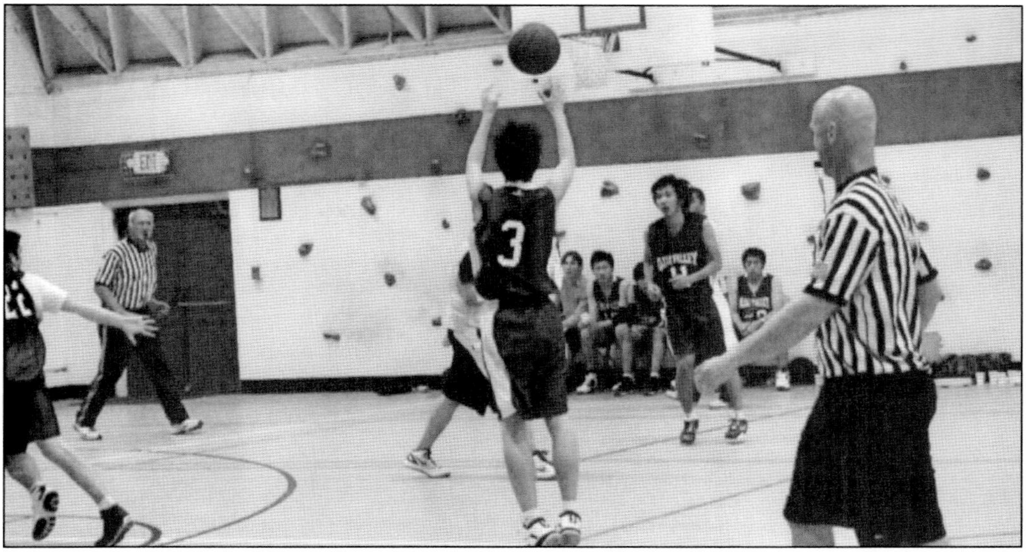

Basketball and Golf. Boys' basketball has become a popular interscholastic sport. For most of OVS's history, basketball was played outdoors on asphalt tennis courts. Routine practice sessions are still held on outdoor courts, and although OVS does not have a gymnasium, arrangements for indoor play have been made with local schools, such as the nearby Matilija Junior High School, to permit the Spuds and Spudettes to host home games. Below at left, Mallory Holt (U12) strains to make the shot during her basketball game against Cate in 2011. Girls' basketball is an extremely popular competitive event, and the girls are eagerly cheered on by the boys, cheerleaders, parents, and faculty. Golf was first offered for boys and girls in 2008. Below at right, Toshiyuki Takeuchi (U10) clears the ball from a sand trap.

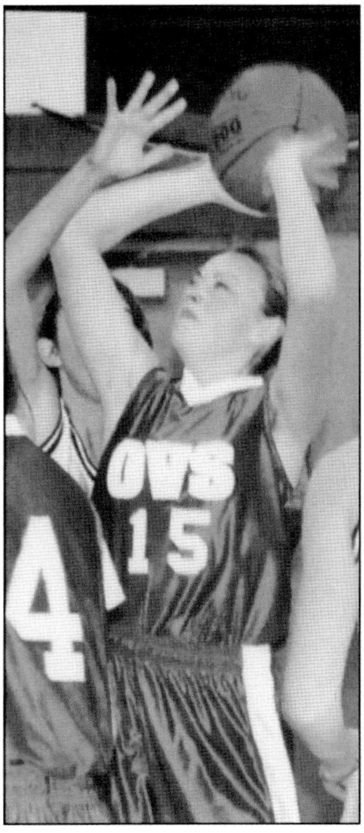

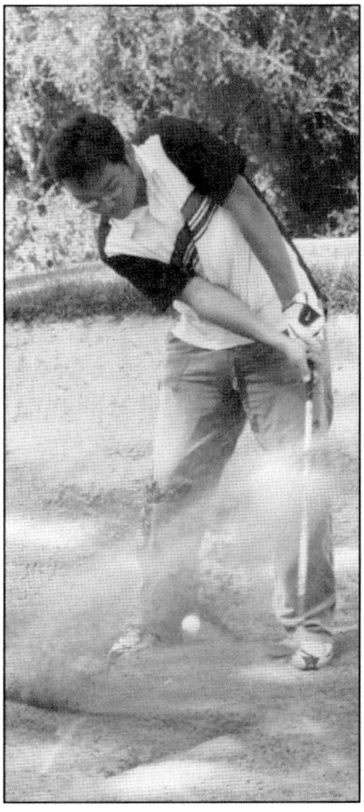

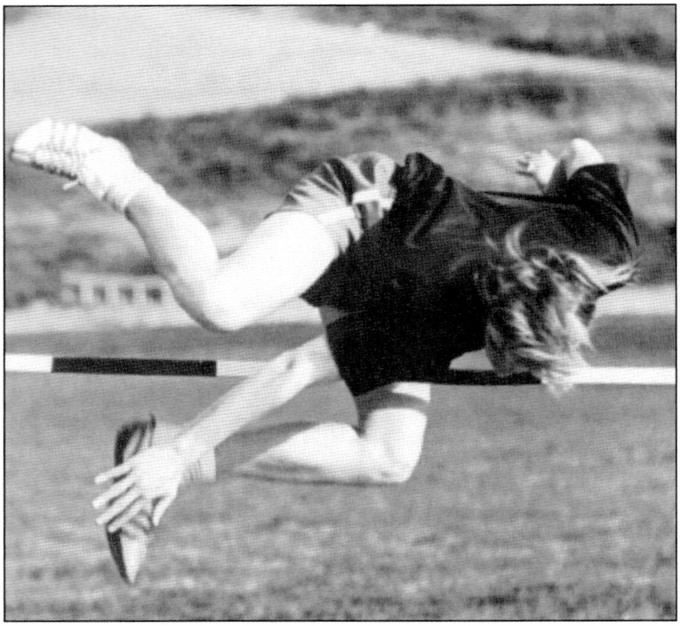

Track and Field. By 1968, track and field was added to the athletic program of other local private schools. Boys and girls who wanted more than the basic court or field sports discovered new opportunities. The foothills of OVS's Upper Campus, with their intertwining trails, provided an excellent cross-country training facility. OVS won the Condor League track championship for the first time in 2008. High jumper Courtney Harris is pictured at left competing in 1968 at one of the first track meets held at Cate School.

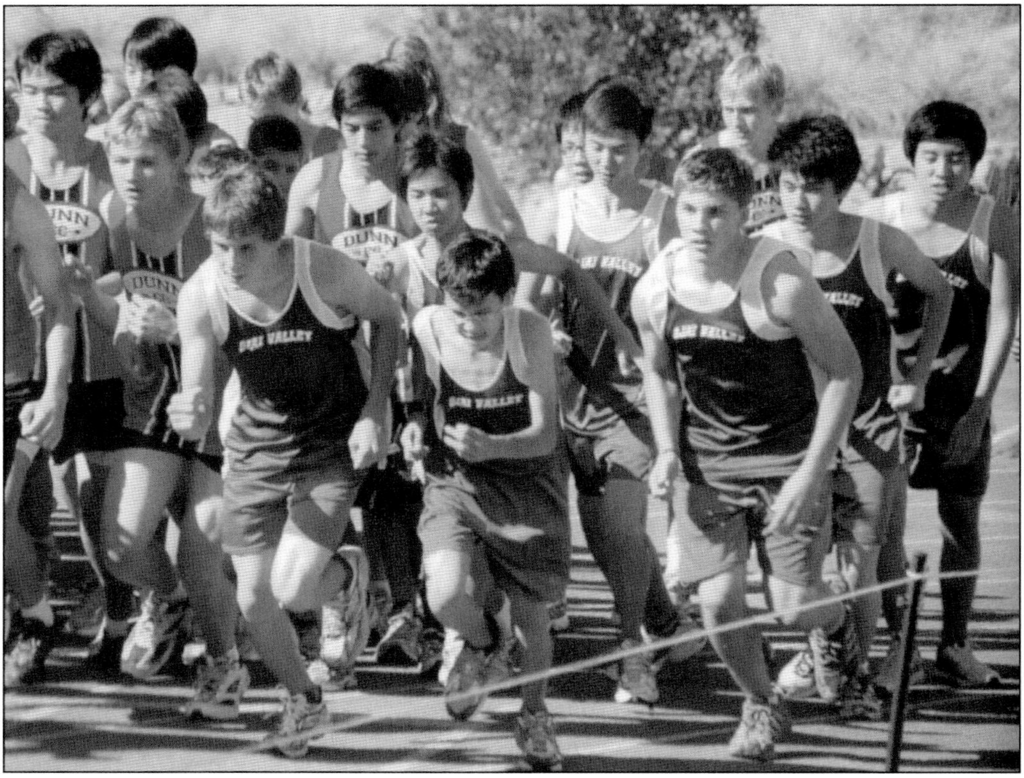

Cross-Country Runners. In this image, OVS gets a jump on Dunn during a 2011 cross-country meet. OVS won league titles in 1980, 1984, 1987, and 1988.

Lacrosse. Lacrosse is an authentic Native American sport that originated in eastern North America and around the Great Lakes. Providing an alternative to basketball, this full-contact sport was added to the OVS athletic program in 1968. Lacrosse teams are made up of 10 players with equipment including helmets, arm pads, gloves, shoulder pads, a small rubber ball, and lacrosse sticks.

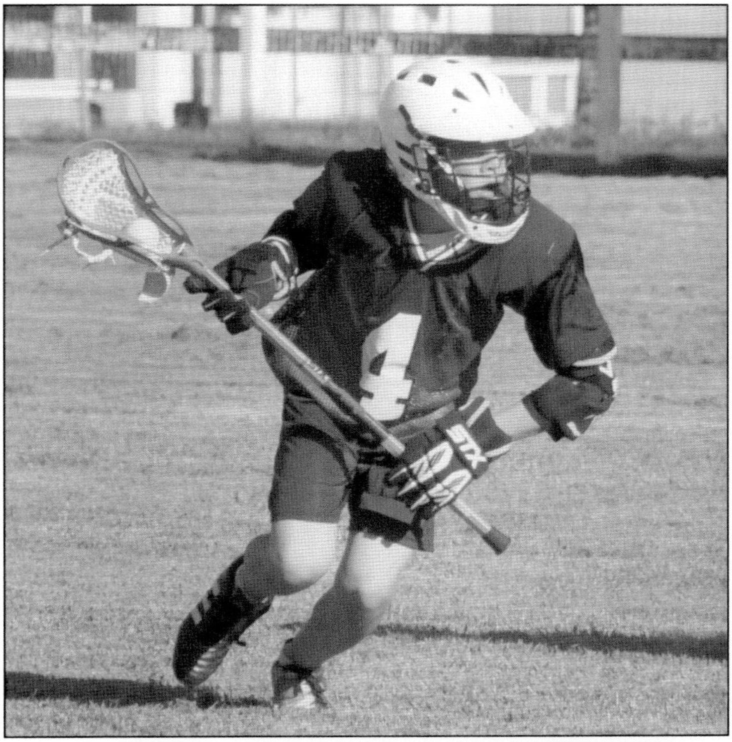

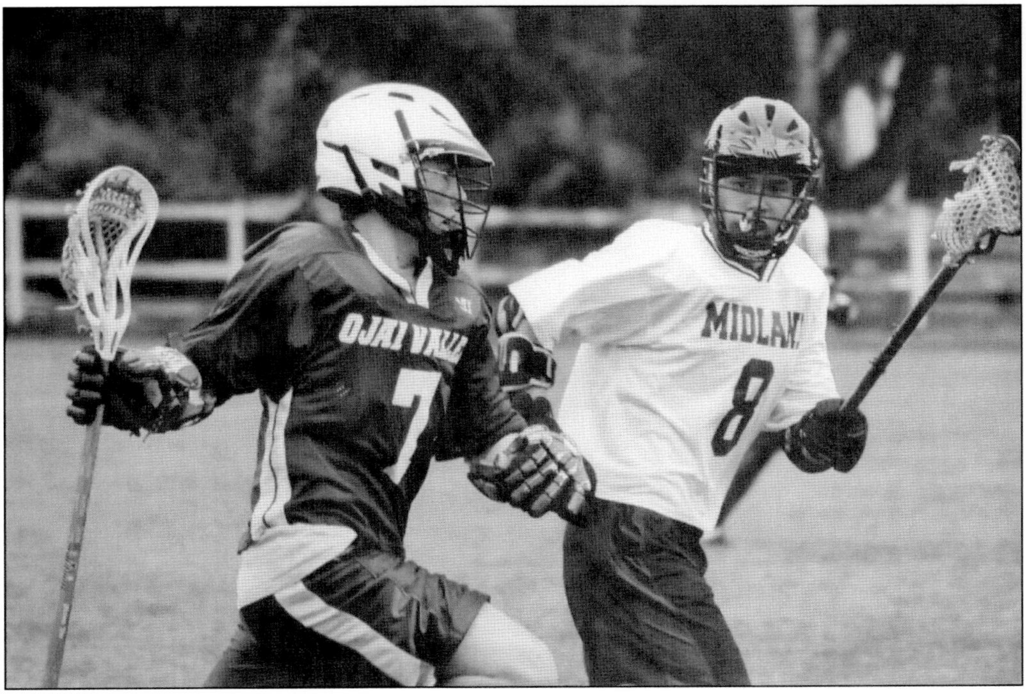

OVS Lacrosse. Lacrosse was a popular Eastern sport, and some students brought their own equipment with them when they came to OVS. Once again, the students had an opportunity to show their teamwork and sportsmanship skills. Ojai Valley School became one of the first independent schools on the West Coast to participate in interscholastic lacrosse.

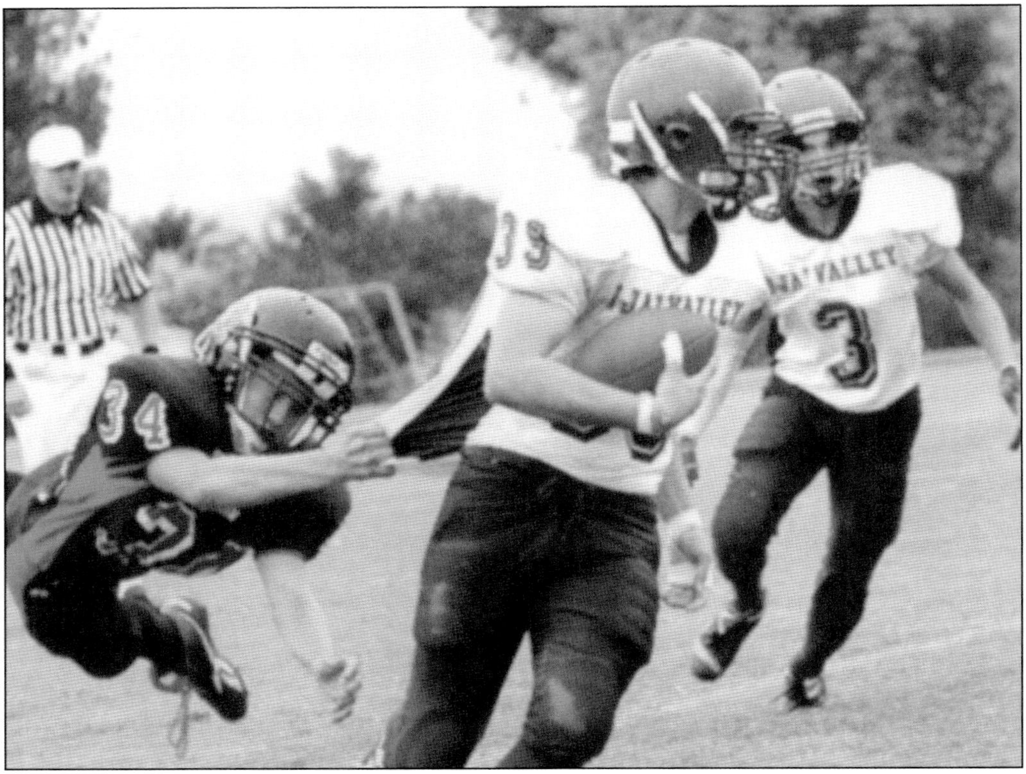

FOOTBALL BEGINS. OVS's eight-man football program began in 2007 and ended after the 2013 fall season. This fall activity was popular with participants and spectators alike. Eight-man football is frequently played at smaller schools that have difficulty fielding a full eleven-man football roster. More running than passing is involved, and scores are traditionally higher. Teaching the fundamentals is imperative in this full-contact sport. Coaches Craig Floyd, John Wickenhaeuser, and Doug Colborn felt home games brought the Upper and Lower Campuses together.

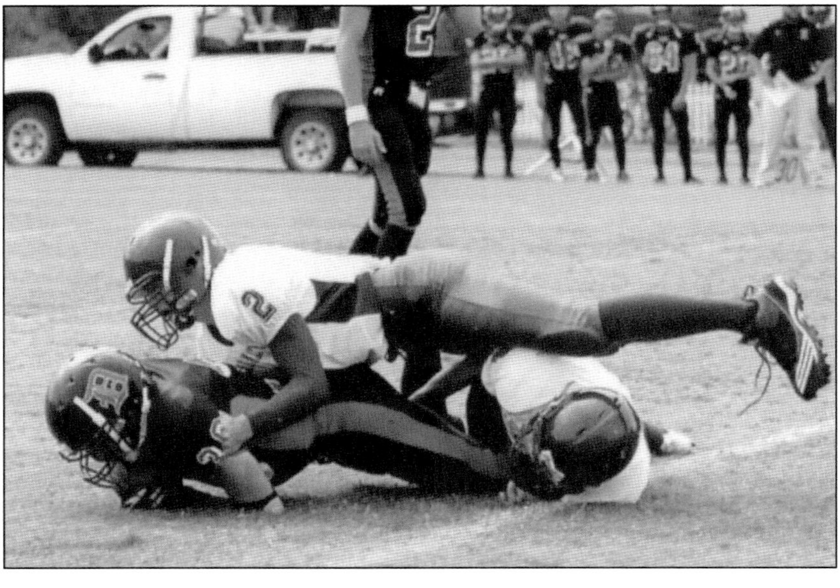

Ten

One Hundred Years and Beyond

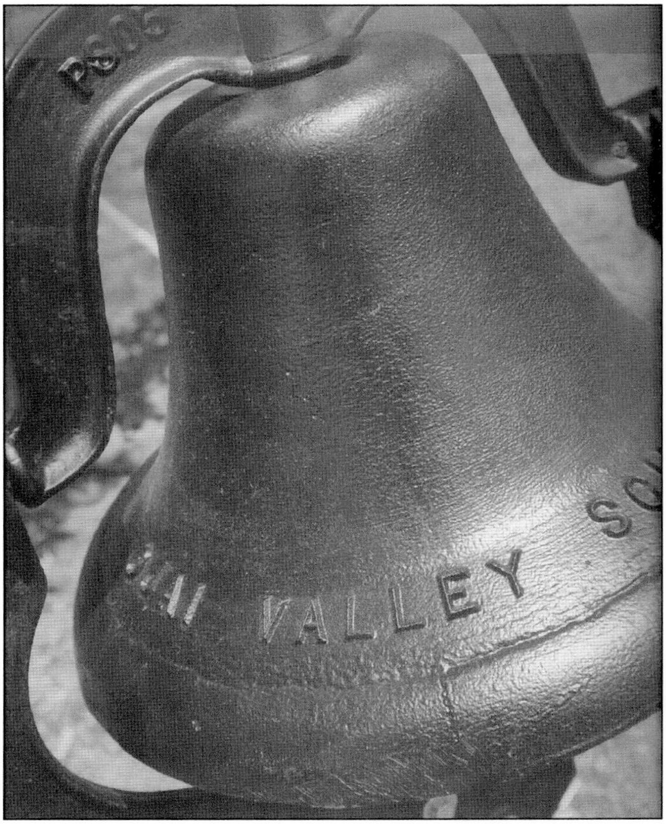

Centennial Celebration. Founded by the Van Pattens in 1911 as a tutoring program and renamed Ojai Valley School in 1923, OVS celebrated its centennial on January 12, 2011, with more than 400 students, faculty, alumni, and friends in attendance. Students enjoyed ragtime music, face painting, maypole dancing, and old-fashioned games such as tug-of-war. In honor of the occasion, a cast-iron bell was presented to the Lower Campus. This bell symbolizes the unity between the Upper and Lower Campuses. More than 1,000 faculty, alumni, and students participated in related events throughout the centennial year.

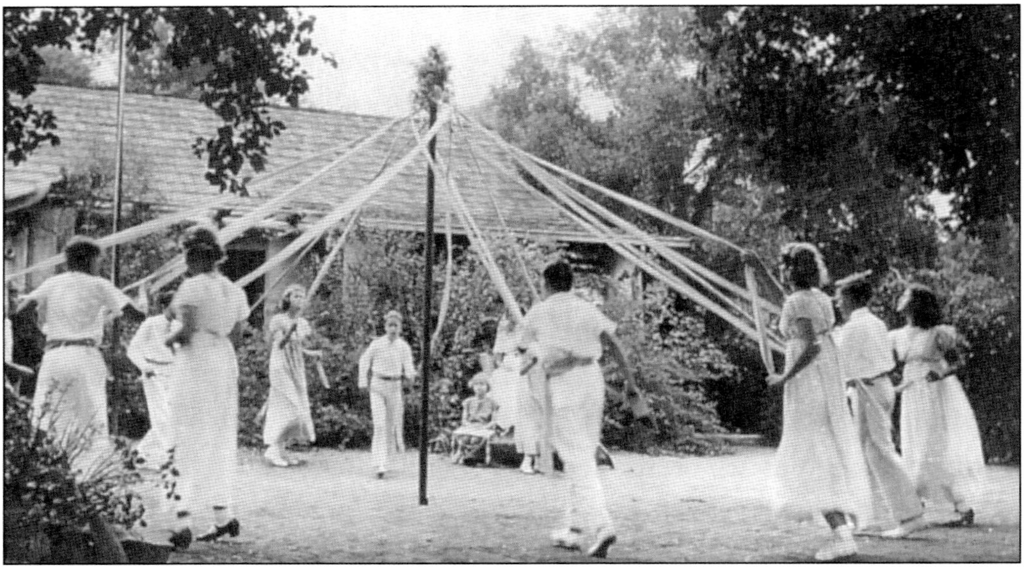

Maypole Dance. The maypole dance originally began as a celebration of the coming of spring and was held on May 1 in Germany, England, and Sweden. Dancers move in a circle, each holding a colored ribbon. As they move around the pole, the ribbons are intertwined in a web. This tradition started at OVS in the 1930s—the maypole dance was performed at the annual May festival on graduation day/the last day of school, as shown in the 1937 image above. This was accompanied by English and Scottish folk dances. Below, elementary children continue the tradition by commemorating the school's 100th birthday celebration in front of the new Greenberg Activities Center in 2011.

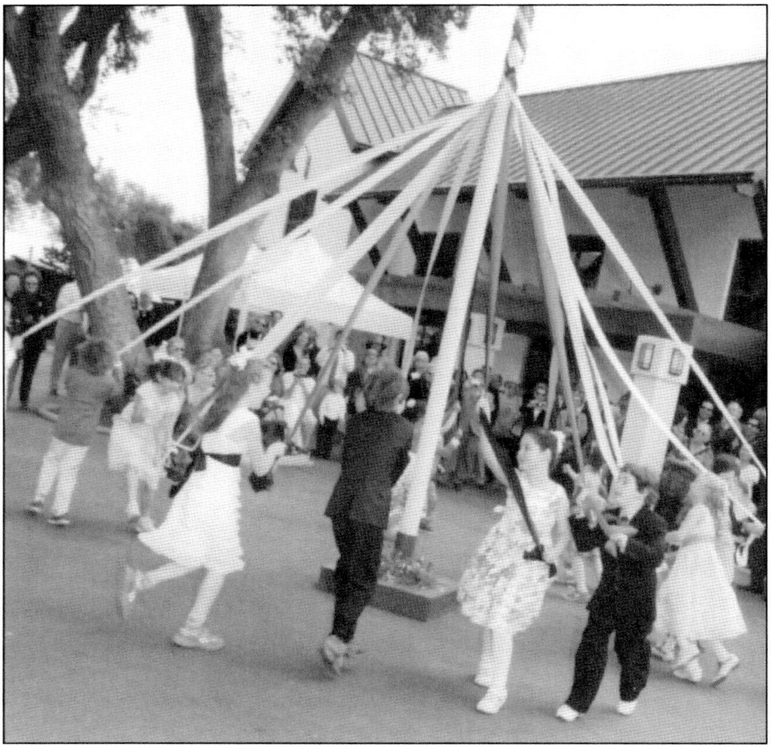

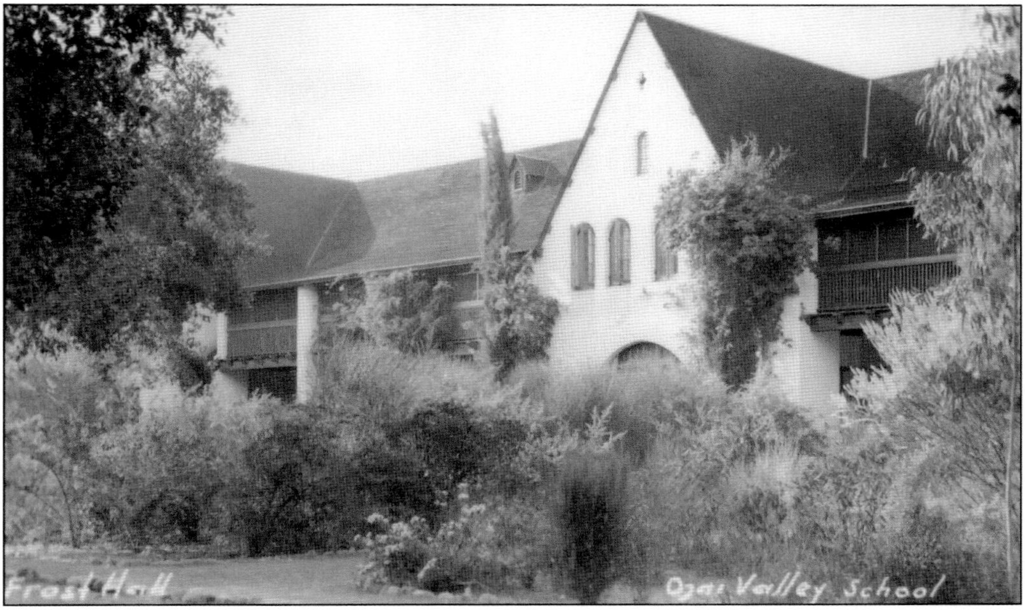

Past to Present. Many changes have taken place during the first 100 years of Ojai Valley School. The enrollment has increased, and facilities (including Frost Hall, seen here in the 1930s and below in 2007) have been upgraded and remodeled, but the basic foundation laid out by Edward Yeomans remains the same. The exceptional faculty is there to guide children and allow them to take risks and learn from mistakes. The educators who have had the honor of being part of the OVS staff are to be commended.

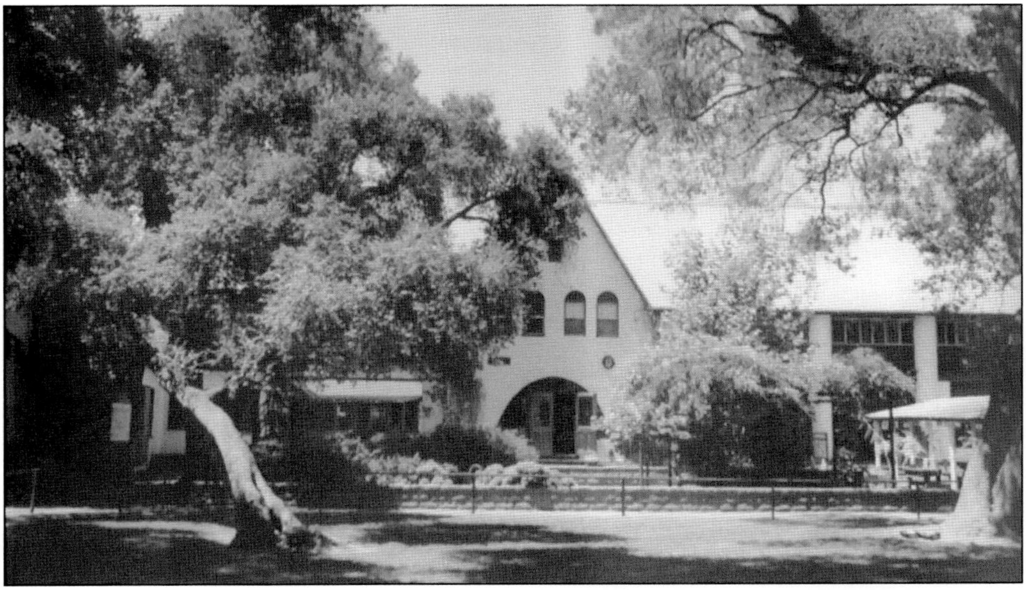

Sustainability. As OVS continues into the 21st century, changes have been made to accommodate and sustain the school's infrastructure, financial security, and facilities. This includes buildings, wireless computer access, playing fields, and stables. The curriculum has been consistently updated to meet evolving university demands and admission requirements. Maintaining the highest standards for faculty applicants and encouraging alumni contributions are examples of the ways in which OVS's continued growth and success are ensured.

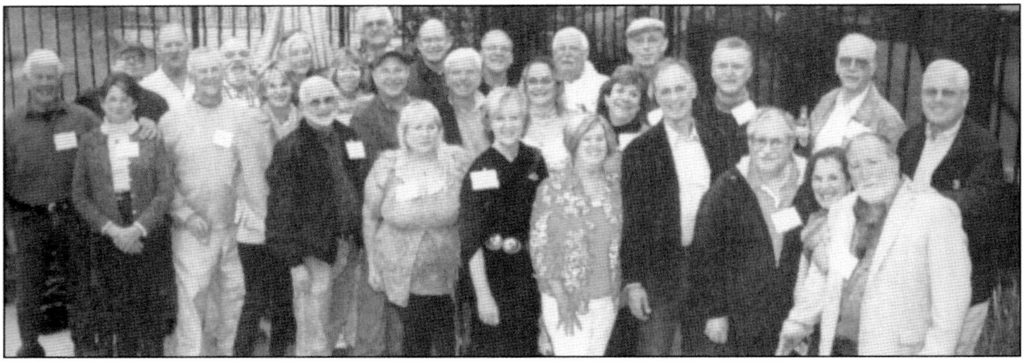

Alumni Gather. At the 100th anniversary of the school in 2011, members of the first three graduating classes gathered to celebrate 44, 45, and 46 respective years since graduation. The centennial alumni weekend was celebrated on June 11, 2011, and the keynote speaker was Thomas Yeomans, grandson of school founder Edward Yeomans. Along with speeches, there were numerous outdoor activities, including hiking, swimming, golf, pony rides, tennis, a ropes course, and the notoriously competitive alumni soccer game.

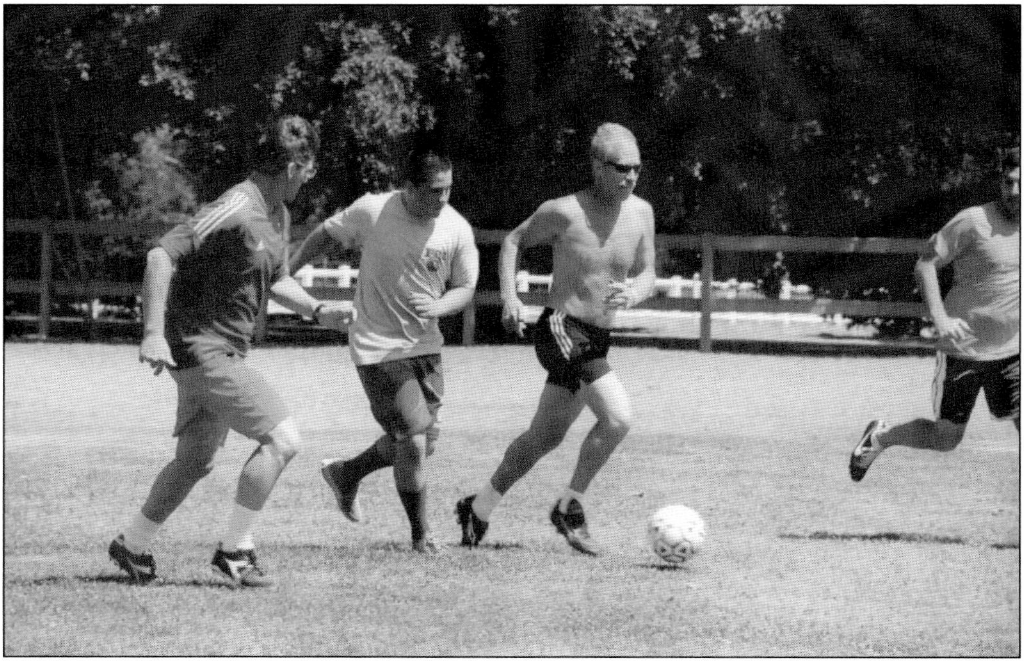

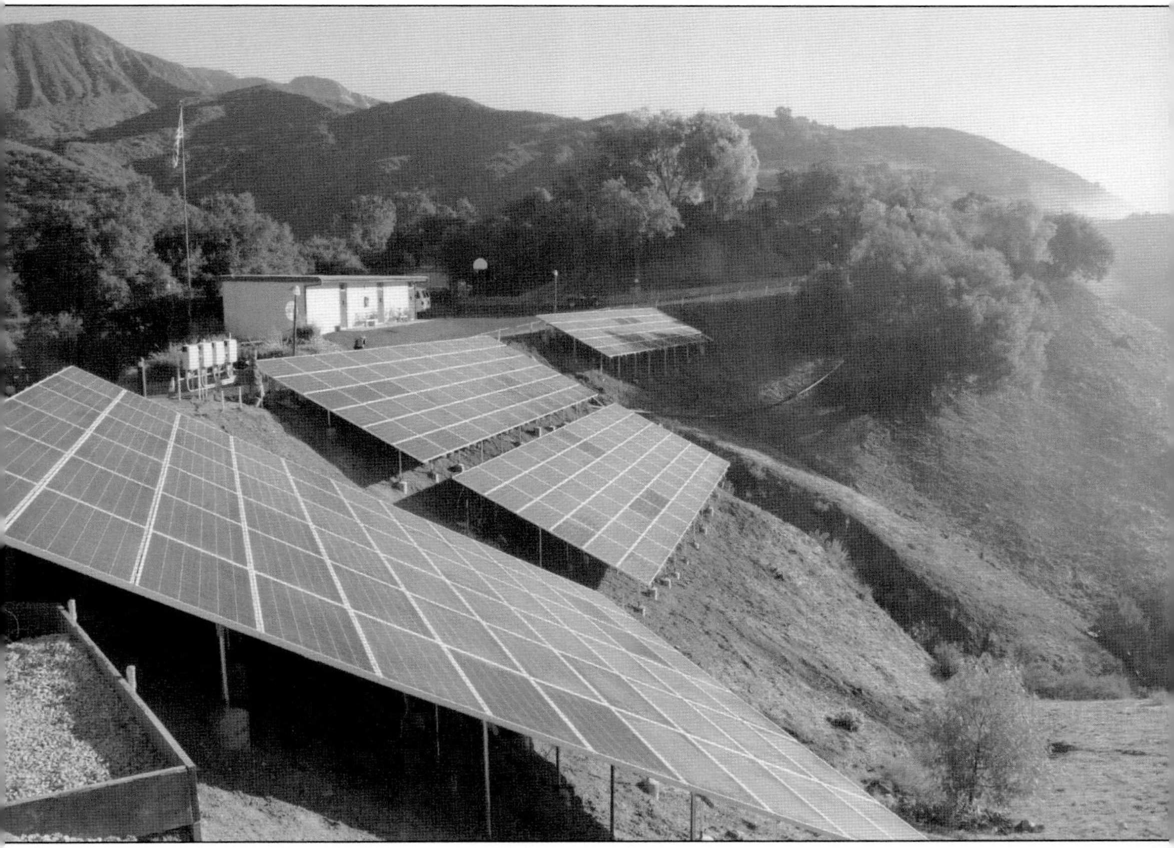

OVS GOES GREEN. Although "going green" has become a popular environmentalist expression in the last decade, respect for the environment was a key aspect of Edward Yeomans's beliefs. Ojai Valley School has taken the concept to the next level as it enters the 21st century. It has completed a solar project that will significantly reduce the school's carbon footprint and create a course toward sustainability for the next 100 years. This photovoltaic system was designed to generate 85 percent of the electricity at the Upper Campus, but it is performing well above expectations. It is one of the largest solar projects undertaken by a school or business in Ventura County. In 2013, OVS was presented the Ventura County Climate Change Action Award.

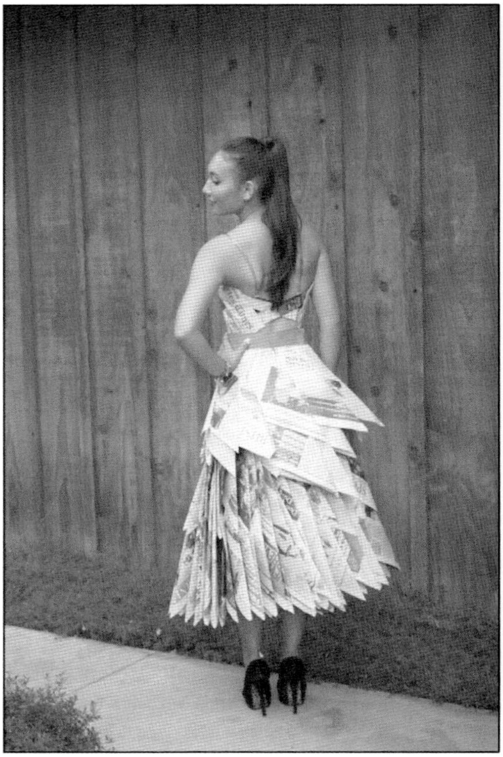

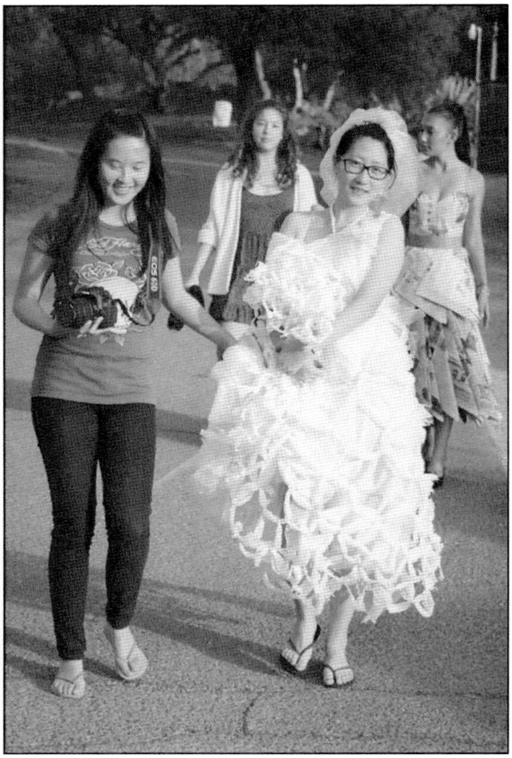

TRASHION FASHION. In 2013, OVS expanded environmental consciousness with its first "Trashion Fashion" show. Teachers, hoping to expand an interest in fashion while also raising environmental awareness, encouraged students to create innovative designs using recycled materials. Here, the artists have turned trash into beauty while demonstrating artistic talent. An exquisite newspaper dress worn by Nakita Moler (U15) and an intricate bridal gown modeled by Shelly Xu (U14) and made entirely out of white plastic trash bags exhibit the possibilities for recycled materials. (Both photographs by Weiwei Wang [U14].)

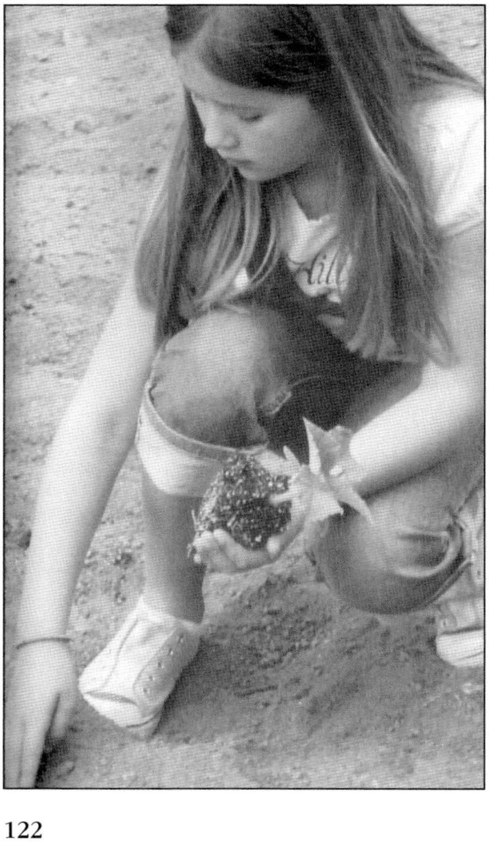

TEACHING GREEN EARLY. The school continues efforts to be ecologically responsible and to pass this knowledge to future generations. These efforts include a state-of-the-art wastewater treatment plant at the Upper Campus, drought-tolerant and native plantings, environmental-education classes and activities for all Lower and Upper campus grade levels, and comprehensive recycling programs.

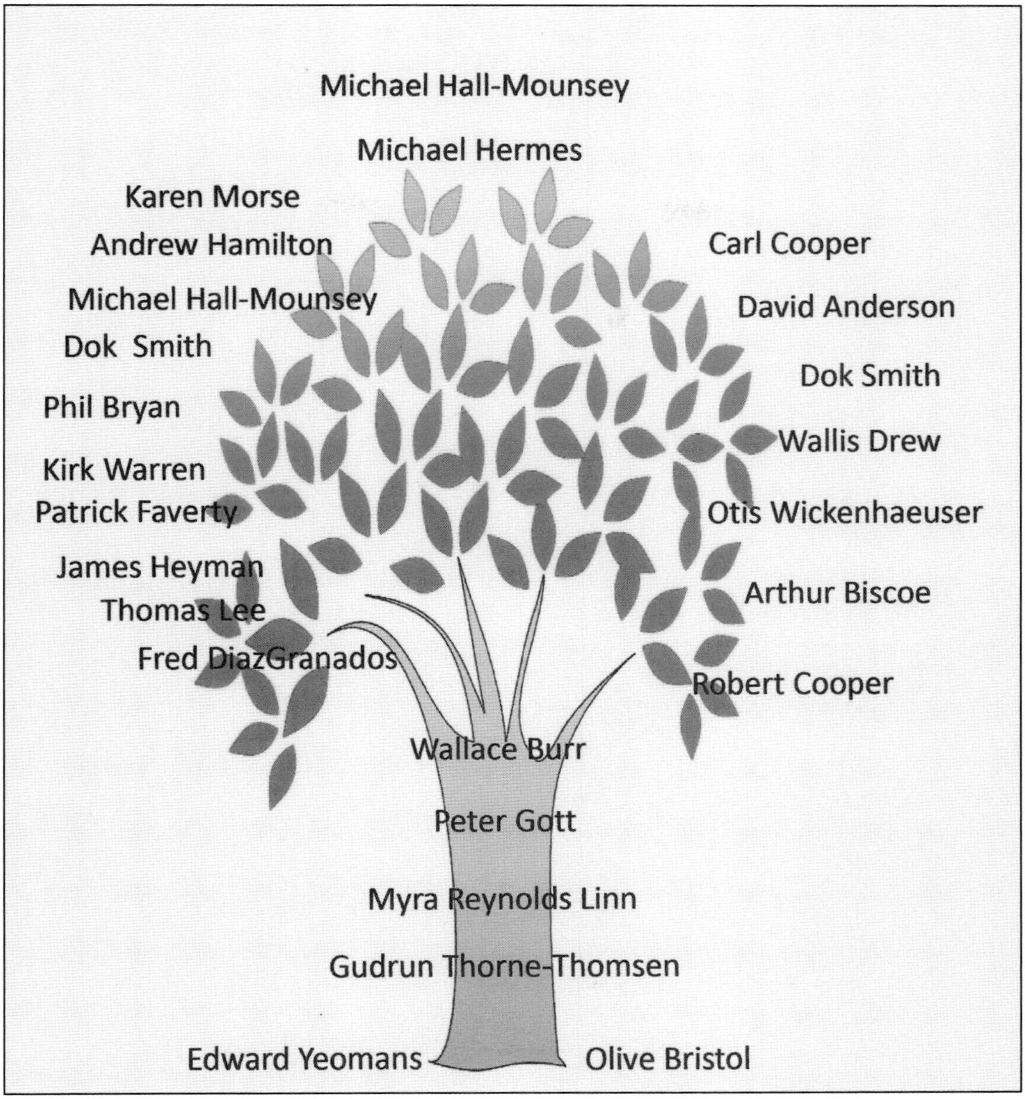

Leadership. Leadership throughout the years of the Ojai Valley School has spread like a family tree. Starting with the foresight of Olive Bristol and Edward Yeomans and expanding to Wallace Burr, whose vision led to the development of the Upper Campus, the institution now known as OVS has grown and flourished from 1911 to the present. The Lower Campus leadership is listed on the left; the heads of the Upper Campus, on the right; and the names of the two presidents who have overseen both campuses are shown at top center.

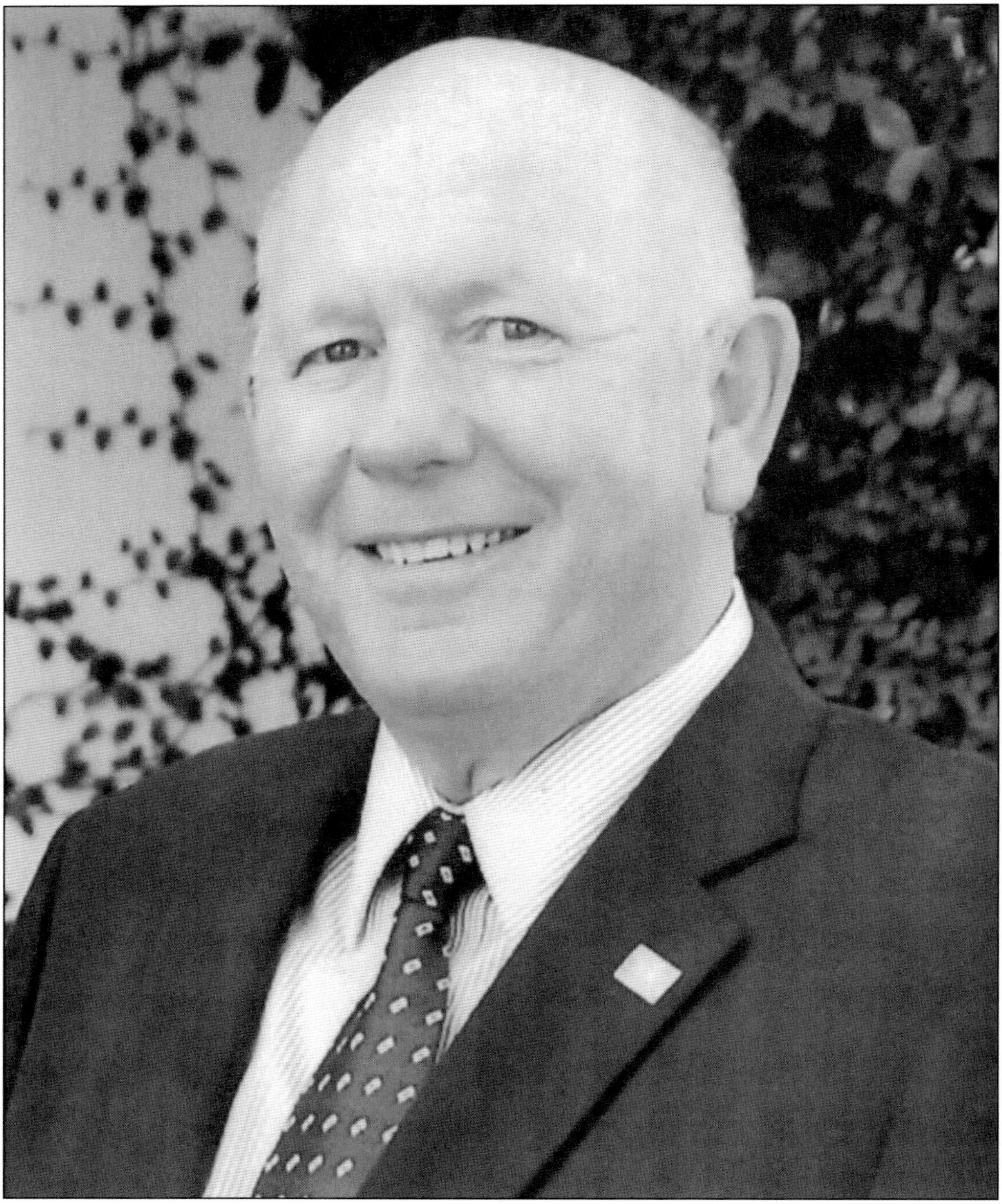

At the Helm. Hired by OVS in 1981, Michael J. Hall-Mounsey has worked hard to ensure the school's future. He was born and raised in England and was educated at St. Paul's College at Bristol University, King Alfred's College in Winchester, and earned his master's in education administration at California Lutheran University. It immediately became apparent to all that he was a highly effective teacher and coach. From 1990 to 2009, he served as Lower Campus headmaster. In that year, after the retirement of Mike Hermes, Hall-Mounsey took over as president of OVS. He believes that "true self-esteem comes from real achievement." Under his stewardship, OVS offers students a myriad of opportunities, including Advanced Placement classes, community-service opportunities, and horse and camping programs. According to Mike Hermes, Hall-Mounsey "has a profound understanding of and respect for the OVS philosophy, and [the school is] fortunate to have him at the helm."

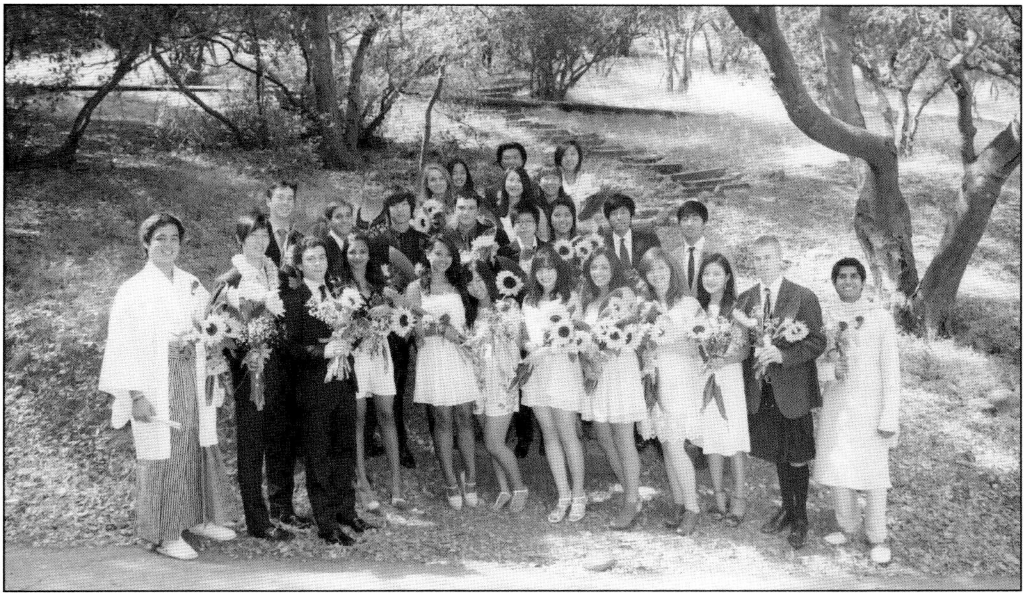

One Hundred Years Later. OVS is an independent, coeducational boarding and day school that serves 190 students on the Lower Campus and 110 students on the Upper Campus, eight miles away. Since its founding, the school has demonstrated all that is best for the education of children. The holistic emphasis, reflected in the *Integer Vitae* philosophy, addresses the whole child. The 2011 graduates, marking OVS's first century, are shown above.

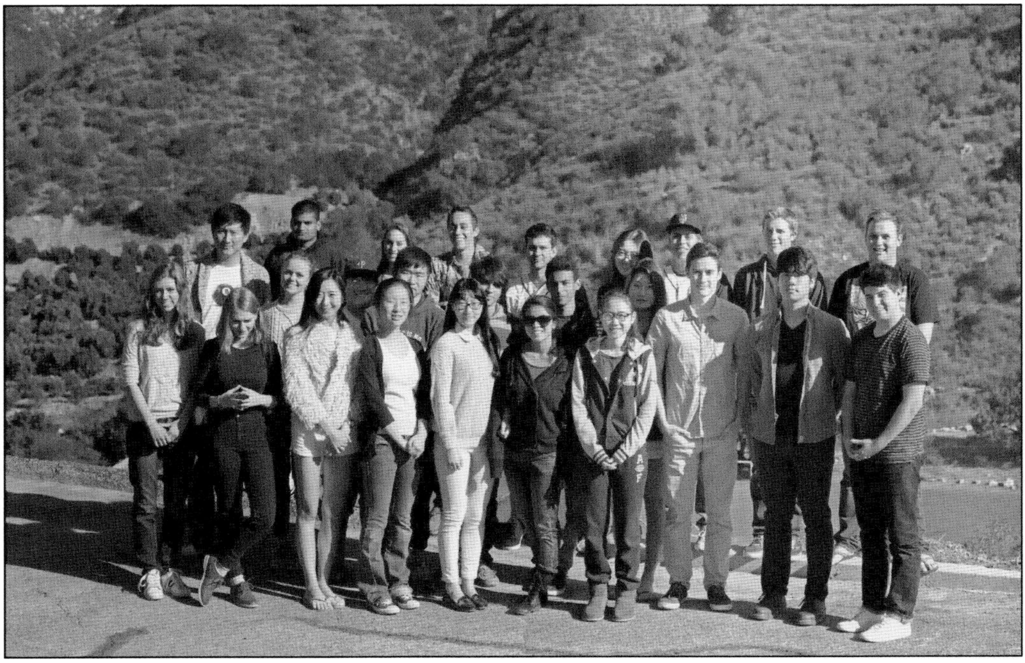

The 50th Graduating Class. As one of the premier coeducational boarding schools in the western United States for prekindergarten through grade 12, Ojai Valley School truly meets the needs of a child with its small classes, individual attention, and family-based environment. These 2014 graduates have developed the academic strength, character, and self-confidence to meet life's future challenges in an ever-changing world. (John Boyd.)

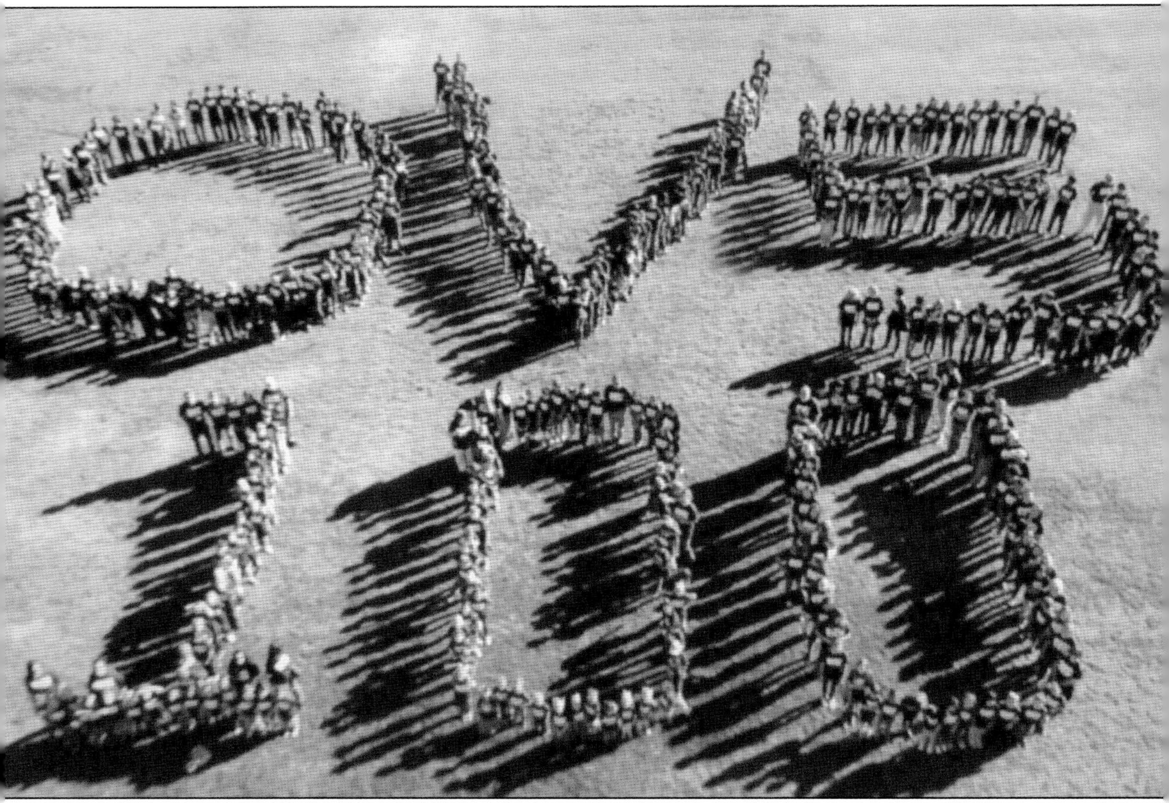

A Unique Institution. As a part of the celebration of 100 years of educational excellence, the students from OVS gathered on the athletic field to show their unity and pride in this unique institution. A quote from the Chinese philosopher Confucius suggests why institutions like OVS are critical to the future of the United States: "If you are planning for one year, plant rice. If you are planning for ten years, plant trees. If you are planning for one hundred years, educate children."

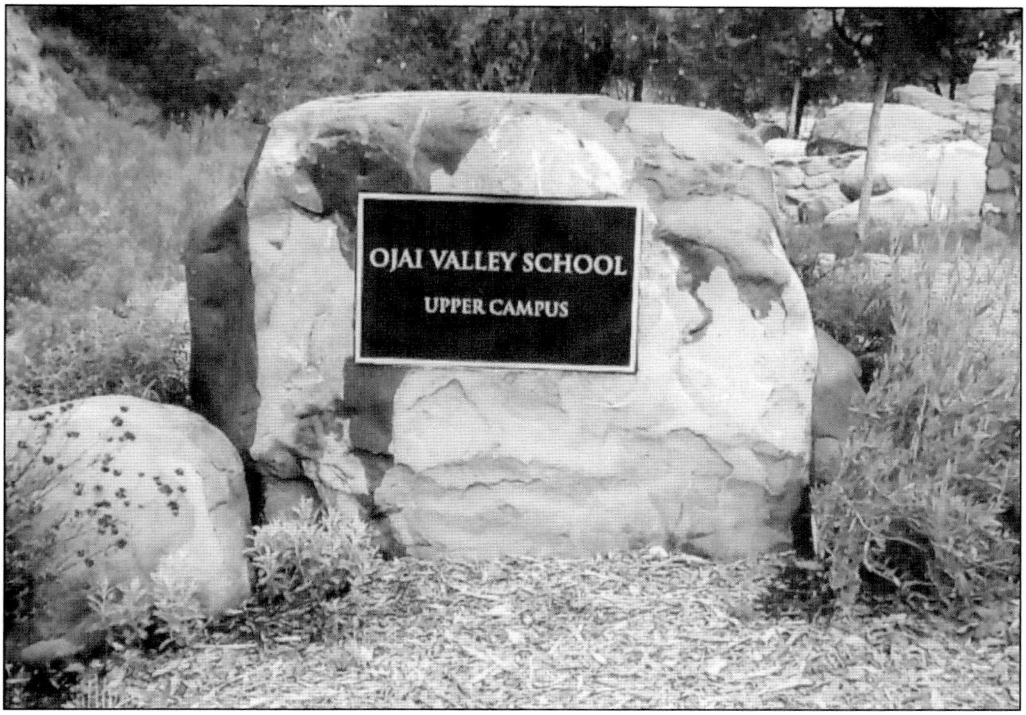

A Welcome Sight. Ojai Valley School, begun as a homeschool and tutor program with Olive Bristol in 1911 and continued as the dream of Edward Yeomans in 1923, has endured for more than 100 years. Almost from his earliest days at the school, Wallace Burr dreamed of including an Upper Campus with grades 9 through 12. Today, thanks to the hard work and vision of Burr, Mike Hermes, Michael Hall-Mounsey, and many others, the Upper Campus continues to thrive after more than 50 years. These gates are a welcome sight to returning students and alumni, who enter with unforgettable memories of a time of growth and challenges in a place of fellowship and peace—their own corner of the world.

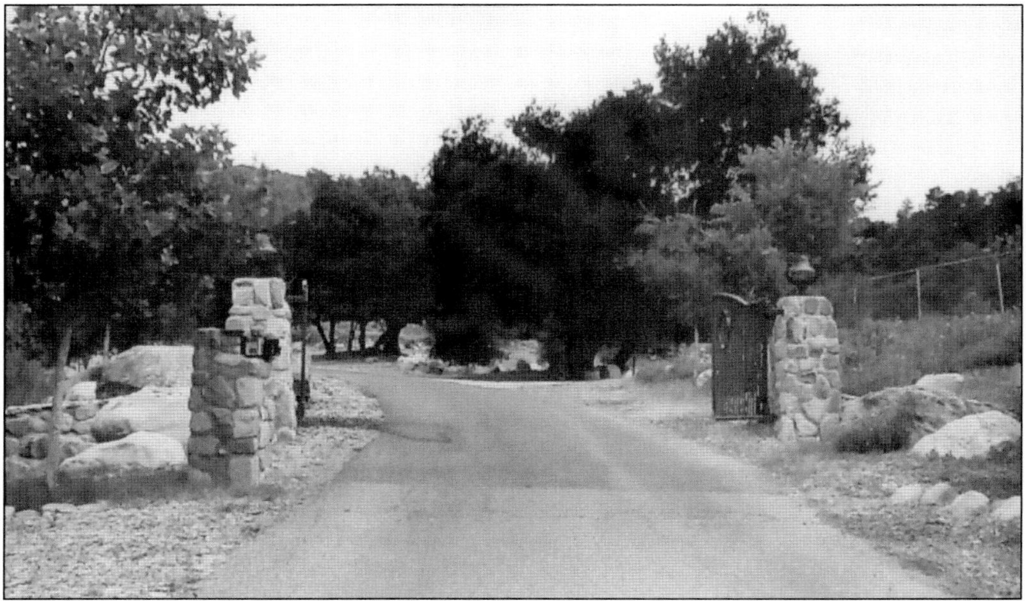